The Theory of Literary Criticism

JOHN M. ELLIS

The Theory of
Literary Criticism

A Logical Analysis

University of California Press

Berkeley • Los Angeles • London

University of California Press
Berkeley and Los Angeles, California
University of California Press, Ltd.
London, England
Copyright © 1974, by
The Regents of the University of California
First Paperback Edition 1977
ISBN: 0-520-03413-9
Library of Congress Catalog Card Number: 73-83055
Printed in the United States of America

1 2 3 4 5 6 7 8 9

For D. G. Mowatt

Contents

Preface

THIS BOOK is concerned with the analysis and resolution of the basic theoretical problems that arise in the study of literature and in literary criticism. It is not so comprehensive in its scope as the by now classic *Theory of Literature*, by Wellek and Warren, which makes at least some mention of almost all the theoretical problems that literary study has ever seemed to raise. By contrast, I have analyzed a smaller number of these problems; but I have done so in order to concentrate on the most central issues of literary theory, those that constitute the essential conceptual framework of literary study within which all others would need to be considered. Rather than leave each one after a brief discussion and pass on to the next, I have sought to analyze each problem in some depth, and in fact to devote to each as much analysis as seemed necessary for its resolution. To go beyond the basic problems of the field, given this aim, would have meant both an impossibly long work and one that obscured the outline of what I have tried to make one sustained and systematic argument.

The reader, on reading my title page, may well feel that he can regard my subtitle as an announcement of a particular approach, i.e., a philosophical one, chosen from the many possible approaches to literary theory that seem to be available at the moment: psychological, linguistic, and so on. I do not think of the situation in this way. Theoretical analysis is, of its very nature, a logical inquiry. Several other disciplines—and the practical experience of critics themselves—contribute material to the inquiry, but the resulting complex is then subject to the general principles of conceptual and logical analysis if it is to become a theoretical inquiry. Literary critics have often shown some resistance to this notion, and have preferred to think of theory of literature as an activity of and for the "literary mind," in terms and language derived directly from the practice of critics. But this attitude only tends to show why it is that there has been so little progress in literary theory; for whatever the field of inquiry, its theoretical problems can be resolved only by carefully controlled conceptual analysis. The results of such analysis may well be couched in terms far removed from the ordinary language of literary critics, and even more remote from literary language itself. They may not delight the sensibilities of the literary mind, but then they do not have to: the literary texts themselves have that function. Criticism should not (it is often said) compete with literary texts; still less should literary theory.

The theory of literature and of literary criticism has, of course, been discussed endlessly for thousands of years. It is impossible to come to terms with everything that has been written on the subject; even the recent literature is of enormous dimensions. Simply to read it all would be problem enough. And then there is the danger, not always avoided by Wellek and Warren, that too much exposition of the views of other scholars results in such a cluttering of one's own argument that its main outline is obscured. Finally, there is the danger, which has always been the bane of literary critics and literary theory, that important issues of principle often become reduced to petty *ad hominem* squabbles between rival practitioners or, worse still, between the disciples of competing ideologues in the field. All these considerations make it difficult to write an analysis of literary theory and, while doing so, to set that analysis properly in the context of previous work in the field.

Fortunately the task is made easier by the fact that the main outlines of the positions commonly taken have been set for some time, without very much variation; they are exceedingly well known, and for my purposes do not need to be traced through their many reiterations. For the most part, I have tried to preserve the clarity of the outline of my analysis and to resist being diverted from central to peripheral issues by avoiding entanglement in the main body of my text with any particular version of these well-known positions. Particular sources are documented in footnotes but, here too, exhaustiveness is neither possible nor desirable, and my selection is usually determined by one or other of several distinct factors: the source referred to is usually a typical version of the position discussed in the text, a classic statement of it, or a particularly influential one. This last consideration explains my fairly liberal use of the recent pamphlets edited by James Thorpe and published by the Modern Language Association of America: *The Aims and Methods of Scholarship in Modern Languages and Literatures* (1963), and *Relations of Literary Study* (1967).

All three considerations are relevant to my frequent references to Wellek and Warren. Otherwise, I have tried to keep some balance between well-known older theorists and very recent work. That a certain amount of fairly random selection of this kind is necessary in discussing literary theory indicates that the field has become repetitive and is not progressing; it seems to be stuck on a small complex of arguments, which generally are not well focused or analyzed but instead have become matters of faith to those on both sides. I shall discuss this aspect of the prevailing scene, and the reasons for it, in my introductory chapter; the rest of the book will consist of a series of related analyses of theoretical problems which will also throw light on this impasse.

The argument of this book is—or is at least intended to be—a systematic chain. On occasion, a link in this chain will be familiar, but it was nonetheless necessary for the completeness of the argument to include it; and to the extent that it occurs in this context used in this kind of way, it is never entirely the same point. Even so, it will be clear at some points of the argument that I am particularly indebted to my predecessors, and these debts are, I hope, sufficiently acknowledged in references. There are, however, more general intellectual debts which I must mention here. Anyone engaged in the analysis of problems of literary theory now must owe a great deal to the important work of Wellek and Warren, a pioneer of its kind. At a more personal level, I was fortunate to have been taught by E. M. Wilkinson. I owe more than I can say to countless long conversations over many years with D. G. Mowatt. And I have also benefited much from discussions with Howard S. Robertson, Brian Rowley, and Hugh Sacker. Several of my friends were kind enough to read the manuscript and to give me many suggestions for its improvement: Michael Warren, William Lillyman, David Mowatt, and Austin Quigley. Barbara Kaun's expert scrutiny of the manuscript was particularly valuable. Finally, I am grateful for assistance provided by a grant of faculty research funds by the University of California, Santa Cruz.

1: Introduction

THE TERM "theory of literature" is sometimes understood in a narrow sense as referring to the question of what literature should do and be for; I am here taking it in the wider sense of its use by Wellek and Warren, in which it covers in addition the whole range of theoretical questions that arise in the study of literature: what literature is, what criticism is, how criticism should proceed, and so on.[1] Much writing has been devoted to these questions, and output continues to be voluminous. Year by year, books appear with titles such as *The Interests of Criticism, The Business of Criticism, An Essay on Criticism*.[2] Yet, in spite of the enormous amount of work that now regularly appears in print, the subject seems peculiarly stagnant and unprogressive, and to be rehearsing old arguments and views rather than opening up any new perspectives on the analysis of theoretical problems.

The basis for the present-day discussion of the theory of literature was laid in the period between and including the two world wars; and, with the possible exception of

[1] R. Wellek and A. Warren, *Theory of Literature*, 2nd ed. (New York, 1956). The first edition appeared in 1949.

[2] These are titles of books by H. Adams (New York, 1969), H. Gardner (Oxford, 1959), and G. Hough (London, 1966).

work in linguistic stylistics, it is difficult to see any serious alteration in the lines of the discussion since the 1940s. Most of the issues argued about constantly since then were first taken to a fairly high level of discussion at that time: the relevance of the artist's intention; the relation of scholarship to criticism; the relevance of information concerning historical background; and so on. Typical and important stances pro and con on all these issues were taken, and a series of fundamental works appeared, each of which seemed to present a distinctive new position that added something to the range of the discussion of literary theory.[3] The end of this lively and interesting period was marked by a series of works that, to a large extent, synthesize an era of thought in literary theory, foremost among them being *Theory of Literature* by Wellek and Warren.[4]

But since then, the terms of the argument have not

[3] For example, the works listed in my bibliography by Eliot, Richards, Empson, Leavis, and others.

[4] Cf. also W. K. Wimsatt's brilliant *The Verbal Icon* (Lexington, Ky., 1954), based on work published mainly in the 1940s, two essays from which were written in collaboration with M. C. Beardsley; and S. E. Hyman's *The Armed Vision* (New York, 1948, 2nd ed. 1955). The reader will note that I have so far referred only to works that appeared in England and America, but Anglo-American theoretical analysis has been so far in advance of anything going on in other countries since about 1920 that the omission of any mention of them is natural. In Germany, W. Kayser's outstanding work *Das sprachliche Kunstwerk* (Bern, 1948) shows its author's considerable knowledge of Anglo-American theory, but just how foreign these developments have otherwise remained in Germany can be seen from, e.g., E. Lohner's excellent "Tradition und Gegenwart deutscher Literaturkritik," in *Sprache im technischen Zeitalter* 3 (1962): 238–248. Things seem no better in France; cf. L. Bersani's perceptive comments in his "From Bachelard to Barthes," *Partisan Review* 34 (1967): 215–232.

changed; much the same points have been made for and against the same positions. This has resulted in a great change in the intellectual climate of the field. Gradually, the intense interest with which new works were greeted has abated, since little really new was forthcoming. Theory has come to seem much duller than formerly. In such a climate it has been easy for the field to actually regress, and for its best work to fall into neglect; this, in turn, has made possible the reappearance of ultra-conservative, obscurantist positions in literary theory in spite of well-established arguments against them.[5] A more serious development, however, has been the tendency to question the value of literary theory itself. This is not just a matter of the widespread loss of confidence that literary theory has much to teach us; more important is the fact that a theoretical position has now become common among literary scholars which involves a considerable restriction of the power and scope of literary theory. The position is referred to by one of its advocates as "wise eclecticism."[6]

In essence, "wise eclecticism" advocates that we should stop trying to rule that one kind of evidence for a literary

[5] Cf. R. D. Altick, *The Art of Literary Research* (New York, 1963). I should also classify some aspects of the contributions to the recent Modern Language Association pamphlets in this way: *The Aims and Methods of Scholarship in Modern Languages and Literatures* (New York, 1963) and *Relations of Literary Study* (New York, 1967), both ed. J. Thorpe.

[6] I take the phrase from G. Watson, *The Literary Critics* (Harmondsworth, Middlesex, 1962), p. 227. Different versions of the same basic attitude are to be found, for example, in A. E. Rodway, "What the Critics Really Need," *Twentieth Century* 172 (winter 1963): 155–163, and W. Righter, *Logic and Criticism* (London, 1963).

interpretation is in principle better than another (e.g., biographical as distinct from structural) and accept that ad hoc decisions will need to be taken in each case. In some cases a particular kind of statement will be the most useful and relevant, while others may demand a quite different treatment. That this position should not imply that everything is equally admissible is the reason for the adjective "wise": the use of good judgment is necessary to give weight to this rather than that, but the application of universally valid theoretical distinctions is not feasible. Typically, adherents of this position attach many positively valued words to the use of such judgment (insight, discernment, perception) and stress the richness and complexity of the literary text in order to undermine further the advocacy of sharp theoretical distinctions, which are then qualified by the corresponding negatively valued words: rigid, dogmatic, simplistic. And if one then asks whether there are any general criteria for good rather than poor uses of judgment, there is usually an appeal to common sense,[7] obviousness, or, quite simply, to soundness of judgment—an evident circularity.

It is not difficult to see how such an attitude arises from the present state of literary theory. It is a response to a stagnant situation, in which further progress in formulating useful distinctions is not appearing, and has not done so for some time. This attitude constitutes both a despair of such progress and a necessary practical attitude in its absence: if sound theoretical distinctions are not available to control our actions, then we have no al-

[7] Rodway, p. 161; Righter, p. 124. Cf. my comments on Rodway's article, *Twentieth Century* 172 (summer 1963): 112–114

ternative but to resort to what our instincts tell us looks sensible. If we take this position, therefore, as an expression of the underlying practical attitude: "theory currently offers little that is useful, and so we shall get on as best we can without its help"—then it is reasonable. But as a theoretical position it is completely untenable; it advocates an end to theoretical controls and to theoretical inquiry. Theory of literature must confront the task of formulating in conceptual terms what causes us to make one kind of move in one situation, but a different one in another kind of situation; it must attempt to formulate and distinguish the aspects of the two kinds of situations that are relevant to their different treatment, and to sort out the factors involved. If it is "wise" to choose one course here, but another course there, what is the basis of the wisdom of the choice? A wise man is one who reads the situation well, and responds to all of its components; theory must, then, concern itself with the analysis of his judgment, and of the situational components to which it relates. "Eclecticism" can only be a temporary practical expedient, which acknowledges that we have not yet been able to analyze the factors involved in decisions to act differently in different situations; it can never itself be a theory. This fact cannot be changed by an appeal to the complexity, nor to the suggestiveness (as against explicitness) of literary texts; complex situations demand complex analyses, not none at all, while the notion that a piece of language can suggest something without stating it still allows us to talk of what is suggested as a product of a linguistic structure. And there is then no reason in principle to suppose that it is beyond

description, and therefore control,[8] given an analysis that
is sufficiently refined. Another frequently claimed theoretical prop for wise eclecticism is the argument that all
contexts (and texts) are unique. Undoubtedly, they are;
but it is a logical error to suppose that their uniqueness
prohibits analysis of them. The notion of the uniqueness
of an organism, a person, or a situation does not reduce
all generality to particularity; on the contrary, all generalization emerges from the analysis of the factors operating in large numbers of unique situations.[9] The statement
that all contexts are unique does not contrast with (i.e.,
clash with or attempt to supplant) the statement that
theoretical analysis should attempt to discern general
principles operating in such contexts. And any claim that
in a given unique situation a particular move is the right
one must begin a general discussion of the factors that
distinguish this situation from one in which the move
would be the wrong one: a theoretical inquiry will have
begun.

If literary theory were noticeably lagging behind a
practical consensus, and if there were a wide agreement
on how to tell good judgment from bad, then the case for
wise eclecticism would be stronger. But this is not the
case in literary criticism; critics disagree with each other
persistently and even bitterly. In spite of the head-in-
the-sand optimism on this score of many of its advocates,[10] there is no practical consensus to which eclecti-

[8] Cf. my review of Righter in *Philosophical Books* 5 (1964):
17–19. This argument raises the important issue of the reference
theory of meaning, which I shall pursue below.

[9] Cf. Wellek and Warren, p. 7: "Individuality can be distinguished from complete particularity and uniqueness."

[10] E.g., Rodway, p. 161: ". . . most of us know from experience

cism can appeal; on the contrary, a situation in which there is so much dispute evidently demands the kind of theoretical analysis that will investigate the basis of the disagreements and ways of progressing beyond them.

The spread of eclecticism is simply one aspect of the decline of literary theory. I want now to turn to factors that may explain why theory of literature has atrophied to this extent in the last quarter of a century, after such a lively and creative period in the preceding quarter-century: at the same time, this discussion will serve to introduce the direction that my own analysis will take in the course of this book.

The impetus of literary theory between the two wars was in large measure provided by a sense that reform was necessary in literary criticism. The theorists of the period have often been identified with the New Criticism; the identification is by no means complete, but its extent shows how much theory at that time was part of a movement for change, an outcrop of that movement, and in turn an encouragement to it. But this fact carried within it an inherent drawback: reformatory zeal alone was not enough to carry on the study of theory after the time when the most urgently needed changes had been accomplished. And so most of the theoretical work done since that of Wellek and Warren has tended to chew over much the same proposals for change; some would have preferred more change, some less, but the

---

the difference between consideration of evidence and self-indulgence or fancifulness." Righter, p. 124: "Even if such criticism is without rules and standards, we nevertheless can recognize the false move." J. Casey's *The Language of Criticism* (London, 1966) is not without this unrealistic optimism; cf. the *Times Literary Supplement* review of his book, August 17, 1967.

horizon of the field has been limited to awareness of those short-term reforms.

It is, of course, true that the practical consequences of theories have been and always will be responsible for a large part of the interest shown in them. That is only natural. But it is also true that theoretical inquiry needs some degree of independence from arguments over immediate practical reforms, even in order to be of some use for practical applications. This is not only a matter of the inquiry's ebb and flow, to which I have referred above. If theoretical analysis becomes too closely tied to practical reform, its whole nature becomes suspect, and the result has been, as I shall now argue, that the analysis of literary theory has been carried on in the wrong spirit, and with the wrong tools.

The question of what background information is relevant to the study of a literary text is obviously an important one for theory of literature. The results of a theoretical analysis of it will be of great use to critics. But theory of literature is kept at a trivial and superficial level if it is pursued only by people whose sole aim in considering such questions is to produce a quick justification for one side or another in a practical dispute over which kinds of books one should read to be a good critic. A firm yes or no will be preferred to any more complex analysis in these circumstances; what should be a controlled logical inquiry is easily reduced to partisan slogans. In any genuine theoretical analysis, the original form of the question asked is commonly transcended very quickly, so that instead of getting a neat answer to it, we find ourselves having to substitute a related but much better formulated and more complex question; again, not uncommon-

ly, we find that the puzzle provided by the question re-
sided in an ambiguity in the way we were asking it. The
development of a theoretical analysis is severely inhibited
if the purpose of the analysis is to justify a particular
reform program, as was largely the case in disputes between New Critics and Historians; for in such disputes
the emphasis was on the choice between two positions,
not on the more fundamental question of the basis of the
opposition and the assumptions involved in its formulation. Time and again, throughout the course of this book,
my analysis will find that the series of choices debated
hotly in literary theory oppose two courses of action,
or concepts of courses of action, which cannot sensibly
be opposed: for example, either we read a work in its
social context or we read it in isolation; either we have
evaluative criteria or we can only do a descriptive analysis; either literary criticism is a matter of judgment
and imagination or it is precise and scientific.

The crux of the matter is this: the shape of the problems must be allowed to develop as the analysis progresses and in the light of what the analysis shows; the
theoretical questions must not be held firm in the shape
in which they first present themselves—in slogans and
practical reformatory demands. Theory must take its
starting points from such criticism, and (mostly) feed
back into it. But, in the meantime, it needs more independence than it has had in order to do anything worthwhile.

Another disturbing aspect of the situation is that this
lack of independence from practical reformatory zeal has
made the field intolerably polemical. Theory has often
seemed to be only a question of providing ammunition
for a literary ideologue's murderous assault on a rival,

and a defense of his own prestige. The result is almost a spectator sport, rather than a field of inquiry. A now commonly accepted procedure in writings on literary theory is the ad hoc discussion of the views of another scholar, whether central or not; by contrast, direct approach to a fundamental analysis of central problems is much less common.[11] Practical reform, which promoted the study of literary theory and made it a lively field for some years, has thus contributed much to the bad state into which theory has recently fallen: one in which it repetitively goes over familiar ground, is trivialized by petty squabbles, and effectively has a very low ceiling put upon its possibilities by too close a contact with practical choices.

If we look at the kind of activity that is involved in the analysis of the problems of literary theory, it becomes evident that its most obvious and necessary features are conceptual analysis and drawing of distinctions. The most relevant techniques and tools are those of logical and conceptual analysis. Literary theory is, in fact, first and foremost theory; the literary theorist is, or should be, first and foremost a theorist among other kinds of theorists. In large measure, their aims and methods are his. He must understand what critics are doing to be able to function properly; but he must perform the job of a theorist, not that of a critic. The performance has much more in com-

---

[11] Even a book such as Casey's, which announces a concern with logical analysis, proceeds in this way—and is severely hampered as a result. "Literary theory is no place for someone who does not like a good argument," says Adams in his preface. Perhaps not, as things stand; but it is certainly instructive that a writer on literary theory feels (probably justifiably) that this needs to be said.

mon with that of other theorists in other fields of theoretical inquiry than with that of critics. I do not wish to
be misunderstood on this point; I am not making an
assertion of the kind made, say, when it is argued that
psychology contributes more to criticism than does any
other discipline, and thus am not countering a claim of
this kind on behalf of psychology with a similar one on
behalf of logical analysis. What I am asserting is that
theory itself (not criticism) is a matter of logical analysis.
As such, logical analysis cannot be contrasted with any
other kind of input into literary theory (e.g., modern linguistics); it must be uniquely at the center of literary
theory and the controlling factor that is used to evaluate
the claims of other disciplines to contribute to literary
theory.

The heavy involvement of literary theory in the arguments of critics about practical reforms has, from this
point of view, been doubly unfortunate. The considerable
progress in logical analysis in this century has been
largely unused by literary theory because the discussion
has been conducted by critics, not theorists. The limitation imposed by reformatory goals was thus reinforced
by a limitation of a different kind, the absence of the most
relevant kind of knowledge and technique.

The difference between having this knowledge and
technique and not having it is not just a question of
knowing the rules of inference that operate, for example,
in syllogisms. If this were all that was in question, as
might be the case given the rather restricted popular notion of logic, then ignoring it would be no very great
danger; few if any arguments in theory of literature
turn on syllogistic inference. The crucial area is that of

the logic of language and of conceptual analysis. Since critics have lacked sophistication in this area, their attempts at theorizing have been unconsciously conditioned by common-sense notions of the logic of language; of these, the most pervasive, and therefore the most pernicious for literary theory, has been the reference theory of meaning.

In my next chapter, I shall pursue the question of the definition of literature, and in the process shall use this example to show in some detail how and why the reference theory of meaning is unworkable; but some brief explanation is necessary at this point of how this theory of meaning has lead theory of literature in some fundamentally unprofitable directions.

The view that words refer to things, and that their meaning and use is determined by this reference, is a natural one at first sight. It seems a rather clear-cut and operable theory. But it is also immediately evident that there is much in language that the reference theory cannot handle; the most obvious, though as we shall see not necessarily the most important, are such things as evaluative words, exhortations, tone and attitude, and, in general, all that this theory treats as connotation (as opposed to referential denotation). A severely consistent version of the reference theory of meaning was the philosophical theory called logical positivism,[12] according to

[12] See A. J. Ayer's classic *Language, Truth, and Logic* (London, 1946; 1st ed. 1936). My text ignores the aspect of Ayer's work which was of such great importance in the history of philosophy and which will always give it—whatever its faults—an honored place there, namely its preeminence in turning philosophy away from a rather empty metaphysical phase. But I think that, sooner or later, another important reason for its status as a great work

which propositions were meaningful insofar as they were verifiable, that is, referred to verifiable facts. Evaluations were expressions of approval and disapproval lacking in objective referential content, and therefore meaningless. Literary critics have not, for the most part, been able to follow philosophers of this school in their ruthlessly honest drawing of the consequences of the reference theory of meaning. It would have been too obviously unacceptable to write off so much that was of such great traditional importance in literary criticism—evaluation, for example. Yet the basic distinction between referential and nonreferential functions of language has been used just the same, with only the former (by definition) subject to any control by verification. How, then, was it possible to avoid the logical conclusion of the reference theory (if applied consistently) that what was not referential was meaningless? The answer is an interesting one: instead of relegating those things with which the reference theory could not deal to a lower status, critics tended to elevate them to a higher one: they were matters of judgment, too complex and rich for simple verification, and too much questions of the mind for direct experience by the senses (reference). In other words, a virtue was made of the fact that no rules could be found which were able to account for or control the use of certain aspects of language. In this way, the defects of the underlying reference theory of language were hidden where, by contrast, the logical

---

will be recognized: by working out with unrelaxing consistency all the implications of the reference theory of meaning, it has performed a very necessary *reductio ad absurdum* of that theory. In a sense, Ayer forced philosophy to go in the direction that it took with Wittgenstein by showing where one must end up if one pursued the reference theory to its logical conclusion.

positivist A. J. Ayer had (though this was not his intent) ruthlessly exposed them in showing the patently unacceptable results to which that theory led. In effect, the casualties of the theory were hidden by promoting them to the honored status of things that were unanalyzable. One could "refer" to certain obvious things about works of literature—rhyme scheme, metre, and so on—but they were trivial by comparison with such important issues as evaluation and interpretation, which could not be referred to and verified in the same way. The concept of literature itself has always eluded definition by referential tests but, in like vein, was thought too rich a concept for down-to-earth simple verifiability. It will readily be seen that the reference theory of meaning leads in this way to the same point as does "wise eclecticism" in literary theory, and that the two concepts mutually support each other: for "wise eclecticism," too, makes much use of the notion that all kinds of issues—and preferably the most important ones in the field—are unanalyzable, and that this unanalyzability, far from rendering them meaningless (as in logical positivism), lends them an almost mystic splendour.

At this point I must enter a disclaimer. By now some readers may suspect that I am about to attempt to make everything in literary criticism and literary theory a matter of clear rules, verifiability, and even "scientific" precision. This is not my intent nor the point of what I am saying. On the contrary: my point is precisely that the reference theory of meaning sees the notion of rules for the use of a concept, and control of its use, in these very limited and inadequate terms, that is, those of direct reference. The fact that the reference theory of meaning is so much a part of our common-sense attitudes makes it difficult to think in other terms, though in the course of this book I shall try to show how the problems of literary theory can profitably be treated in different terms. If (to return to the hypothetical objection that I have raised) to extend analysis and logical control into areas that do not seem to be subject to control appears to trivialize those areas, this can only be because the very notion of analysis that is employed here is a trivial one; and this is precisely what happens when the reference theory of meaning is used. The reference theory employs such a limited kind of analysis, accounts for so little and excludes so much, that for any issue to be treated according to such a logic is for it to be trivialized; and the trivialization will seem the greater by contrast with the grandiosity that is generally attributed to those areas of language that this theory cannot handle, as a means of covering up its omissions. Analysis demeans nothing, unless the notion of analysis has first been impoverished.

The reference theory of meaning has been questioned by philosophers and linguists, the most notable of the latter being J. R. Firth.[13] The most important figure among philosophers in this regard is Ludwig Wittgenstein, whose logical analysis of the reference theory is already classic.[14]

[13] There are evident similarities between the directions that Firth's thought took in the 1930s and Wittgenstein's thought during the same period. B. L. Whorf, from a different direction, also undermined the reference theory by his insistence that language not only refers to, but also organizes our environment. See *Language, Thought, and Reality. Selected Writings of Benjamin Lee Whorf*, ed. J. B. Carroll (Cambridge, Mass., 1956).

[14] Cf. L. Wittgenstein, *Philosophische Untersuchungen/Philosophical Investigations*. Bilingual ed., trans. G. E. M. Anscombe, 3rd ed. (New York, 1968).

The idea that Wittgenstein (and, by extension, modern logical analysis) can be important for literary theory is by now not entirely new. It is certainly true that virtually all literary theory has ignored such developments; but in the last decade a few volumes have appeared which have announced a concern with the use of these developments for literary theory, e.g., those by Righter (*Logic and Criticism*), Casey (*The Language of Criticism*), and Weitz (*Hamlet and the Philosophy of Literary Criticism*).[15] Yet these works have done little more than point in the right direction.

Of the three, Righter's work is the least useful. His view that criticism is "illogical" but still of value in being rich and suggestive could easily have been shared by Ayer himself; it is certainly much closer to logical positivism (and to conventional literary theory) than to Wittgenstein, who is interested in extending the logic of language into such "illogical" areas. It is a fundamental misunderstanding of Wittgenstein to abstract from his work only the fact that certain nonreferential aspects of language are valuable and interesting (which Righter appears to do) without recognizing that the reason for his interest in them has much to do with his dissatisfaction with the theory that separated them off from simple descriptive discourse in the first place. Righter's own version of that separation is an extreme one,[16] so that his stance is in reality a conventional one within which the veneer of Wittgensteinian language is in no way integrated into a theoretical position.

[15] M. Weitz, *Hamlet and the Philosophy of Literary Criticism* (Chicago, 1964).

[16] E.g., Righter, p. 132 and p. 145.

Weitz, by contrast, shows that the reference theory creates many problems in theory of literature, and that literary critics make many different kinds of statements that are not referential. He also shows that impasse results if these different kinds of statements are discussed as if they were referential (i.e., with a logic appropriate only to the reference theory of meaning). But here he ends his book where it should be just beginning. We do not get any analysis of the problems of literary theory in the light of what he has shown, i.e., that one gets nowhere with reference-theory logic. Where, then, do we go from here? On this point, Weitz's concluding position is that critics do many different kinds of things, and that they are misconceived and misjudged if all are thought of in referential terms. By concluding in this way, Weitz, like Righter, seems to enlist Wittgenstein in support of the already prevalent critical laissez-faire; yet he would scarcely have done so had he seen that he had reached not a conclusion but a starting point. For the important question remains untouched: how does one conceive of these various critical activities if not in referential terms? What is their logic if not a referential logic?[17]

Casey's book, alone among the three I have mentioned,

[17] Weitz sometimes moves in this direction, but only in small steps. For example, he asserts that even if there are no "true or false" interpretations, they "must nevertheless submit to criteria of adequacy" (p. 262). But this stopgap notion of "adequacy," the only substitute forthcoming for true/false referential logic, is never analyzed. Here, as in general in Weitz's book, we have the feeling that Weitz is much clearer about what Wittgenstein would have found wrong with literary theory than about the more important issue of setting it right. The weakness of existing literary theory is to some extent exposed; anything to replace it has yet to appear.

enters the real field of the argument, and makes one or two interesting and relevant points. Yet it, too, is finally disappointing and leaves most of the field still untouched. The fundamental motive behind the book is the right one: to extend the notion of rules for, and control of, critical language. Here, Casey unquestionably grasps the spirit of Wittgenstein, unlike Righter and Weitz. But this having been said, it is also clear that Casey is uncertain of how to proceed; his work lacks a clear focus. Because of this, he allows himself to adopt the prevailing *modus operandi* in literary criticism: a series of ad hoc discussions of the positions of well-known critics, a procedure that lets him get bogged down in minor issues with critics who are nowhere near the level of logical sophistication to which Casey rightly aspires. Any possibility for a sustained argument relative to a precisely defined thesis or issue is thus lost and the book meanders somewhat purposelessly. It treats only one or two issues in literary theory, and those only in a piecemeal, unsystematic way, illuminating them with odd remarks more than with an argument.

None of these three works, therefore, has contributed in any important way to the performance of the fundamental task that I have outlined. In order to introduce some further definition of what that task is and how it should be approached, I shall make one further point on how not to approach it.

Both Casey and Weitz offer summaries of Wittgensteinian theory prior to an application of that theory to literary problems.[18] No doubt there are cases in which a

[18] Casey's summary is actually not a good one; cf., once more, the remarks of the *Times Literary Supplement* reviewer (n. 10 above).

straight transfer of a piece of Wittgensteinian doctrine will suffice. But I am doubtful about how much will be achieved if no more than this is done; it is Wittgenstein's analytic technique, not his dogma, that we must borrow from him. His actual doctrines may not offer us anything, in a given case, that solves a problem in literary theory; but his characteristic way of solving problems is always relevant, and this characteristic approach is in a real sense the necessary practical version of his most important theoretical doctrine, his rejection of the reference theory of meaning. When, for example, Wittgenstein confronts a proposition asserting some kind of theory, and attempts an evaluation and interpretation of that proposition, his initial approach is likely to be in the form of the question: what distinction is being made by this proposition?[19] This first move is significant. It is not the interpretation of the individual words in the proposition, or the clarification of their reference that Wittgenstein begins with; nor is it the gathering of evidence for or against the proposition. For these kinds of initial moves would result from an underlying assumption that the proposition is primarily talking about (referring to) something, and that one's energy could be turned to finding out what it talks of, and then finding out whether or not what the proposition ascribes to the thing under discussion is true.

Wittgenstein's move implies a different stance. Propositions, above all propositions that are puzzling enough to be made the subject of theoretical analysis, are primarily designed to achieve something for the speaker:

[19] For example, Wittgenstein, p. 7: "When we say: 'Every word in language signifies something' we have so far said *nothing whatsoever*; unless we have explained exactly *what* distinction we wish to make."

they organize things just as much as referring to them. In asking what distinction is being made by a proposition, Wittgenstein is asking for the purpose that it is designed to achieve; and this purpose is primarily to be sought in a contrast between what it wants to avoid and what it wants to pursue. If a proposition is designed to achieve something, it must exclude other things, and so make a choice between various ways of organizing a situation. Wittgenstein's characteristic way of exploring the meaning of a theoretical proposition is to make explicit the possible distinctions it might be trying to make, and the possible contrasts from which it derives its meaning.

This point can be made clearer with a simple example of a common proposition in literary theory. It is often asserted (or denied) that a literary text should be studied in itself. (The denial commonly also states that a text should not be studied in a vacuum.) A closely related assertion is that literature should be studied as literature. These propositions are superficially simple in structure and seem to make definite enough assertions. An analysis on reference-theory lines would tend to make them all look intelligible enough as they stand: it would see the last as true by definition. It might even find both the first two propositions true as well, though they are used to oppose each other in practice. But that they are so used is their whole point. Wittgenstein's approach to all three would surely have been this: for all the seeming clarity of meaning of their individual words, for all the simplicity and directness of their structure as assertions, they have said precisely nothing until it has been explained what distinction they are really designed to make. We can puzzle ourselves for a long time wondering what reading a text in a vacuum would be like—would it mean not knowing the meanings of any of the words, for example, since words get their meaning outside a text? And we can puzzle ourselves greatly, too, as to what reading a piece of literature *not* as literature would be like—should we have to pretend that a short story was an anecdote told us by our best friend, or that a poem was a rather strange letter from an aunt? All such speculations would, of course, be unnecessary. The relevant contrast intended by the speaker in these cases is always to do with the reader's knowledge of biographical and historical circumstances of the composition of the text. The meanings of the original propositions, out of the context of their use, are most uncertain; only when we have made explicit the contrasts and distinctions that are implicit in their use can we get on with examining the issues. But when we do so, we find that the relevant intended distinctions are dubious ones. It turns out to be the case that the major issue involved in the examples that I set out above is the demand that literary texts be read in the light of the circumstances of their composition; but to talk of reading a text in a vacuum rather than in the light of the circumstances of its composition is not to make a clear distinction nor a necessary contrast. Likewise, to talk of reading literature as literature is not to make an assertion that contrasts clearly with any of the intended alternatives. I shall go more deeply into the analysis of these particular issues in the course of this book; for the moment I want only to show a particular example of a general fact about literary theory, and one that makes Wittgensteinian analytic technique essential for the field. It is that the problems of literary theory commonly involve slogan-like assertions in which the forms of the assertions themselves do not make clear the real point of what is being asserted and what denied; and that when the underlying distinction is brought out, it is commonly the case that two assertions are being held to be in contrast with each other, where the one is not the opposite of the other.

A further example will illumine one of the most important ways in which this lack of genuine contrast can pass unnoticed. When it is asserted that literature is a social document, the reaction of literary critics suggests that something of considerable moment has been said. That statement is felt to contrast with "literature must be studied as literature," which is likely to be said as a counter to it. But instead of allowing this dubious contrast, we could respond to those who make such assertions just as Wittgenstein might have responded: Literature is a social document indeed. It is much else besides. But what you have said means nothing until you tell us why you singled out that statement from the others with the same structure: "Literature is. . . ." Surely you are making some point which is more specific than the statement you made: you have in mind some particular importance for this statement about literature, probably that it is in some special way more important than others that could be made. And you have in mind not just social relevance in general (which would set up no implicit distinction, since everything that happens in a society can be said to be social) but a very specific way in which literature relates to society through the social context of its composition. Until we know all of this, we do not know what you are saying.

In this example we can see the importance of keeping

an eye on the word "is"; it can seem to introduce mere statements of fact, as such undeniable, without creating the need for any special evidence as to their importance. But, commonly, its use creates an implied distinction between this and other facts such that its force is "is importantly," or even "is first and foremost." To ask what distinction is being made forces these implications to the surface and even reveals the fact that the word "social" in the assertion discussed above is generally used to imply "uniquely relevant to the social circumstances of its composition." And yet how innocent, simple, and straightforward the form of the statement "literature is a social document" appears![20] That kind of apparent simplicity is only one of many hazards involved in analysis of the definition of literature, to which I now turn.

[20] This issue is pursued below in more detail, e.g., pp. 133ff.

2: The Definition of Literature

THE QUESTION, What is literature? has, understandably enough, loomed large in the theory of literature.[1] It is evidently a basic question; to ask oneself what one is dealing with would seem to be essential for any critic or theorist of literature. And yet, it is apparently also common to confess that the question is unanswered or even unanswerable. To take a random example: Hazard Adams considers it a vital question but immediately confesses that he cannot answer it and "I know of no book that does."[2] It has, in fact, become quite common for critics and theorists alike to raise the question, only to go on and assert that we all know what we mean by literature even if we cannot define it.[3] But in so doing they are all opting to remain with their intuitive notions and

[1] Cf., for example, the essays that devote themselves to it entirely, by L. Lerner, *The Truest Poetry. An Essay on the Question: What is Literature?* (New York, 1964), and J. P. Sartre, *Qu'est-ce que la littérature?* (Paris, 1948). Wellek and Warren (*Theory of Literature*) devote an early chapter to the problem, though this is more a survey of previous answers to it than an attempt to solve it.

[2] H. Adams, *The Interests of Criticism*, p. 1.

[3] E.g., G. Hough, *An Essay on Criticism*, p. 9.

to avoid theoretical inquiry into them, a procedure that will work only if those institutions are agreed upon on all sides and if they stand in no need of correction. The first proviso is obviously false, the second will turn out to be equally false on examination. Defeatism on the question is by now understandable. Complacent defeatism is not.

The question itself has a deceptive simplicity and contains a number of logical puzzles, which must be unraveled before it can be answered. But before going on to do so, it is as well to get some idea of what depends on the answer. The major interest in the question lies in the fact that large numbers of other issues of literary theory depend on it, and many disputes in literary theory proceed with very firm (but not defined) appeals to a notion of literariness. The dispute as to whether a particular kind of approach to a literary text is a "literary" approach or not is one of the great battlegrounds of literary theory. Wellek and Warren build into the very structure of their book *Theory of Literature* a kind of distinction between literary and nonliterary approaches in their terms "intrinsic" and "extrinsic." Now these and comparable distinctions must beg the question until we have a definition of literature that will allow us to give some substance to the notion of a treatment appropriate to literature, for the point at issue in disputes as to whether an approach is "literary" is precisely how we should understand "literary" treatment, and therefore ultimately: What is the nature of literature? Historical scholars, too, thought that they were making appropriately literary statements. But it was not only the side whose slogan was "literature as literature" which begged the question. Many critics have argued that if all approaches that were not specifically literary were ruled out, nothing would be left, which is to assert that there is no specifically literary approach to a literary text. This view, too, begs the question of definition and always avoids the definition argument, which alone could bolster such a position.[4] Not surprisingly, with both sides appealing in effect to a non-existent statement of definition, this argument never progresses: it becomes tediously repetitive and bogs down in slogans. From this, it is evident that the complacent view that we all instinctively agree and know what we mean by "literature" is inadequate; we may be able instinctively to use the word correctly, but are not necessarily able to explain how we use it and to abstract the principles involved in its use. It is in this sense that we do not all know what we mean by the word "literature," and from this lack of explicit agreement derive some of the important problems on which we persistently disagree.

Nowhere in current theory of literature is it clearer than in the dispute over the problem of definition that the reference theory of meaning is the barrier to progress; it is still the basis of all thought on the subject. This has meant that the search for a definition has been exclusively a search for the characteristics of literary texts to which the term "literary" refers, characteristics that distinguish them from nonliterary texts. From a common-sense point of view, such a procedure has seemed reasonable. Particular attempts to do this have sought these characteristics in three possible areas: (*a*) specific "literary" ingredients in the texts, (*b*) specifically "literary" organization

4 E.g., G. Watson, *The Literary Critics*, p. 221.

of ordinary linguistic material of the texts, (c) the authorship of the texts by specifically "literary" authors, i.e., poets. Without yet entering into the basic flaws of this whole way of approaching the question, it can easily be shown that none of these three works. The first view attempts to find isolable features of literary language. Modern linguistics provides an important group of adherents to this approach, including especially those linguists whose allegiance is predominantly to transformational grammar. The latter have tended to view poetic language as being essentially a deviation from the normal grammar of a language.[5] But this is a quite unworkable approach; many literary texts do not deviate from ordinary diction or grammar, so that this kind of definition can never be logically necessary. Conversely, the kinds of linguistic features usually suggested as the deviations (archaisms, rhyme, metaphor, alliteration, suggestiveness, rhythm, and so on) are all found quite commonly in ordinary language,[6] so that they cannot be logically sufficient (distinctive). Indeed, they do not seem to be very central to literature, and it seems that all this energy is being devoted, in fact, to defining poetic license—the permitted extensions of ordinary language—not the language of poetry. Some texts exploit the possibility of poetic license, some do not—but to say that these features are defining of literature is most implausible.

[5] See, for example, several of the essays collected together by D. Freeman in his anthology *Linguistics and Literary Style* (New York, 1970), notably that by J. P. Thorne: "Stylistics and Generative Grammars," and M. Bierwisch, "Poetics and Linguistics."

[6] Cf. R. Jakobson's examples in his "Closing Statement: Linguistics and Poetics," in *Style in Language*, ed. T. Sebeok (Cambridge, Mass., 1960), pp. 350–377.

Isolable features cannot, therefore, be used to define literature. But much the same arguments succeed against the second case, that which seeks a definition not in linguistic features but in their organization. If appeal is made to the organization provided by dramatic or fictional form, for example, then it is again easy to show that plays can be indistinguishable linguistically from transcriptions of conversations, just as short stories can be indistinguishable from ordinary real-life anecdotes. If, on the other hand, the appeal is to vague notions such as a greater degree of organization,[7] then it is possible to argue again that this is neither necessary nor sufficient: many nonliterary texts are highly organized, and many literary texts are simple in structure. Moreover, with the concept of organization, definition has moved toward evaluation rather than identification of defining features, for this concept is a large part of what is often thought of as the aesthetic superiority of a text. I shall return to the question of evaluation both in criticism and in defining literature; for the moment, it is sufficient to note that the introduction of evaluative notions in covert form into a definition effectively undermines the attempt at a referential kind of definition and thus already begins

[7] Here the problem of form and content is raised for the first time. I analyze it below, chapter 6. Wellek and Warren (p. 13) tend to favor this argument from tighter organization ("Poetic language organizes, tightens . . ."), but they accept a referential framework for the problem of definition and so are committed to some such argument from the beginning. To reject "tighter organization" as part of a definition does not, of course, mean that it is not commonly the case that literary texts display highly organized language. Cf. below, p. 181, where this point is considered, though not within the framework of definition.

to show the need for a different kind of logic.[8] For example, it is not at all clear what could count as a test of tight organization. The test would have to be specific to literature, for we expect all sorts of other linguistic performances—political speeches, government reports, and so on—to be well organized too. The usefulness of a notion such as "organization" in saving a referential framework in the definition of literature is directly related to the vagueness of its reference, it seems. And so definition by reference to features of the text is preserved only by making it unusable; in general, a theory the only plausible versions of which are very vague is suspect on that ground alone. I do not mean to suggest here that critics are clear that they want to preserve something called the reference theory of meaning; my point is that they have an expectation of what a definition should be which corresponds to that theory, and that to preserve their sense of what a definition should look like, they are forced to take positions that covertly abandon it.

The third[9] way of distinguishing literary texts from others is by postulating special authorship or authorial

---

[8] Hill insists that ". . . literary excellence is not the same thing as the defining characteristic of the species. . . . Definition should be based on formal characteristics, since only a formal definition is readily verifiable" and ". . . utterances which are not characterized by stylistic characteristics which set them off from casual utterances are not literature." (A. Hill, "A Program for the Definition of Literature," *Texas Studies in English* 37 [1958]: 46–52). This is the most honest and forthright statement of the referential position on definition of literature that I have seen.

[9] I omit here any consideration of the view that literature covers all of the written documents of a civilization, which simply avoids the issue of distinguishing literary from nonliterary texts. Cf. the arguments against it by Wellek and Warren, pp. 8–9.

intent, but it is even weaker than the first two. Either we are forced to accept as literature all that is offered as such, or we restrict the category to the products of poets. In practice, we are more likely to think of the situation as the reverse; only when we have decided that a text is "literature" do we accept that its author is a poet. Too many people write verse for us to do otherwise.

It is tempting at this point to bring in the notion of value to solve the problem of definition: literary texts are those texts having literary value. But, within a referential framework at least, this does not get us very far; in fact, the definition appears to be circular, referring to "literary" to define "literature," but not, in turn, explaining "literary." And it cannot appeal to the consistent advocate of a solution on reference-theory lines who is likely to insist that the definition must distinguish one class of texts from others by reference to their structural properties. The rejection of evaluative notions from a referential standpoint is correct as far as it goes—but, as we shall see, its correctness is the final proof that the form of the question is wrong. Only a different logical framework can disentangle the issues involved in the definition of literature.

Whenever an impasse occurs in a theoretical inquiry, it is very likely that the *form* of the question asked must be reexamined; to continue to search for another answer to the same kind of question usually results only in an accumulation of yet more unworkable theories. Often an assumption buried in the form of the question is the reason for the impasse; and once this assumption is found it usually supplies an immediate explanation of the blockage, after which progress in the analysis is possible.

The general form of the question asked so far has been, What is literature? And to judge by the answers usually given, it can be assumed that the question has been thought to be equivalent to, What are the defining properties of literary texts? In what follows I shall argue, first, that both forms of the question are unsatisfactory, in that they confuse the demand for a definition of a class with the quite different question of factual information about the class, and second, that the appropriate form of the question, to begin with, should be this: What circumstances are appropriate to the use of the word "literature"? These two arguments result from one logical point: that not all statements of the form, X is Y (in reply to, What is X?) are to do with a definition, and that, conversely, not all definitions have to do with statements of that form. In other words, factual properties are only sometimes relevant to a definition, and definitions are only sometimes in terms of factual properties. After discussing the form of the question, I shall try to establish a definition of literature that is an answer to the correct form of the question.[10]

[10] M. Weitz (*Hamlet and the Philosophy of Literary Criticism*) goes badly wrong when, having perceived that many terms in literary theory cannot be defined in terms of necessary and sufficient properties, he then goes on to say that in a term like "tragedy" we have a "concept whose very employment requires that it have no defining conditions" (p. 306). This seems to relate to his equating "necessary and sufficient properties" of tragedy with the "necessary and sufficient conditions of its [the word's] use" (p. 307). This is not Wittgensteinian thinking; Weitz is opposing referential definition to no definition at all, instead of to another *kind* of definition, and in so doing he seems to be assimilating the kind of definition that Wittgenstein advocated to a referential kind of definition instead of making of it the necessary alternative to the referential definition. Words without rules for their appropriate

There is an important ambiguity in all sentences of the form, X is Y.[11] Sometimes the verb can be glossed as "is defined as" or "means." If we ask, What is X? and the verb "is" can be so understood, we are asking for the meaning of the word in question, its use in the language that we are speaking. We are here asking only for a fact about that language, not for the kind of fact usually involved in the question, What is the temperature? This question we take to be a demand for a fact about the world at a given time, not for a statement of what "the temperature" means: it is not a demand for a definition. Yet it could be a demand for a definition, and we might

---

use would be meaningless. To be sure, the notion of "tragedy" has changed from time to time during its history, and those changes have produced pseudo-disputes over its "real" meaning. But the logic of definition can easily deal with historical attempts to broaden or narrow the rules of use of a term (as with "tragedy"), without any resort to such implausible notions as the lack of *any* rules of use.

[11] H. Adams agrees that the question "What is literature?" is ambiguous: "Unfortunately it is an ambiguous question. It may mean, What things will we call literature? Or it may mean, Assuming we know what objects we are talking about, how are we to define the word? in terms of what these objects do, how they are made, or what they resemble?" (p. 1). But defining "the word" is a question of finding out what objects we are talking of: the ambiguity of the question is thus not precisely located here. Adams's first question is that of a stipulative definition, which does not come into question here in any case. Hill, on the other hand (p. 47), begins in very precise and relevant fashion by the assertion: "First it is assumed that definition differs from description. Definition should enable the student to recognize all members of the class defined, and to exclude all nonmembers of the class; it has no other purpose." Description, by contrast, concerns characteristics of members of the class which are not to do with recognition. Only Hill's rigidly referential framework prevents him from making better use of this important distinction.

take it as such if uttered, for example, in a foreign accent and bewildered tone, or by a child who could not yet count. With all statements involving "is," we must, therefore, be careful to distinguish what is intended as explanation of a word (i.e., a definition) and what is merely a statement of fact that says something informative about the thing or things concerned, the meaning of the word being already assumed.

The example I have chosen—What is the temperature? —is one in which it is relatively easy to distinguish the two senses of "is." Before going on to discuss specifically, What is literature? I want to discuss a more difficult case in which it is much easier to confuse statements that define a category with statements that give the results of research into the already defined category.[12] Certain broad categories of the social sciences are the subject of much empirical research in order to discover common features within the category: for example, the category of educationally subnormal children. Research can take many directions, going, for example, into physical conditions or social backgrounds. It is quite possible that such research may turn up features that are very important

[12] One problem here is that we have begun to extend this confusion into the very use of the word "definition" and to use it to refer to important facts about a category rather than definitions; e.g., as in such statements as "Aristotle defines man as a rational animal. . . ." Cf. also such sentences as: "Happiness is a fried egg." Dictionaries commonly give both explanations of words and information (i.e., both kinds of statement), and even talk about how the thing designated by the word is used. It is doubtful, however, whether most dictionary compilers realize that their statements about the use of a thing are often themselves defining —they probably think of them as being simply useful extra comments and elaboration.

within the category, and the occurrence of these features may approach coexistence with the extent of the category. And in that case researchers begin to make statements of the form: "educationally subnormal children are children from culturally deprived backgrounds." And from here it seems only a short step to saying that we have "defined" educationally subnormal children. But this would be an error. In the results of research and description, we have information (perhaps central information) about the category, but this is not a definition. The definition of the category is still, as it was before this research began, in terms of the performance of the children. We have found facts about the children, not made a definition of them. The category, and its definition, had to be assumed to exist before research into it could ever begin; and so it was not the meaning of the category that was under investigation, but facts about its composition.

From this example emerges a very important point for the definition of literature: namely, that to begin seeking a definition by investigating the possible common features of the category is a misconception. That sort of empirical inquiry may be beside the point, for there is no guarantee that such common features would have anything to do with a definition. When we seek a definition, what we are seeking is not a statement of the features held in common by the members of the category, but the appropriate circumstances for the use of the word and the features of those circumstances that determine the willingness or unwillingness of the speakers of the language to use the word. Factual research into such a definition is possible, but it will be research not into the common features of the category, but into the responses of speakers of the language to appropriate and inappropriate uses of the word. This will dictate very different tactics to those used before: instead of looking to the center of the category (that is, its most typical and unproblematic cases) and for broad features running through it, it will be more profitable to look at its edges, its marginal members, and to find out what factors cause speakers to hesitate as to whether the word is appropriate or not in a given case. It is from such decisions on the part of the speaker that we can abstract the principles on which instances are included within or excluded from the category. Literary theorists who have sought a definition of literature in common features of easily agreed instances of "literature" have tended to regard the problem of marginal instances as something to be shrugged off with the comment that all categories have blurred edges. To be sure, all categories have shaded edges; but we learn most about those categories by examining the critical decisions made at their edges.

So far, I have tried to establish that common features are not necessarily part of a definition simply because they are common. But my reader may still be puzzled that I think it essential to speak of the "appropriate circumstances" of the use of the word "literature" rather than, say, the *relevant* common features of the category; my argument shows that there may well be common features irrelevant to a definition, but not that we need dispense with the search for features of the members of the category which bear on the speakers' willingness or unwillingness to use the word. It might seem that the discrimination of speakers of the language must be a matter of the concrete differences between objects, and hence that there was no need to substitute the idea of "appropriate circumstances of use of the word" for "relevant common features," since the two ideas should amount to the same thing. But they do not, and I shall attempt to show the difference between them. I shall argue that a definition need not be in terms of any common features at all, and that in some cases—among them literature, educationally subnormal children, and so on—performance is the key area for a definition. If I am correct, then the error of confusing factual statements with definition has (in the case of the definition of literature) been compounded by the error of assuming that properties must be the relevant factor in definition. The two errors are natural partners: for the assumption that empirical characteristics must be involved in a definition must lead, when the search for them has been frustrated by their unavailability, to the introduction of factual statements irrelevant to a definition to fill the resultant vacuum.

It is quite natural that some definitions can be made simply in terms of common properties; for example, all triangles have a common property of being three-sided figures. People use the word appropriately in circumstances of three-sided figures; there is, in this case, no difference between the two formulations referred to above. Whether we look at typical or marginal examples, we get the same answer. But this example comes from the artificial world of geometric constructions; the everyday world is different. In that sphere there are very many cases in which we do not reach the same answer, with the result that one formulation ("appropriate circumstances of use") can be used in all cases, while the other cannot always be relied upon. The word "weed" is a typical case in which the difference shows up.

We experience no difficulty in using a word like "weed"; it represents for gardeners a hard fact of the real world. Weeds can exist, we persecute them and may even pay someone to remove them for us. We suffer annoyance or even economic loss if we lose the battle against them. No one can say that they are elusive things. But when we try to define the word "weed," things are more problematic, and the concept can well appear elusive. Anyone who has tried to explain to his children what weeds are and has watched them then decimate his garden in the belief they are helping him will know that it is incredibly difficult to do. At which point we tend to say (just as we do when finding difficulty in defining literature) that we all know what weeds are, and when the children grow into adults, so will they. But the concept is evidently not taught by means of a catalogue of its empirical properties, and here, too, it is like "literature." We never seem to be able to explain what these concepts mean, but people learn how to use them and then, having done so, shrug off any notion that they might not understand what a weed is or what literature is. In both cases, however, disputes do arise about practical instances and people remain puzzled by them.[13]

We should certainly look in vain for physical proper-

---

[13] A celebrated example of this kind of dispute in ordinary language is provided by the categorization of a tomato as fruit or vegetable, normally carried on in terms of botanical properties of the tomato instead of the only relevant factor, the human decision to group crops in certain ways according to their use by human beings. It is because the tomato is not entirely typical of either pattern of use that its membership of one of the categories is made a matter of contention—not because of its own qualities.

ties characteristic and defining of weeds. A particular
kind of leaf, or a particular family of plants? Clearly not.
A particular size? Neither necessary nor sufficient. Especially easy seeding and hardy plants? This is an interesting attempt, for it gets at why weeds are a nuisance
to us. But it must be seen as a descriptive statement, the
result of research into the category rather than a definition of it. It is neither necessary nor sufficient; not the
latter because there are many hardy plants that are not
weeds, and not the former because we would not fail to
call something a weed merely because it was less hardy
than average. It is an important descriptive statement to
say that the category of weeds contains prominently a
number of hardy plants, but that is not an explanation of
what a weed is defined as. It may seem a counsel of despair to exclaim, when all attempts to explain to a child
the difference between weeds and nonweeds have failed,
"Weeds are plants that I want removed!" But only from
the point of view of the reference theory of meaning has
there been any failure, for the exclamation gets to the
point of the category: weeds are plants that we do not
wish to cultivate.[14] The reason for the child's inability
to use the concept is that he does not yet understand the
social convention as to which plants are not wanted.
From a referential point of view, the definition seems absurd. It commits at least two sins: circularity (weeds are
plants to be weeded out) and inclusion of value judg-

[14] I borrow this example from P. H. Nowell-Smith, *Ethics* (Harmondsworth, Middlesex, 1954), p. 72, though my treatment of it
and conclusions from it concerning the theory of meaning differ
in important respects from his. E.g., I should not say that "To say
that dandelions are weeds is not to *classify* them at all."

ments (weeds are unvalued plants). But in fact this concept, like most concepts that we use in ordinary language, is defined not in terms of physical properties, but of the use that society has for a group of plants. If we object to the classification of a plant as a weed, our objection relates not to the physical structure of the plant, but to the way in which society regards that plant. The basis of the category of weeds is primarily (and as a matter of its definition) a question of the grouping of all plants that society treats in a certain way, and only secondarily (and not as a matter of definition at all) is it a question of any physical similarities between members of the class which might lead to such treatment by the society. Weeds are a matter of hard empirical fact in our lives: they are indeed tangible and have distinct physical qualities that cause problems for us. And this is why we naturally commit the error of looking for the definition of a weed in those qualities that affect us, in its tangible attributes. But the source of the concept lies in our determination to cultivate some plants that (for a great variety of reasons) we can use, and to eradicate others. The category of weeds is composed, therefore, of those things for which we see no use and which we have agreed to eradicate; but if we made different decisions, the membership of the category and therefore the physical attributes of its members could well change without the concept "weed" changing in the least.

If we ask the question, why is sorrel a weed, there will be two distinct answers, and I want to distinguish them carefully. The *reason* for the inclusion of sorrel within the category of weeds is that it is a plant that is not wanted, i.e., not considered horticulturally desirable. But the *cause* of the inclusion of sorrel within the category of weeds by means of such treatment of it in society is a matter of its physical structure. While there is only one reason for the inclusion of a plant in the category of weeds, there may be many different causes (in the sense of "reason" and "cause" which I have used here) located in many different kinds of physical characteristics. This means that the composition of the group may be extremely varied in terms of physical structure and this, in turn, is why we do not necessarily find structural features possessed exclusively by all members of the class. What, in effect, happens in categories of this kind is that human beings reduce a very complex empirical situation to a simplified one in which objects having very little in common may be treated as equivalent for certain human purposes; categories are set up which project, above all, human needs and human decisions to treat things in certain ways for their own reasons. They organize the world rather than describe it. Research into the structure of the category may discover a distinct physical type within it, or several distinct types, or conceivably very little typology at all: the purpose of the category is the only necessary binding factor. The reference theory of meaning, on the other hand, assumes that physical structure is the binding factor.

The category that I have been discussing may seem unusually amorphous. It might be objected that this category is a marginal case, and that most concepts, including the concept of literature, could not be quite so inefficient; if they were, language could not work in any reasonably efficient way. In fact, however, the logic of this category is the same as that of "literature," and it is a logic typical of linguistic concepts: it is words like "triangle" that are marginal and exceptional. We are commonly deceived by the familiarity of our own evaluative organization of the world into thinking that we are describing the structure of the world instead of setting up in our language an organization of it reflecting our own needs and values. I chose the example of "weeds" first of all because it is relatively easy to see it as organizing rather than describing our world: it is not difficult to see that there is a certain sense in which weeds do not exist until we make them into weeds. But we tend to feel that, for example, trees exist quite apart from our wishes and that only solipsistic philosophers would question the fact. Yet on closer inspection it can be seen that the category of trees is much the same as that of weeds. If, for example, we attempt to define the properties of trees, as opposed to bushes, it proves rather hard to do. We first think of shape: a strong, distinct trunk set off from the rest of the plant. Yet a woody plant of this shape and no higher than six feet would be classed as a bush, though a much larger one of the same shape would be a tree. Moreover, what we think of as a bushy shape (no distinct stem) is classified as a tree if sixty feet in height. This makes height seem to be the operative factor. Yet if we take a woody plant of, say twelve feet in height, its classification depends on shape, and it will be a bush or tree accordingly. The reference theory fails us again: neither characteristic is defining, nor is the combination of the two, since they do not operate uniformly and in the same direction. The puzzle is resolved by the same means as the puzzle of the concept "weed": the basis of the distinction between bushes and trees is one of our making, of our

use of them. The point of these categories, which com-
bine shape and size as outstanding characteristics in
such a strange relation to each other, lies once again in
our having distinct attitudes to and uses for them; trees,
for example, are used for timber, bushes for hedges.
And so, for a tree, either a distinct stem or a size sufficient to guarantee substantial thicknesses in the absence
of a distinct stem, is necessary. The distinction is not
botanical but one involving two different uses to which
men put woody plants. In the strictly botanical situation,
this distinction plays no part in setting off one family of
plants against another; it is simply part of the system of
values of our language, an expression of our demands of
the world. Here, as elsewhere, we group experiences according to what we want from them, not according to
their nature. The two factors may coincide—but if they
do not, the former takes precedence.

To return now specifically to the concept of literature:
its logic is, in fact, identical with that of the concept of
weeds. Literary texts are not defined as those of a certain
shape or structure, but as those pieces of language used
in a certain kind of way by the community. They are used
as literature. This sounds circular, just as the description
of "weed" sounded circular, and so the notion of "using
as literature" must be expanded. What we are looking for
is the characteristic use of these particular texts as opposed to other pieces of language. We ordinarily use language as a means to a specific end, to achieve given purposes in our everyday lives. We find out things we need
to know and tell others things we need to communicate
to them. We use such language for a purpose that is relevant to the immediate context of the utterance of that

language. It is a specific context in which a specific person addresses others for specific reasons to do with that context. After the purpose is achieved, the language can be forgotten; its purpose is over. The piece of language is revived after the context is over and done with only if, for some reason, that context is revived, perhaps as an object of study, or perhaps through its relevance to a future specific context. Thus, we study historical documents after their original context is past in order to find out about that context. Such language is still used within a directly utilitarian framework. When, on the other hand, we treat a piece of language as literature, we characteristically do something quite surprising: we no longer accept any information offered as something to act upon, nor do we act on its exhortations and imperatives. We do not generally concern ourselves with whether what it says is true or false, or regard it as relevant to any specific practical purpose. In sum, we no longer respond to it as part of the immediate context we live in and as something to use in our normal way as a means of controlling that context;[15] nor do we concern ourselves with the immediate context from which it emerged,[16] and so are not taking it up to learn, in our normal way, something about that actual everyday context. Assertions about literature

[15] Though scientific treatises do not refer to one particular context, they present no real problems from the point of view of the distinction I make here; in that they refer to a specific class of contexts, and are directly of use as information relating to that class of contexts, they must clearly be categorized as ordinary, rather than literary, language uses.

[16] This statement, though ordinarily true in a fairly obvious way, needs further discussion and elucidation where texts from earlier periods of history are concerned. See the discussion in chapter 5.

similar to these may well, in themselves, be familiar; but what is here of the utmost importance is that they are not simply true statements about literature, but constitute the *definition* of literature: literary texts are defined as those that are used by the society in such a way that *the text is not taken as specifically relevant to the immediate context of its origin.*

Ordinary pieces of language, then, function in the context in which they originate, perish after that context is gone, and only reappear afterwards as part of that context when it is under study. But the characteristic use of texts as literary is one that lifts them out of the context of their origin and no longer assumes that they are part of the practical give and take of any particular context. They are read widely in the community outside their original context and are not referred to that particular context or to any other. A man may express a lament over something that has happened to him and arouse sympathy among those who hear him. So far this is all the ordinary use of language. But when what he has said arouses an interest among those who have no necessary sympathy for him personally, then it has begun to become one of the literary texts of the community; that is to say, the character of the language and what it says has now become an important concern independent of what can be inferred from it to an actual situation. Whenever the ordinary use of language to communicate to someone in a specific context is no longer evident, and the piece of language is no longer regarded as one having interest only for its original utterer, those addressed by him, and those (present or future) who have interest in that whole situation, it is being treated as literature. And here, "being treated as literature" means not just "used as literature is used," but actually "established as a literary text": the class of literary texts is the class of those to which we respond in this way.

In speaking of this characteristic use of literary texts, I have consciously avoided some possible formulations of it. For example, I have avoided saying that in our response to a literary text the emphasis is on the message itself;[17] or that it is on the use of language; or that literary texts are admired rather than used for practical purposes. All of these are formulations of the kind of distinction I have been making which are inadequate and restrictive to the point that they have naturally caused many critics to want to question whether such a distinction should exist at all. To say that we admire literary texts (rather than use them for any practical purpose) has seemed too trivial to be appropriate for the extremely serious experiences with which they are concerned; to say that we are concerned with the use of language has seemed to contrast with concern with the content of what language says, and so again must seem to avoid the seriousness of the fundamental ideas and issues that these texts contain; while the notion of a "message," on the other hand, suggests simplification. These notions have

[17] I am thinking here of Jakobson, p. 356, who goes on to make this idea depend on formal properties of the language concerned, e.g., paronomasia. Actually, it need not imply this, since the formulation is not in dualistic terms; "the message for itself" can easily be taken to refer as much to content as to poetic (in this sense, superficial) devices. But even so, it would still have the drawback of implying sender and receiver, and therefore a particular context. I should make clear, however, in spite of these misgivings about Jakobson's formulations, that I am not out of sympathy with much that is basic in his argument.

been associated often with an aestheticism that preferred
to think of a pleasurable rather than a meaningful experience of literary texts. I shall pursue these issues in
their more appropriate context in the following chapters
on evaluation and on textual analysis; I mention them
here only to make it clear that the definition that I have
formulated avoids this kind of restriction ("aestheticism")
on the quality of, or issues present to, our concern with
literary texts. The definition has in no way restricted the
possible content of that concern other than to specify that
the original context of origin is not relevant to literary
texts in the way it is with ordinary language. To show
that literary texts are not taken to relate to the context
of their origin, as other pieces of language do, is not to
remove them from the context of life itself, or to remove
from them any issues that the larger context may involve.
To put the matter more bluntly: the definition that I have
reached is a necessary consequence of adopting a logic
of definition that (unlike the logic of the reference theory
of meaning) is appropriate for the concept of literature.
It has, as yet, nothing to do with the dispute between the
two opposed views of "aestheticism" and "literature is
about life"; and it neither originates from nor results in
a decision to side with the former view against the latter
in a dispute that, as I shall attempt to show, is a thorough-
ly mistaken and unnecessary one.

As is the case in the category of weeds, the membership of the category of literary texts is simply what is
currently agreed to be usable in this way by members of
the community. The proviso must be made here, however, that the agreement seems never to be quite so clear
as in the case of weeds, though there is still substantial

agreement. Part of the reason for this seems to be that the case of weeds is fairly finite: no new members of the class of plants occur so that no new categorizations become necessary. On the other hand, new linguistic texts are constantly being offered for use as literature. We have already noted that the composition of the category of weeds, and the typical physical structure of its members, could change without change in the meaning of the word; the same is equally true of literature. Because of the constant supply of new possibilities, there will be a steady stream of new instances accepted for inclusion and old members discarded. We should note here a central principle: in an important sense, texts are made into literature by the community, not by their authors. To be sure, authors endow them with the qualities that are the causes (in the contrastive sense used above) of their being so treated by the community. But it is the agreement of the community that makes them into literature, in that the category is defined as those texts used in this way by the community, not as those texts offered for that use. The notion may in one way sound paradoxical, but in another way it receives support from common sense. The membership of the class of texts "English Literature" cannot seriously be thought to include my (or anyone else's) schoolboy verse. Such things are attempts at literary status and usage, but the texts are rarely accepted outside the context of their originators to become part of the literature of a community. Many are offered; but few are chosen.[18] The converse is also

---

[18] This throws great doubt on the notion of studying, as literature, the forgotten literary compositions of an historical period. Only on the view that everything composed with intent to

true: just as the class of literary texts cannot be equivalent to the class of those texts offered for literary treatment, neither can it be confined to a selection exclusively
from that class. Many texts not so offered are included;
for example, Gibbon's *Decline and Fall of the Roman
Empire.* Here, indeed, is a very good example with which
to test my definition of literary treatment. For, when we
begin to regard Gibbon as literature, we characteristically stop worrying about the facts of Roman history;
we cease to regard the book primarily as historical information, neither do we relate it to the context of the
remaining evidence for what actually happened in Rome.
Truth or falsity relevant to the specific historical context is no longer the main point, for Gibbon's is no longer
the book for that purpose; we now read it as a narrative
with its own kind of rationale.

An interesting misconception about the definition of
literature is shown in the claim often made by literary
historians and biographers that their work, if well organized and otherwise well written and executed, becomes artistic and hence a piece of literature and literary
art.[19] This claim actually rests on a number of theoretical

---

be literature actually achieves membership of the class of literary
texts can this be done—and that view is an error. I pursue this
point below, chapter 7. The revival of a forgotten text not as
object of study but as a literary text in its own right is, of course,
nothing to do with this issue.

[19] E.g., R. Spiller, "Literary History," in *The Aims and Methods
of Scholarship in Modern Languages and Literatures,* p. 55: ". . .
the products of research can have meaning only when they are
organized around the insights and aesthetic controls of the artist—
in this case, the literary historian." Also L. Edel, "Literature and
Biography," in *Relations of Literary Study,* p. 70: "Such a biography achieves its primary purpose of being a work of lit-

errors. The first of them is that to which I have already pointed: the error of assuming that literariness consists in textual properties, instead of the decision by the community to use the given text in a characteristic fashion. There will certainly be many well-executed biographies and literary histories that are never admitted to the category of texts used in this way, and few that will be so used. The second error of this view consists in an exceedingly restricted view of empirical science, in which anything going beyond mere cataloging of the facts of research is thought of as artistic rather than scientific. I shall discuss below in much greater detail the role of this restricted notion of empiricism in other areas of literary theory;[20] for the moment, it suffices to say that to organize one's material well and to abstract relevantly from it should be standard procedure in any field of research; we cannot seek "literariness" in such things.

In this chapter I have attempted to set the discussion of the definition of literature on a sound basis by extricating it from the reference theory of meaning. Much depends on the results obtained thereby, and upon their being distinctly at variance with those results to which the reference theory of meaning leads.[21] The chief points

---

erary art." Apart from the two major theoretical points made in the text, one further observation may be made: even in the event that a biography came to be treated as literature, it would not *necessarily* be its excellence as a biography that was the cause of this development. A text may function as both a biography and a piece of literature, and be judged differently in the two quite different uses.

[20] See below, chapter 6.

[21] For example, a very recent article attempting to show that the intentional fallacy is not a fallacy (Peter D. Juhl, "Intention and Literary Interpretation," *Deutsche Vierteljahrsschrift für Lit-*

that I have attempted to establish will be relevant to many other issues of literary theory that need reorientation; I shall therefore set them out in summary form to end this discussion of definition.

The category of literary texts is not distinguished by defining characteristics but by the characteristic use to which those texts are put by the community. Literary texts are those used in a way that is characteristically different from other uses of language. This invalidates much of the work of those linguists who attempt to find distinguishing characteristics of poetry and poetic language: in practice, they are really dealing with the permitted extra stock of expressive devices (poetic license), which literary texts may or may not exploit, and not with the nature of literary texts.[22] The occasional and peripheral is here promoted to the central and defining. Contrary to the view that value must not be brought into a definition[23] (which, it is often said, should

---

eraturgeschichte und Geisteswissenschaft 6 [1971]: 1–23), has as one of its main assumptions the assertion that "There are, I think, at least two important distinguishing characteristics of imaginative literature . . ." (p. 11). Chapter 5, in particular, will show numerous other ways in which the issue of definition has confused other questions in theory of literature.

[22] Cf. a very exposed version of this in Freeman, *Linguistics and Literary Style*, p. 15: ". . . a set of linguistic characteristics which uniquely specifies *poetic* language as opposed to *nonpoetic* language. . . ." Linguists working on literature have shown that all the careful and precise research in the world cannot make up for an initial theoretical mistake.

[23] This is perfectly consistent with the facts of experience in doubtful cases; when speakers of English reflect on whether they should call a particular text "literature," they always talk of its literary value. As always, it is at the edges of the category that its underlying prescriptive power becomes apparent.

be a matter of observable characteristics), the definition of literature must, like the definition of weed, bring into a definition in a very central way the notion of value: the category is that of the texts that are considered worth treating in the way that literary texts are treated, just as weeds are the members of a category of things that are thought worthy of the treatment accorded to weeds. In both cases the definition states an element of the system of values of the community. The membership of the category is based on the agreement to use the texts in the way required and not on the intent of the writer that the text shall be so used. Texts not originally designed for this use may be included, while texts that were consciously designed for this use may not be included. The question, What is literature? is not then, as Sartre treats it, a matter of why writers write and what they are attempting to do; it is concerned with the acceptance of texts as literature by the community. We must distinguish the question of definition from the question of factual research in the ambiguous question, What is literature? The former is concerned with the distinctive use which indicates that a text is for the purposes of the society a literary text, the latter with empirical analysis of those texts (the category already having been established) and thus with information about literature. We should distinguish the *reason* for the inclusion of a text within the category (the fact that it can be and is used in the way characteristic of the category) from the *causes* of its inclusion (its empirical characteristics, which must be presumed to be the reason for its suitability for this use). Analysis of the texts is to do with causes of inclusion, not with the reason for inclusion, and thus not with

definition. Analysis of the empirical characteristics of
literary texts is the beginning of an analysis of the function of literature, in the sense of its role in the life of
the community, and to this point in particular I shall
return in later chapters. I have avoided the formulation
of the characteristic use of literature as, for example, its
being contemplated for its own sake, precisely because
this might suggest that literature had no important function in the community. That literature is language that
no longer functions in a particular context does not mean
that it does not have a general social function; on the
contrary, it indicates precisely that its function has become a more general one in the life of the community.[24]

[24] This issue is not clarified in the account of Wellek and Warren, p. 17: "The nature and the function of literature must, in
any coherent discourse, be correlative. The use of poetry follows
from its nature: every object or class of objects is most efficiently
and rationally used for what it is, or is centrally. . . . Similarly,
the nature of an object follows from its use: it is what it does."
Wellek and Warren want to move toward the view that literary
works can have many uses (as historical documents, etc.) but that
they are centrally literary in nature and that historical treatment
is not literary treatment; this is recognizably a position within the
"criticism vs. history" controversy. But they still tend to think of
the textual characteristics as defining, with the result that the
phrases "follows from" and "must be correlative" do not pin down
the correct logical relation between the nature and the use of
literature, which must be one of identity. A further important
complication arising from the way in which Wellek and Warren
link the nature and function of literature must be noted at this
point: though the nature and function of literary texts are the
same thing if the word "function" is understood in a limited sense
as referring to a text's overtly functioning and being treated as a
literary text, there is another, quite different sense of function
which concerns the social importance of literature; in that second
(and perhaps more appropriate) sense it is nothing to do with
definition. The two senses of "function" here are related to the

Finally, the failure of all referential definitions need not lead us to take the view that no definition of literature is possible, or the more extreme view that literature is, in principle, an undefinable concept.

These are the main points of principle that emerge from an analysis of the issues involved in a definition of literature. The succeeding chapters of this book will, to some extent, show how these points can be developed and built upon in other areas of literary theory, and will confirm their validity from quite different lines of argument.

---

distinction I have made between "reason" and "cause"; I pursue this question further in chapter 8.

3: The Aims of the
Study of Literature

THE WORD "study" is used here in the broadest possible sense: I mean by it any kind of concern with literature that goes beyond the mere reading of literary texts. It will thus include criticism and any other kinds of statements that are designed to illuminate or inform us in any way about literary texts. I want to consider the possible uses and purposes of this kind of activity; what it can or what it should do, and how it should proceed to achieve its purposes.

There is an important preliminary distinction here, which is commonly overlooked by literary critics. It has often been said that the purpose of criticism is to render the text more enjoyable to the reader, to encourage and excite his appreciation of the text, to explicate it, and to point out to him what he might otherwise have missed—in short, to enlighten and increase the enjoyment of a public less well read than the critic himself.[1] Sometimes, the critic himself is included as one who

[1] Cf. e.g., Rodway, "What the Critics Really Need": ". . . its [criticism's] function is to enlighten some reading public less well-equipped than the critic" (p. 160).

benefits by his critical activity, which is held to deepen his relationship with the text under discussion; and no doubt that, in turn, enables him to do an even better job for the public. This view sounds reasonable enough, and it is certainly not false to say that criticism helps the critic himself and the reading public to appreciate literature. But as an answer to the basic question, What are the aims of literary study? it avoids the issue; it does not approach the question of what it is that literary study should concern itself with, and instead only suggests the appropriate recipients of the results of those concerns. It is all very well to say that criticism should increase the understanding of literature, but this leaves untouched what must be the whole point of talking about the aims of criticism: what is the nature of this increased understanding and how is it to be pursued? In any field of knowledge, it is possible to make a distinction between the knowledge itself and the uses to which it is put. To ask what are the aims of the field is to ask a question that may seem to relate to the uses of the knowledge sought rather than its character. But the logically prior question (and the more important one), asks what kind of knowledge we are seeking. As an example of an answer to the more important question, take, for example, the common view[2] that the aim of criticism is to recreate the original circumstances of composition of a text—to ascertain why it was written and for what audience. As we shall see, this view is problematic; but it is certainly an answer (whether correct or incorrect) to the kind of question that

[2] E.g., S. M. Schreiber, *An Introduction to Literary Criticism* (Oxford, 1965), p. 16; cf. also H. Gardner, *The Business of Criticism*, pp. 18ff.

must be faced before we are in a position to know what kind of help criticism can give to a reading public.

The transmittal of results, then, is a limited, practical question: the tactics and language appropriate to a given audience should obviously be chosen, but to pursue such considerations would not be of central relevance to theory of literature. Accordingly, I am only interested here in the question of the aims of literary study in the sense of the character of the knowledge worth seeking. Before leaving this issue, however, I must point to some further disadvantages under which literary study has labored as a result of failing to distinguish the two kinds of questions involved.

When the aims of a study are formulated in terms of the application and use of its results, questions of presentation become entangled with issues of principle. An impressive literary style becomes one of the marks of "good criticism," and the need for direct entertainment in presentation produces demands that all technical language be avoided.[3] No doubt a clear presentation is always useful in any field, whatever the audience; and, equally, uncontrolled jargon is always to be avoided, anywhere. But the avoidance of any specialist language would effectively restrict students of literature to the terms of ordinary language, and any distinctions that they found to be necessary as a result of their investigation, but which were not already present in ordinary language, simply could not be made. Meanwhile the promotion of rhetorical effect from being an issue of presentation to being a basic aim of criticism, has certainly had much to do with the prevalence of pretentious but empty criticism. The

[3] Rodway, p. 160; cf. my "Reply to Rodway," pp. 113–114.

communication of knowledge originally formulated in a specialist language (and precisely statable only in those terms) to a more general audience is a problem in any field, and there is no reason to believe that literary study is in principle an exception, even though the practical problem appears to be much less severe than it is in other fields. At the moment, the gap between research and popularization hardly exists in literary study; but the theoretical distinction must still be made, and may become a practical necessity at any time.

Even if there were agreement that practical usefulness for enhancing public enjoyment and understanding of literature was the only justification of literary study, the basic question would still remain: What constitutes an understanding of literature, and how can it be revealed more fully for public enjoyment? But in any case, I do not think that any field of study can be defined exclusively in terms of relevance to a practical purpose, or that it can operate successfully if it has always to answer to an immediate demand for practical usefulness. What is found may be fairly quickly useful, never useful, or eventually useful; but one can never know which of these it will be until found, for the character of a discovery is not knowable in advance. The process of extending knowledge is, by definition, getting at things that one does not yet know about, and this means that one does not know whether or in what way they will be useful.

In any field of inquiry, knowledge is evaluated in terms of its being central or peripheral in the field, a criterion that takes precedence over immediate practical usefulness. If a student of literature discovers something central and important to the field, he cannot be criticized for not having provided a direct contribution to the enjoyment of literature. In practice, the direct connection between knowledge and enjoyment is often challenged by readers who say, for example, that a critical analysis of a poem actually disturbs their enjoyment of it. To this, critics generally reply, rather magisterially, that no genuine appreciation of a poem can be disturbed by analysis, that it can only be deepened in that process. But such a response is quite unnecessary. Whether a reader is helped or not by a piece of knowledge is an individual matter: I suspect that most people are, but some are not. That critics are commonly trapped into making this an absolute matter is another indication of the problems they run into in making the uses of their results the rationale for the results themselves.

The distinction I have been making does not imply that knowledge is always, in literary study or elsewhere, a pursuit justified for its own sake, with occasional useful benefits that are not the true researcher's concern. My point is that "knowledge for its own sake" is an argument that transcends this particular inquiry, and is just as acceptable or unacceptable in physics as it is in literary study; it is just as easy (and logically the same point) to argue that we would be better off leading a simple life without washing machines as to argue that we should retain our natural, untutored responses to literary texts. Literary study and physics can both be justified as useful fields of research, in that they are prominent in human experience, and likely to be worth investigation; only if the demand for practical use is too direct, as has certainly been the case in literary study, does a field suffer from the practical interest in it by having restrictions placed on the kinds of questions that it can ask, or the kinds of answers that it can give.

So far, I have argued that the aim of literary study must be the investigation of literary texts; this proposition might seem a truism unless seen in the light of the particular distinction I have been making between this as a primary aim, and such secondary matters as facilitating appreciation of literature.[4] But the proposition is still insufficiently analyzed; one distinction has been made, but many more are necessary: What kinds of statement must be sought, and how?

It is at this point that a characteristic vagueness in literary theory is frequently to be observed. James Thorpe, having alluded to all sorts of possible ways of proceeding, then observes that the literary scholar's purpose is "to reach a greater understanding of literature."[5] The use of this kind of phrase takes us not in the direction that literary theory must go, but the reverse; with Thorpe we move from particular statements to an unanalyzed, vague one, instead of the other way around. Thorpe's statement avoids theoretical analysis; the purpose of literary theory should be to go beyond such statements and to begin

---

[4] This notion of literary criticism as a branch of knowledge and study is clearly present in Wellek and Warren, *Theory of Literature*, p. 3, and in Kayser, *Das sprachliche Kunstwerk*, p. 11; but in both these cases the predominant distinction was between the notion of an intellectual inquiry and the individual's (emotional) response to the text.

[5] J. Thorpe, *Aims and Methods*, p. viii. W. Sutton's "Literature and criticisms are social functions," (*Modern American Criticism*, [Englewood Cliffs, N.J., 1963], p. 289) is equally vague and unhelpful; and G. Hough's "Criticism is a natural activity for the literate man," in *An Essay on Criticism*, p. 4, similarly avoids probing the aims and function of criticism.

making distinctions. We need to ask in precise terms: What advances the understanding of literature? What kinds of statements are involved? and What is their logical relation? It seems clear that in practice, many different kinds of statements are made, and that these are categorized as the result of many different kinds of "approach," such as psychological or historical. But, again, in practice it has proved extraordinarily difficult to sort out the logical relation of these different kinds of statements. This has evidently been another of the factors that has produced a laissez-faire atmosphere in criticism; there are many different kinds of approach, it seems, and all apparently help to promote the greater understanding of literature. Wise elders in the field tend to counsel tolerance of any approach but at the same time (rather inconsistently) warn against possible irrelevance to literature;[6] meanwhile, an occasional outburst against such lack of theoretical discrimination comes from a convinced advocate of one approach.[7]

---

[6] Cf., once more, Thorpe, *Aims and Methods*, p. viii.

[7] See, for example, F. Crews's essay "Literature and Psychology" in *Relations of Literary Study*, and his "Anaesthetic Criticism," in *The New York Review of Books* 14 (1971): 31–35 and 49–52. The destructive parts of Crews's arguments are superior to anything that he offers in the way of a constructive alternative; there is, for example, much to admire in his diagnosis of the amateurism and gentlemanly (but self-protective) civilized restraint, which he thinks relevant to the avoidance of theoretical issues and the choices that result from them on the part of literary critics. His point that the general tolerance of all approaches often amounts to an intolerance of anything that is sharp and challenging is well taken. To embrace all new ideas with the same enthusiasm is indeed to avoid coming to terms with any of them. On the other hand, it must be allowed that another real factor in the situation is a genuine and unsolved theoretical puzzle about the logical

Where can we find a secure beginning, a standard of
relevance in the light of which the various kinds of statements about literature generated by various different approaches can be evaluated? It is tempting, and usual, to
place literary texts at the center of our attention, and

---

relation of many different kinds of critical statements, for which
Crews offers no solution; some critics, to be sure, are happy to
protect themselves by being tolerant of everything and, so, intol-
erant of any sharp and challenging assertion, but others might well
appreciate something on these lines that was really convincing.
Crews is inclined to see all resistance to his Freudianism as being
in the former category; I should think that there must be many
who find his positive assertions unconvincing, as I do. That the
prevailing atmosphere in literary theory is one of "civilized restraint," as Crews terms it, probably accounts for the tendency
in Wellek and Warren to avoid sharpness of formulation; they
often interrupt an analytic argument of great promise and show a
strange unwillingness to draw any conclusions from it which
might seem to be a lapse from an overall stance of seeing all
sides of the problem. In this kind of atmosphere, it took courage
for R. Cohn (an example to which my colleague M. Kanes kindly
drew my attention) to offer his view of Mallarmé as one that
strove to be authentic, rather than only one among various possible interpretations of that poet (*Towards the Poems of Mallarmé*,
[Berkeley and Los Angeles, 1965], p. 7). There are, of course,
logical problems in such a view, of the kind pursued below in
chapter 6. But Cohn's intent in putting the matter so provocatively
is obviously to avoid the prevalent manner of civilized restraint by
invoking standards of relevance to Mallarmé's work, and he is
probably correct in saying that the opposing view is held by individuals "who do not, I am convinced, care much about Mallarmé." Critics often go beyond a mere reluctance to discriminate
between various kinds of statements to a position of enthusiastic
wallowing in the resultant intellectual mire. E. Heller, for example, asserts that criticism of literature "cannot be taught, but
only 'caught,' like a passion. . . ." (*The Disinherited Mind*, [Har-
mondsworth, Middlesex, 1961], p. ix); this is a *reductio ad absurdum* of critical laissez-faire in its rejection of any standards
for an intelligent statement.

then to say that we are looking for statements that are relevant to them, that elucidate them, explain them, and so on. We are to make statements about literature—and what could be a more simple, direct beginning? But unfortunately, this beginning masks a central logical error, the diagnosis of which is the key to our puzzle: it lies in the assumption that the nature of any phenomenon in itself can define the framework of an investigation. It is, as we shall see, another of the errors that the reference theory of meaning encourages us to make: too much reliance is placed on the physical characteristics of things, and too little on their characteristic use. If we ask the data to provide their own framework of investigation, all we get is a large number of different frameworks and no way of choosing between them, or evaluating their competing claims.

Let us first turn from the study of literature to a consideration of some other established frameworks of investigation: physics, economics, psychology, for instance. All of these frameworks tend to concern data that we think of as central to them: atoms, money, people. But these disciplines are not restricted to this material, nor is the material exclusively theirs; the framework of investigation is not defined by the material that it considers, but by the nature of its characteristic concern with that material.[8] The relatively central nature of some kinds of material is a product of the nature of that concern, not a defining feature of it. From the standpoint of eco-

[8] The pseudo-disputes among undergraduate majors in various fields as to whose subject is the most basic usually result from the insight that everything in human life can be treated in economic terms (or psychological terms, and so on), without the further insight that the same is true of all other fields.

nomics, everything is relevant, not just money; a break-through in physics can become an important economic "fact," the wealth of a nation may reside partly in its art treasures, and the ecology of wild life reserves may become a strong economic factor for an African country whose big game is a tourist attraction. It is not difficult to see that psychology could take hold of the same range of phenomena and make of them psychological facts about human involvement in art, in animals, in danger and/or leisure, even in money. For a physicist, moon research may be basic research into the physical structure of the world; for a political scientist it may be part of American foreign policy and relations with Russia. Examples can easily be multiplied, and a few easy examples can be seen as we approach the field of literature. Shakespeare is poetry for students of literature, but perhaps part of the British economy for economists. The important general point here is that almost any piece of empirical material can be construed in terms of several different fields of inquiry, and all frameworks construe data in their own terms, not terms imposed by the data. It follows that it would obviously be nonsense to say that any framework of investigation could be defined as "any and all statements about a given phenomenon"; the definition of a framework of investigation must be in terms not of restriction to certain kinds of material but in terms of a particular kind of analysis of and concern with that material. It would even be dangerous to specify that a certain kind of analysis would always be concerned centrally with certain kinds of material, and conversely that certain kinds of material would only reach central importance in a certain kind of framework of investigation. As to the former case, economic analysis is possible even in societies without money; as to the latter, the oratorical style of political figures can have central political importance.

The notion that the facts of a field are its building blocks and establish its status as a field comes partly from a misconception about the facts themselves: a historical fact, for example, is not just anything that happened, but, as Carr[9] has argued, only an event held to be significant for certain purposes. What we think of as historical facts (1066, for instance) are already lifted out of the continuum of millions of actual events by the concerns of a historical framework of investigation. Goethe put the point with great precision when he asserted, in a celebrated aphorism, "dass alles Faktische schon Theorie ist," that any statement thought of simply as a "fact" had already been interpreted and formulated in the light of a theory. If, then, the "facts" of a field ever seem to establish the field, that is because they have already been established by the field; they have been selected and formulated in its terms, since facts are facts only in the context of a given field of inquiry.

We cannot, then, derive our standard of relevance to literary study from the texts themselves: merely talking about the texts is not any guarantee that we are involved in a literary framework of investigation. A framework of investigation can never be defined as "statements about this phenomenon." The eruption of Mount Etna can be considered as a geologically interesting event, an ecologically and biologically interesting upheaval, or an economic event; but the only framework that can afford to

[9] E. H. Carr, *What is History?* (New York, 1961), pp. 6ff.

simply define its parameters as "statements about the Mount Etna eruption" is a popular book, aiming to interest and entertain the general public. Any serious study must place the event in a definite framework of investigation.

When someone takes in his hand a literary text[10] and makes statements about it, he may be involved in one of a number of different kinds of inquiry. He may be a historian, interested in the text as one written at a particular time and giving evidence of certain characteristics of that time. He may be a biographer, interested in building a picture of a particular man (the author of the text) and therefore using the text to help him build that picture. What he cannot intelligently do is have no aim in mind in studying the book; because then his framework of investigation would be, in effect, "any statement about this text"—a nonsense framework, and one that cannot avoid statements that even the most eclectic critics would regard as trivial and irrelevant, for no context within which the book had ever appeared could be in principle excluded. I do not wish to be misunderstood here: I am not yet discussing the question of whether historical knowledge or any other kind of knowledge is relevant within the framework of literary study. My point is only, at this stage, the logical one that the given framework provides its standards of relevance, and that no piece of material can of itself provide those standards. Historical state-

[10] I have used a similar argument in dealing with Schiller's writings on aesthetic theory, which have also been used in many different ways; there, too, I have objected to the virtual definition of a field of inquiry as "statements about these texts." Cf. my *Schiller's "Kalliasbriefe" and the Study of his Aesthetic Theory* (Paris and The Hague, 1969), pp. 22–29.

ments may or may not be relevant to a literary framework of investigation (a point to which I shall return), but they would have to be distinguished from the same statements made within a historical framework and justified in a different way.

R. Spiller,[11] for example, asserts that "Shakespeare's works as a whole may be taken as a reflection of and comment upon the political thinking of Elizabethan England," and that "Goethe provides a critique of the German Romantic philosophy." Let us concede that these may be true statements. Shakespeare and Goethe may well be taken as relevant to and among the facts of political history and the history of philosophy. But from the mere truth of these statements it does not follow that they are relevant to the study of literature, unless the study of literature is defined as "statements about literary texts." For Spiller, it is enough that the statements involved are true. He has defined a field in terms of phenomena, rather than the characteristic treatment of phenomena. And this is yet another logical error that is basic to "wise eclecticism"; for to assume that the standard for a relevant statement in literary study is merely that it should be about a literary text is to bring about a situation where many different kinds of statements are made, and no intellectual framework exists to determine their relationship. The net is cast so wide that the field has become shapeless and lacks the capacity to distinguish what is central and important from what is not: that a statement exists and involves literary texts in any way is the only touchstone of relevance. Under these circumstances, no progress is possible.

[11] Spiller, "Literary History," p. 49.

An appeal to the greater understanding of literature[12] is in practice a common means of evading a standard of relevance and so, in effect, of defining the field of inquiry as "statements about these texts." Meanwhile, resistance to the acceptance of a standard of relevance tends to focus on an apparently negative side to such a standard; to decide that certain statements are less relevant than others or to pronounce them irrelevant to our inquiry is to risk losing something, and surely, it is said, the more we know the better. It may seem unnecessarily austere to exclude what seems interesting because of an excessive concern with demarcation. But it is not at all difficult to show the positive advantages for literary study of insisting on a clear standard of relevance, as well as the considerable disadvantages of not observing such a standard.

When we group together statements that are within the same framework of investigation and which, therefore, have the same basic aim, we achieve much more than mere tidiness; only through such a clear decision to pursue a particular aim can an inquiry be taken to a higher level of complexity. A shotgun approach of "statements about literary texts" results characteristically in a large number of isolated statements about the texts which do not interact and have no relation one to the other; but if comparable statements are taken together they generate

---

12 Sutton, p. 283: "All possible sources of illumination are needed." This attitude is present throughout J. Thorpe's introduction to *Relations of Literary Study*, and his introduction to *Aims and Methods* is full of exhortations to use all methods to achieve "a greater understanding of literature." Cf. also W. Scott's compendium: *Five Approaches of Literary Criticism* (New York, 1962). A recent German example is J. Hermand's *Synthetisches Interpretieren* (Munich, 1968), e.g., p. 167.

more complex and interesting statements through their relations to each other. From this kind of grouping together of comparable statements a methodology of the field arises;[13] individual statements are seen both in the light of the general logical and conceptual problems of the field which have emerged in the past, and in contrast to other possible statements in the field, a contrast from which they derive their significance.

In the kind of literary criticism that concerns itself with a variety of different statements about literary texts, those that might be relevant to a literary framework are often very undeveloped statements—of necessity so, since they are made and then dropped in order that the critic can go on to something else. Some typical kinds of incipient literary statements might be that a given poet wrote symbolic poetry or that he used natural imagery. These undeveloped statements have often passed in criticism when surrounded by "interesting" facts about, for example, the context of the origin of the texts. Stripped of these surroundings, they would seem trivial. Something more specific would be needed to gain our interest. If we were to avoid wandering to other kinds of statements, these would look inadequate, and so we should pursue more complicated questions within the relevant framework. What particular kinds of symbolism or natural imagery, and for what purposes? We should immediately begin to make contrasts between this particular version of such things and others, and try to reach distinctive statements

[13] Cf. again my *Schiller's "Kalliasbriefe"* for a demonstration of how this argument applies to that particular example, and how vague, general, unfocused, and "interesting" collections of assorted statements have inhibited the investigation of Schiller's aesthetic theory in its most relevant context, that of aesthetic theory.

that apply specifically to the material under consideration; and so a precise focus in studying literature leads to
statements that are more developed, interesting, and
sophisticated. The procedure of "shotgun" criticism has
always been to discuss literary texts in noncontrastive
general terms, which could apply to any one of a hundred
poets, and then to move to specific statements from a different perspective (usually biographical). This procedure
gives the illusion of having dealt in specific terms with
the particular poet's work, but the relevantly distinctive
and specific things are ignored. And here we see the real
source of the insistence that knowing all sorts of things
about a text is interesting; the statements made specifically about the literary text as literature have often not been
at all interesting, and the resultant vacuum has been filled
by other means. If the relevant statements were genuinely
interesting, it would never seem satisfying to break the
thread of those statements with something irrelevant to
the main framework of the inquiry, and so to stop the development of the argument within that framework. "The
more we know about literature, the better," does, therefore, turn out to have a very negative side: in that it
breaks down the principle of relevance, and turns the inquiry toward idle curiosity and away from the development of initial elementary statements within the relevant
framework, it ensures that we will know less about literature in the more important sense. It is of no use here
to say that we are free to return, after such excursions,
to more relevant statements; those who pursue them do
not think of them as excursions at all. Judged by the
same kind of standard, the excursions themselves would
also look uninteresting: the facts of economic history that

we are commonly offered, or those of political history, or psychology (comments on the author's personality) would not seem remarkable if related to those fields in any systematic way.

We must, then, determine a framework of investigation and a standard of relevance to that framework, use that standard to group together statements that are comparable and can be meaningfully contrasted, and develop those statements in the light of the accumulated knowledge and methodology of the framework. The popular view that in literary criticism all knowledge about texts is useful and all approaches to the texts contribute to the greater understanding of literature, accompanied by its tempting appeal to such virtues as manysidedness and tolerance,[14] only results in muddle and confusion, less real knowledge, and a level of intellectual interest rarely above the lowest possible.

In this chapter, I have argued first that literary study cannot be controlled by the question of its use to readers of literary works, and thus that its aims should not primarily be thought of in those terms; and second, that if it is to progress and develop, literary study must not define itself as "statements about literary texts" but as an intellectual framework of investigation to which some kinds of statements about literature are relevant, given the standards of relevance that emerge from that frame-

[14] Many pointless disputes in literary criticism are caused by the attempt to contrast statements from different intellectual frameworks as if they belonged to the same framework. But it is not a virtue of the kind of "tolerance" I have referred to that it forbids such disputes; for that same kind of tolerance allows the two kinds of fundamentally different statements within the same framework in the first place, and so invites the mistaken contrast.

work. The question now arises, What is that framework? and What are its standards of relevance? Given the definition of literature set out in the preceding chapter, the framework of investigation may be stated as follows: the study of literature must be concerned with those aspects of the society and of its literary texts which are relevant to the society's characteristic and defining use of them. This framework of investigation poses a large question, but it provides a standard of relevance that can be used to begin the task of breaking down critical laissez-faire and "wise eclecticism."

This formulation of the aim of literary study is an end to this chapter, but it is the essential beginning to the remaining chapters. These deal, in succession, with different parts of the framework defined: the evaluation of texts as literary texts; the information relevant to their meaning as literary texts; the structure and meaning of literary texts; general statements about the composition of the category of literary texts; the social function of literature; and finally the relation of this framework of investigation to others. I turn first of all to a consideration of the logical problems involved in talking of what it is that makes a text valuable as literature.

4: Evaluation

PROBABLY NO AREA of theory of literature has received
more attention than that of evaluation of literary works.
On the other hand, no area of literary theory is (or ought
to be) so dependent on advances in logical theory and in
theory of value. And this is why the most heavily culti-
vated area of literary theory has been the least effectively
handled in the past. That intricate logical problems occur
here is indicated by the fact that we constantly encoun-
ter two very plausible but apparently contradictory points
of view; on the one hand it is often argued that as critics
we are above all concerned with literary merit,[1] while the

[1] A wide variety of scholars of differing general viewpoints on
literature and literary criticism take essentially this position; for
example, Crews ("Anaesthetic Criticism," I) complains that: "Actual criticism, in the familiar sense of making a case for the superiority of some works to others, is frowned upon as amateurishly
subjective." Other formulations are by Hough (*An Essay on Criticism*), p. 3, who includes prominently within the tasks of criticism
"to establish as far as may be a true judgment of literary matters," and Schreiber (*An Introduction to Literary Criticism*), p. 2,
who sees the critic's first task as "to distinguish between a good
book and a bad one." And the 1952 report of the Modern Language
Association Committee on Research Activities, of which R. Wellek
was a co-author ("The Aims, Methods, and Materials of Research
in the Modern Languages and Literatures," *PMLA* 67) also thought

equally common contrary view is that critics should stop
worrying about the problem of value and instead concentrate on interpretation and analysis.[2] The resolution
of these two views, each of which seems by no means
unreasonable, is extremely difficult.

The starting point for the discussion of the problem of
value looks uncertain enough within literary criticism;
but logic and value theory have not seemed to offer any
very firm orientation points either. Many moral philosophers.[3] have taken positions that have amounted to the
assertion that value is irreducible and unanalyzable; from
that standpoint, there would seem to be little point in trying to analyze the problem of evaluation in literary study.
On the other hand, logical positivists such as A. J. Ayer[4]
have held value judgments to be simply emotive expressions, without meaningful content; once more, not an encouraging conclusion for the literary theorist out to re-

that "The essential nature of literary criticism turns on value
judgments" (p. 29).

[2] N. Frye has argued (in his "Literary Criticism" in *Aims and
Methods*, ed. Thorpe) that judicial (primarily evaluative) criticism
is the province of journalists, and that academic criticism is more
usefully directed at the interpretation and analysis of a body of
texts that has already been evaluated by the community at large
as being worth such analysis. In practice, he may well be right
that the more useful results are obtained by critics who have a
consciously analytic intent rather than an evaluative one. But that
does not solve the theoretical problem of the contrast between this
view and the opposing one.

[3] See, for example, Nowell-Smith's (*Ethics*) exposition of typical
viewpoints on ethics in his early chapters.

[4] Ayer, *Language, Truth, and Logic*, pp. 107ff. Ayer argues that
"fundamental ethical concepts are unanalyzable," though his reason for this assertion is not that they are simple and indivisible:
"the reason why they are unanalyzable is that they are mere
pseudo-concepts."

solve one of his major puzzles. More recent work[5] on value theory has tended to stress that value words are to do with persuasion, appraisal, and commendation rather than with description. Again, this solution, correct or not, must be disappointing to the literary theorist, since it offers him no help in resolving his dilemma. Expression of admiration for something is one thing; but talking about what it is that distinguishes that thing from others that do not arouse such admiration seems to be something entirely different, and it is this quite different issue that the literary theorist wants to get hold of and analyze.

None of this looks very encouraging, and meanwhile the briefest look at our ordinary critical practices in regard to evaluation shows up more and more contradictions, which must be resolved. We praise a given work for a definite and generalizable reason, but allow that great works break all the rules too.

When dealing with any theoretical impasse or area of apparent theoretical confusion, it is always helpful first to look at the train of thought from which the problems originate. In literary criticism, there are indeed assertions of value that seem very solid. Shakespeare seems without doubt to be a much better writer than his contemporary Kyd, and we assert this without stopping to consider the meaning of what we have said; why should we, when it is so noncontroversial? This example sets the basis of the problem: in making this assertion we seem to have

[5] E.g., R. M. Hare, *The Language of Morals* (Oxford, 1952); and more specifically within the sphere of aesthetics, this kind of view of value has been taken by B. Harrison, "Some Uses of 'Good' in Criticism," *Mind* 69 (1960), and H. Eichner, "The Meaning of 'Good' in Aesthetic Judgments," *British Journal of Aesthetics* 3 (1963).

done something analogous to using factual descriptions in any other contexts. We have made a meaningful and useful distinction concerning the material that is the basis of our study. This train of reasoning can be carried even further. The thing that distinguishes Shakespeare from Kyd must not only be a real thing to talk about but must be central to our study: it must be what makes it important to talk about Shakespeare at all. This simple picture is, unfortunately, entirely called into question when less clear cases are dealt with. When two authors are considered who are more nearly equal in reputation, the situation becomes problematic. The clearer first case gave the illusion that we were dealing with solid fact, but the less clear case, when it comes to a dispute and a search for criteria that can be appealed to for the purposes of that dispute, makes us aware that we have no idea what that apparently solid fact was or how to talk about it and conceptualize it. Elsewhere, assertions of fact can be referred to a criterion of their truth, and doubtful cases make us puzzle over whether the criterion is fulfilled adequately; but here we puzzle over the quite different issue of what the criterion is.

The search for criteria has been going on for a long time, but without any results that all sides agree to be successful. If the criterion was sought in a certain kind of content, the distinction between literature and life was in danger, for mere content might too easily be duplicated in a real-life sequence of events.[6] A theory radically

[6] Such proposals are often surprisingly vacuous in any case: see, for example, B. Jessup's version of the "great art is art with serious content" view in "What Is Great Art?" *British Journal of Aesthetics* 2 (1962). It is obvious that many other things besides great art (even poor art) have serious content. Cf. my comments

opposed to this one, and designed to avoid the objection
fatal to it, stressed the organization of elements in a work
of art: formal excellence was seen as the needed criterion.
Over the years, many versions of this alternative theory
have been proposed, among which the "organic unity"
theory has had much currency: according to this view,
great works of art were organic unities and their greatness
lay in the degree and kind of organization of their dis-
parate elements.[7] This theory avoided one kind of objection (that of the non-uniqueness of content) but ran
into precisely the opposite objection, and for that reason
has never been universally accepted either; for if critics
who were concerned to defend art for art's sake were dis-
mayed at content criteria, critics who took art to be concerned with the important issues of their lives did not like
formal criteria, which seemed to deal only with the beauty
of appearance but never with the weight and importance
of the work. Characteristically, the ideal of aesthetic
value has been "beauty" for the formalists,[8] and "greatness" for those more concerned with content and relation
to human life.[9]

---

on Jessup's argument in "Great Art. A Study in Meaning," *British
Journal of Aesthetics* 3 (1963): 165. This paper is the first published version of some of the ideas developed in this chapter,
though it will be apparent that I have now considerably modified
some of them.

[7] This view goes back at least as far as Schiller (see my *Schiller's "Kalliasbriefe" and the Study of his Aesthetic Theory*); for
a modern version of it, see the work of Harold Osborne, e.g.,
Theory of Beauty (London, 1952), and *Aesthetics and Criticism*
(London, 1955). On the history of the concept, cf. G.N.G. Orsini,
"The Organic Concepts in Aesthetics," *Comparative Literature*
21 (1969).

[8] Cf. my *Schiller's "Kalliasbriefe,"* pp. 118ff.

[9] This point assumes importance in chapter 8; meanwhile, it

One attempt to solve the puzzle is the claim that when we talk of the value of works of art, we must also have recourse to extra-aesthetic criteria,[10] that is, to criteria not primarily to do with works of art. But this is an attempt to have things both ways, in which the notion of the value of works of art evaporates. When dealing with any category of things, we may talk of the value of those things as members of that category. But it is logically very strange to do so by referring to criteria that are not part of the value of the category. This is not yet to deny that the factors commonly referred to as "extra-aesthetic" factors may be relevant to the value of works of art; it is only to make the point that to describe them in such a way (if they are indeed relevant to the value of works of art as such) must indicate that the notion of aesthetic value employed here is inadequate; if relevant, these must indeed be included as aesthetic factors.

Clive Bell[11] is the author of a celebrated attempt to have things both ways by arguing that great art is that which has significant form. The formulation used here refers both to formal aspects of the work (so satisfying the concern of the formalist, "art for art's sake" group) and to the significance of the work (thus attempting also to satisfy those more concerned with the human significance and meaning of the work). Both form and content seem to be included. But this, too, turned out to have

---

also links with my discussion in chapter 5 of the social context of literature, and with that in chapter 6 of the relation of form and content.

[10] This issue is interestingly discussed by Wellek and Warren, *Theory of Literature*, pp. 234ff; but their discussion of value in general is somewhat inconclusive.

[11] C. Bell, *Art* (London, 1927).

severe logical drawbacks, as Beryl Lake convincingly demonstrated.[12] They are, in fact, the same kinds of logical problems that any theory of the kind I have been discussing must involve, and it is to the logical status of all of them that I now turn.

The point of all of these theories is to find a criterion of aesthetic value, and, in this sense, an explanation and even an analysis of what great art is. The desired end result is the ability to point to actual properties of this work of art rather than that work, such properties being discernible and discussible in a reasonably clear way. Evaluation of works is then analyzed into descriptive statements about them. It is unnecessary here to discuss the details of these various theories, and in this brief exposition I certainly do not claim to have done justice to them; in many ways they are interesting in their own right, but mainly in ways that do not concern me directly here. It will suffice, for the purpose of my argument, to show that they all fail in three important respects to achieve the kind of logical status that they are designed to achieve. From this will emerge the point that concerns me most of all: the starting point from which all originate, and the logical ambitions that are common to all, are in principle mistaken. Once again, I shall argue, it is the initial posing of the problem that creates the impasse.

The first problem in these theories is that they are impossibly vague. Their aim is to clarify the notion of aesthetic value, but the end results are notions that them-

[12] B. Lake, "A Study of the Irrefutability of Two Aesthetic Theories," in *Aesthetics and Language*, ed. W. Elton (Oxford, 1954).

selves stand just as much in need of clarification, such as "significant form" and "organic unity." The pinning down of descriptive properties has simply not occurred when the results are as undescriptive as this.

The second recurring problem is circularity, and the covert support of a theory by a piece of arbitrary definition. The standard test of this is to produce possible counter examples to a given theory, and see how its practitioners deal with them. Clive Bell's theory rules them out by definition: anything that does not have significant form is just not good art. Thus we have the circle: great art is art with significant form, but form is only significant when we have great art. The vagueness of the terms is an aid to the circularity here; it is often the case that the property suggested as the touchstone is so far from being clearly visible that it itself is clarified by reference to the notion of great art, rather than (as was intended) the notion of great art clarified by reference to organic unity or significant form.

The third and simplest argument against such theories is that they do not reduce value to description, but instead invariably replace one evaluative term with another. Even if it were true that the two evaluative concepts were related, it would still be clear that the meaning of the basic evaluative terms (such as "good," "great") has not been explained in the way that had been sought, that is, by non-evaluative criteria.[13]

In literary criticism, texts are commonly pronounced to be valuable as literary texts because they are well written, deal with important issues, use imagery and symbol-

[13] Cf. the point argued more fully in my "Great Art. A Study in Meaning."

ism in a subtle way, and so on. It is clear that these reasons
are themselves all evaluative terms, albeit of narrower
scope; instead of pointing to the work *in toto* and pronouncing that to be of high value (which is what the
general aesthetic value judgment does), we point at part
of the work, or an aspect of it, and do the same thing.
Logically, nothing different has occurred: we have not replaced one kind of statement with a different kind. We
have not said, "this is good for the following reasons," but
only something like, "this aspect is good, and insofar as
it is good, the whole has some goodness in it." No elucidation of goodness in terms of another kind of statement
has taken place. And this is, in essence, true of all the
various kinds of theories of value I have been discussing:
judgments of unity or of significance of form are concerned with the value and success of certain aspects of
works of art; the shift from the large notion of aesthetic
value to such concepts is not that from analyzandum to
explanation, or from value to that property which is the
basis of value, but only from the general value of a work
to a specific aspect of its value, and from assertions as to
the value of the whole to assertions as to the value of
parts of the whole.

Sometimes this fact about "criteria of value" (namely,
that they are not criteria for the value of the whole, but
only partial evaluations of the whole, and thus logically
on the same footing as general evaluations themselves)
is difficult to see, but it is always there, nonetheless. Consider, for example, the cases in which critics judge works
of literature "nobly simple" in style. Now in other cases
a text in a similar style might be judged plain and un-
adorned. A more complex style might be termed "rich"

or alternatively "overburdened with ornament." If we reduce all of these instances to facts, they become neutral and do not distinguish the good and the bad, and are in no sense criteria. If we choose those formulations of the facts which seem to indicate that the text is valuable, it is not because they fulfill criteria of value, but because they are partial evaluations of the text.

An analogous point arises in moral philosophy. An unusual degree of explicitness of speech can be evaluated positively as plain, honest speaking, or negatively as rudeness. Rudeness is not a matter of plain unevaluated fact, and so it cannot be a factual criterion of the behavior of a "bad" man. If we say rudeness is morally bad, we are in fact saying that bad direct speaking is bad. No one can deny this—but that shows how uninformative such a statement is.[14] Similarly, to say that richness or subtlety of language is a *criterion* of a good piece of literature is a logical error, and one to which literary critics are very prone.[15] "Good (or effective) complex language is good," is the only thing asserted by such statements.

Our problem has been reduced to the following: the search for criteria of value originates from a desire to explain judgments of value. But if such criteria are genu-

[14] P. Foot ("Moral Arguments," *Mind* 67, 1958) discusses the notion of rudeness, but without seeing that more than description is involved in pronouncing someone rude. Casey (*The Language of Criticism*) discusses Mrs. Foot's argument, but in a rather inconclusive way.

[15] That Righter misses this crucial point is shown by his statement that one could accept the "description" of James's style as rich and subtle and "still not admire it" (*Logic and Criticism*, pp. 80–81). See also Nowell-Smith's treatment of the same issue from another standpoint, pp. 73–74.

inely descriptive, they explain nothing, and do not even support partial judgments. If, on the other hand, they are evaluative, they are no longer criteria that explain judgments, but only smaller scale judgments, more limited in scope than general aesthetic value judgments but not logically distinct from or explanatory of them. Neutral facts neither entail nor are entailed by value judgments.[16] And here, on the whole, the problem of discussing what it is about literary texts that makes them great works of art or inferior ones has rested—on a depressingly inconclusive note.

A completely different way of approaching aesthetic value judgments has arisen, which shirks the job of looking at the texts and thinking about how the good ones differ from the others; instead, it concentrates on the responses of people to these texts, and describes aesthetic value in terms of these responses. No doubt this direction is tempting for those who despair of the ever less intelligible formulae of traditional aesthetics;[17] but it was from the outset certain to be unsatisfying.

---

[16] Cf. my "Great Art. A Study in Meaning," p. 166: "No purely descriptive phrase guarantees any value, and if it appears to do so, this is because the phrase used is already in part evaluative." The gap between statements of fact and evaluative statements ("is" and "ought") was established long ago by David Hume. Recently there have been many attempts to break down the distinction. I remain convinced that none of this discussion has established a link between descriptive and evaluative statements in the sense required by traditional moralists and aestheticians: cf. my discussion of recent attacks on the distinction in *Schiller's "Kalliasbriefe,"* p. 88. My conclusion, in brief, is that most of this discussion turns on the blurring of an important distinction: that between the process of valuing and the description of that process.

[17] Some interesting general dissatisfaction with traditional

The extreme subjectivist position is one of translating "Shakespeare is great" into "I like Shakespeare," that is, into an expression of approval. This obviously does no justice to the fact that we are talking about Shakespeare rather than our wishes; the difference between Shakespeare and Kyd is to be sought not in our preferring one to the other but in the fact that there is some difference in the quality of the two. And it is possible to say "I do not like Shakespeare, but he is a great writer." Such a sentence might be reformulated as "Many people like Shakespeare but I do not." But that would make the original subjectivist proposition highly problematic; it looks as though it is a proposition with an implied subject which is variable.

Many much more complex reductions of evaluative propositions on subjective lines have been attempted, but they turn out to be all subject to much the same objections. Recent theories that evaluations are essentially commendations, appraisals, predictions of approval by others, or exhortations to them to do so, all suffer from the same gap—a glaring one which will always stand in the way of their being accepted as adequate theories: there is an obvious difference between talking about Shakespeare and talking about actual or potential responses to him.[18] Ayer's decision to regard value judgments merely as emotive expressions is an extreme re-

---

aesthetics is expressed by W. Kennick, "Does Traditional Aesthetics Rest on a Mistake?" *Mind* 67 (1958).

[18] Cf. Harrison, and Eichner; in a reply to Harrison: "Description and Critical Appraisal," *Mind* 73 (1964), I argued that Harrison had greatly underestimated the extent to which a text could be described, rather than merely appraised.

duction of this whole line of argument, but a useful one; in following an argument to its logical conclusion, Ayer makes us aware of the need to rethink the whole direction that it takes.

This impasse, like others we have encountered, has its roots in the influence that a basically referential approach to language has had on our attempts to grapple with theoretical issues. The search for the property to which an assertion of aesthetic value refers either leads to the identification of properties of such vagueness that only their grandiose phraseology defends them against the immediate recognition that they are valueless as solutions to a problem, or, in the case of the really consistent reference theory adherent, the logical positivist, to the view that such judgments refer to no properties at all and are hence devoid of meaning.

I now turn to my own approach to the meaning of value judgments on literary works, and the relation of the judgments to those works. My discussion of the definition of literature has a bearing on this issue, since it has prepared the ground for a reorientation of the problem of value which is essentially similar to that needed in the case of definition. Just as a work of literature must be seen primarily as a text that performs a certain task and is treated in a certain kind of way, rather than a text having certain qualities, so a good work of literature is primarily one that performs that task well and is eminently suitable for its characteristic use as a piece of literature. This reorientation may not at first sight seem too exciting; it may not seem to assert anything more than a truism. But, as we shall see, it constitutes a different point of departure in the analysis of judgments of value which can lead somewhere, and even dispel some of the confusion and defeatism in which traditional theories of aesthetic value result. And, paradoxically, this line of reasoning can at last make the actual qualities of works of literature relevant to a judgment in a useful way, in spite of its seeming initially to exclude mention of those qualities.

To talk of the value of literary texts is, in the context of present-day discussion of the question, to enter a world of such confusion that a simple explanation seems difficult; but the structure of such an explanation can easily be seen from an example removed from the sphere of theorizing on aesthetic value. My earlier example of the category of weeds and bad weeds makes the elucidation of certain principles of evaluative categories simpler. The relation of facts about physical structure to the character of the category and to evaluation within it in this case presents few problems. Weeds are plants that we categorize in a way concerned exclusively with the use we have for them. Judgments of value within that category (identification of particularly troublesome weeds) are still recognizably to do with our use of them. Such judgments isolate cases where the factor of our atttiude to the plants (on which the category itself is based originally) is taken to an even higher point—these will be weeds that are particularly irritating to gardeners, ones that have high status as weeds. If weeds are plants that we wish to avoid, bad weeds are plants that we doubly wish to avoid. Now it makes perfectly good sense to say, "This is a particularly bad weed because it is especially hardy, seeds very easily, and so on." It is perfectly acceptable to relate such facts about the structure of a particular weed to its evaluation as a weed. But now suppose we make the move made so often in aesthetic theory and ask whether these are criteria for the identification of bad weeds; the answer must be that they are not. A plant exhibiting these features may be categorized as a flower or vegetable and even be rated a particularly useful one for precisely those same reasons. These facts about certain particularly bad weeds cannot therefore be considered "criteria" of badness in weeds, though they are relevant to the badness of the weed. Even within the category of weeds, not all plants exhibiting these qualities in high degree need be rated very bad weeds; the plant concerned might be rare, susceptible to frost, easily rooted out, or be easily exterminated with a kind of selective poison that was harmless to other plants, and therefore not be evaluated as a particularly troublesome weed.

Logically, we have reached exactly the same position we reached earlier in the question of definition; and, in fact, the matter of evaluating things within a category is logically very similar to that of placing them in the category in the first place. Both categorizing and evaluation within the category are done on the basis of performance. The important thing to note is that in neither case is it possible to look for criteria (especially single criteria) that determine the inclusion or relative evaluation. The reason for the inclusion of a weed in the category weed is quite simple: it is a nuisance. And the reason for evaluating it as a particularly noxious weed is, equally simply, that it is a considerable nuisance. It is these single considerations that give such categories their unity and uniformity. But there are causes of the fact that they can perform in the way that the category requires, and equally of the further fact that they can perform particularly well in the way that the category requires. These causes may be various, just as we established in the case of definition. Two things included in the category as highly valued members of it may well have nothing in common in their structure. This means that any aspects of physical structure which can be isolated as causes in a particular weed are in no sense criteria, either for membership of the category or for evaluation within it. On the other hand, the analysis of the membership of a category gives us information about those things that can perform in the desired way, and the analysis of the top end of the category (the highly evaluated end) gives us information about what makes for their high evaluation. We may or may not find considerable patterning in these facts, though it seems highly likely that we will do so. But suppose we find a complex of factors that occur frequently, features displayed by most bad weeds. If, as we may be tempted to do, we make them a kind of index of what a bad weed is, we commit an important logical error. A particular instance of a bad weed may not show such features, and instead may achieve its effect through quite different ones; and the only effective ranking is that derived from actual performance. In this case, no amount of tallying physical factors will lead logically to a statement of value. It might make an estimate of value likely; but we must be careful over logical priority here. In any case, where performance conflicts with an estimate derived from factual observations and the comparison of a particular weed with other weeds, the former must prevail.

I conclude from this example that it is possible to talk of the physical structure of a weed and be talking in a way that is relevant to the question of its evaluation as a weed, though that is not the same as defining a weed or talking of criteria for the badness of weeds. The same logical error of the reference theory of meaning is responsible for the search for criteria of value on the one hand, and for defining properties on the other. This example shows the same logical structure as that of aesthetic value judgments.

It is essential to begin by saying that great works of literature are those that are particularly successful in performing as works of literature, rather than by assuming that they have a quality called aesthetic value, which we must then try to locate. The unity of the notion of aesthetic value lies in the common factor of performance, not in any necessary common structure of the texts. The reason for the assertion of aesthetic value lies in the performance; but the causes of that assertion must be distinguished from the immediate reason, and have to do with the actual qualities of the text.[19] The causes may be many and various, and to talk about them is genuinely to talk about the value of literary texts, though not in terms of criteria. There can therefore be no inference from past instances of causes to possible future ones; each work is evaluated on the basis of its performance in

[19] This is the same distinction between reasons and causes found in chapter 2, in relation to definition. I used it in analyzing evaluation in my *Schiller's "Kalliasbriefe,"* p. 91, and earlier in my 1965 University of London doctoral dissertation on the same subject, p. 132. Wittgenstein uses the distinction between reason and cause for a different (though not entirely unrelated) purpose in the *Blue Book*; see *The Blue and Brown Books* (New York, 1958), pp. 14–15.

the role of literary text, and then analysis can try to find out what facts of its structure relate to that performance. But to say that a particular work has structural features often found in successful literary works, and therefore is a good literary work, is to ignore the possible diversity of those features.[20] If in this kind of argument from experience we are trying to set up universally valid criteria, we are in error.

It is worth noting that, once more, the two senses of "is" confuse the issue. When we ask, What is great literature? we may interpret the request in two ways, and the confusion of the two has caused chaos in critical theory.[21] To take the example of a radio: when we ask What is a good radio? we may be asking for a definition of the meaning of the phrase or we may be asking the empirical question of what a good radio set is in terms of its physical structure. The first is answered by replying that a good radio set is one that can receive the signals we want with a reasonable degree of faithfulness; in other words, it does well the job we want it to do. The second would require us to go into the physical features of a radio set that does its job well. The first does no more than explain what the use of the phrase "good radio" is. The second, on the other hand, may involve much

[20] Cf. *Schiller's "Kalliasbriefe,"* p. 91: "This is not to deny that a good deal of theory, consciously or unconsciously . . . contributes to judgment. Reflection may well change our view of works of art. But the judgment still stands in no need of, and is logically distinct from, direct theoretical justification." Cf. also p. 92, concerning appeals from past experience of physical structures which were successful to all cases including future ones.

[21] Cf. *Schiller's "Kalliasbriefe,"* p. 90.

technical material, and the explanation may well change from one set to the next, and from one technological advance to the next.

In the case of works of literature, the same ambiguity occurs: the demand for an explanation of the use of the words (the problem of definition) may easily be confused with that of the empirical facts involved. Conceptual analysis is something we can sit down and think about; but empirical research is quite different. If we want to find out what great literature is in the sense of finding out what its structural properties are, then the answer is that we cannot sit down to perform conceptual analysis on the problem: no theory thought up in the armchair will suffice, and no inventive formula will be of any use. The answer to this question is that one must go and find out; one must investigate large numbers of works of literature and think about the features that they display. If our analogy with weeds is anything to go by, these features will be many and various,[22] and there is no logical limit set on the number of important recurring factors that we may find.

Since these points all have a deceptive simplicity and, when stated baldly, even an obviousness that can lead one to wonder how they can have been disputed, I shall,

[22] To take a random example of how this logical point is commonly violated in discussion of literature, cf. the statement by J. Thorne ("Poetry, Stylistics, and Imaginary Grammars," *Journal of Linguistics* 5, 1969: 148), that deviations on a deep rather than surface level characterize good poetry: ". . . herein lies the essentially poetic character of poetic language." I shall discuss the bearing of this kind of view on the problem of style in chapter 6; its relevance at this point lies in its being one more example of the search for the single criterion of value.

at the risk of repetition, list the major logical errors of treatments of value that derive from the reference theory of meaning. This will provide the distinction between one conclusion and a different one, which we need in order to evaluate the point of a statement such as "great literature is literature that functions particularly well as literature," since this might otherwise not seem in any way controversial. The errors of reference-theory treatment of aesthetic value are, then, as follows:

1. The assumption that there is a single criterion of value,[23] which derives from confusing the single reason for inclusion within a category with the many possible causes of the inclusion.

2. The assumption that aesthetic value judgments refer directly to a fact or facts about the structure of works.

3. The confusion of factual research with conceptual analysis: logical analysis is the method of the latter, but extensive empirical work is necessary for the former. The confusion of the two has made conceptual analysis insufficiently analytic, while empirical work has been insufficiently empirical. The results, typically, have been oversimplified empirical statements; for if these empirical statements had done justice to the complexity of the empirical facts, it would have been too obvious that they

[23] One reason for this has been the feeling that if value was to be "objectively valid" (i.e., indisputable) it must lie in one hard and fast standard; to accept a multiplicity of relevant factors would have seemed like surrendering to a subjectivist view of "each to his own taste," since many kinds of value could exist independently. But the fear of losing the guarantee of value in this way is quite unfounded: the guarantee of value is just that something is valued. Cf. my *Schiller's "Kalliasbriefe,"* pp. 118–120, for further discussion of this and other factors which have tended to promote a search for a single criterion.

could not be definitions or criteria. Such statements, therefore, served to advance neither conceptual analysis nor empirical research, and hindered both.

4. The assumption that facts about works which are relevant to literary value must be viewed as criteria of value, with all that that implies.

5. The assumption that if we merely analyze a literary work descriptively we are not dealing with the question of its value.

I must further clarify the last point of these five. It is not just the point made already by Hyman, or by Wellek and Warren,[24] that even when doing a descriptive analysis of a piece of literature we are involved in evaluation through our choice of text to analyze, since we have judged it worth the time and trouble involved. This point is certainly a reasonable one. But mine is a more basic point, and not just a matter of the critic's action implying his own value judgment. My point is that descriptive analysis is an investigation of the value of a text purely as that, and that it is the only possible kind of investigation of value. To return to my example of weeds: if we rid ourselves of such notions as "the criteria for a bad weed," and similar notions that embody the misconceptions of aesthetic theory, the position is really quite simple. We can look at bad weeds and find out what it is about them that makes them such a nuisance; and unless we make the mistake of supposing that all such things must be true of all weeds, there is absolutely no mystery about the situation. I do not mean here that the task

[24] S. E. Hyman, *The Armed Vision*, preface; Wellek and Warren, *Theory of Literature*, p. 241.

does not demand careful scrutiny and hard work; it does. But there is no danger of entrapment in any logical dead end. We may perfectly well make the statement that this weed is particularly bad partly because it seeds more easily than any other. Likewise, there should be no logical difficulty when analyses of works of literature reveal features that appear to be among the causes contributing to the value of those works as literary texts. Again, this is a situation without mystery or logical problems. It is only when we introduce faulty logical notions into that situation that problems appear: for example, Is this a criterion of value that we have found? What does aesthetic value really consist of? What is the standard we must apply to literary works? When, therefore, we are analyzing a literary text, we are always dealing with the features of its structure which are the cause of its being valued highly as literature: we are dealing just as much with value as a man is who examines the physical structure of a particularly obnoxious weed. The descriptive literary analyst is therefore contributing directly to the analysis of the value of the work, and indeed is doing the only kind of analysis of its value that is possible. Only the intrusion of notions of absolute value has managed to persuade critics that they are doing otherwise. They are, in fact, conducting an investigation into the structure of the membership of the class of great literary works, and therefore no descriptive critic should concede that he is avoiding discussion of the value of works: he is already doing just that.[25] The demand for information as

[25] I shall pursue this point further in chapters 6 and 7, which deal more directly with the function of descriptive analysis.

to what good literature is can be a factual question, if it is construed as asking about the structure[26] of the texts in question. Analysis of texts is an *investigation* of what is valuable as literature—but not a *determination* of literary value.

From a logical point of view, there is one further error of traditional aesthetic theory which supports the other errors that I have noted. It can be summarized as an unwillingness to analyze the notion of value and evaluative categories, and a tendency to cling to simple assertions of value as if these were the end product of the investigation of value rather than the starting point for analysis. The issues involved have become so clouded by aesthetic theory that, once again, I shall first turn to an example from another sphere to explain this characteristic logical error.

Imagine a discussion on this question: Which are the greatest kings in English history?[27] Conceptual analysis gets us no further than the fact that great kings are kings fulfilling well the functions of kings, and presumably the function of a king is to rule his country well. And here we still have some unanalyzed notions of value in the conceptual explanation. What actions on the part of kings do we normally take to be relevant to their stature as kings? The answer seems to be that we are normally impressed by the following kinds of rulers:

[26] My purpose here is not to contrast "structure" and "meaning," but only to refer to any and all features of a text. My reason for doing so will be apparent in chapter 6.

[27] This is an example I used, though in a slightly different way and for a different purpose, in "Great Art. A Study in Meaning," p. 168.

(1) Kings who built up the power of their country
(2) Kings who made their subjects happiest
(3) Kings who significantly altered the course of the history of their country
(4) Kings who ruled with conspicuous wisdom and humanity
(5) Kings who presided over and encouraged great cultural and artistic achievement

The model I have used so far to relate factual statements to judgments of value evidently works well with this example too. The greatness of a king depends on the single fact of his being important and outstanding in the sequence of kings of a country. That is the sole *reason* for his categorization as a great king. But the *causes* of that categorization in his person and deeds may be many and various; so various that some of those causes may in fact exclude the others. It is doubtful whether the first two factors can coexist in the same reign, for example. Again, there is no one criterion of greatness, nor are the various factors criteria. But a problem continues to arise even after we have stopped chasing the single criterion of greatness. Suppose the argument still went on as to who really was the greatest of the English kings. What would be the point of such an argument? It is quite possible that all participants in such an argument might be in agreement as to the facts of the reigns concerned, and as to the judgments of those facts. What can be the issue that is being disputed? This question takes us to the purpose of general judgments of value.

If we analyze the act of evaluation that is involved in such judgments, we find that it is concerned with various kinds of valued performance which are all reduced to a single value scale. On the face of it, this reduction might seem a rather inefficient operation. Analysis reveals that many factors are involved, and after such analysis we can make much more intelligent and precise judgments about those individual factors; but the kind of reductive summary involved in assertions that a particular king was the greatest one treats several unrelated issues at once. The key to our choosing to make such a reductive summary judgment, in this example as in the countless others like it in our ordinary language, is that we may need to act. The practical point of the dispute over the stature of kings can only be a matter of the number of hours to be devoted to one rather than the other in the history books and curriculum. In making the reductive summary judgment that X is more important than Y we are committing ourselves to a course of action. Absolute value judgments are, paradoxically, not things of finality and mystery; they are essentially pragmatic, concerned with practical matters.

Consider now a situation in which the relative stature of two kings is being discussed, and the two participants have made a careful analysis of all the factors involved. After agreeing between themselves on their careful analytic account, each, without any practical need of his own to devote more or less time to one or the other in a classroom or in any other context, then argues that one or the other is the greater, and this becomes the point of the whole argument. Something very strange is happening here. The two are preferring, as a superior kind of statement, the vague reductive summary of the general value statement to their much more careful analysis. They have the impression that the general kind of value statement really gets to the heart of the matter, is somehow more real, than their more analyzed statements. But, as we have seen, the reverse is the case; the summary general statement is always a matter of a practical decision in a context that has nothing to do with the actual qualities of the material under discussion. The general evaluative statement is a vague one, imprecise but often useful in practical situations. We should make it the starting point for a much better analysis. But what happens in this example is that the reverse direction is taken. The vagueness of the general evaluative statement is given a mystic status; instead of being regarded as a logically second-class statement, useful for practicality rather than truth, and to be used as a gateway to something better, it seems to be accepted that analysis must lead up to the vague general statements; in this way the latter are made the final and most important stage in the investigation, instead of the first and least important stage. This mistaken reversal leads to much sterile and pointless argument about judgments in the summary reductive form.

To return to the case of literary judgments: to take a body of texts that displays very great diversity, and to categorize the whole field on the basis of a judgment allowing only one factor and one dimension—good or bad —is to simplify a very complex situation. There is nothing wrong with doing so for particular purposes; indeed we sometimes cannot avoid this simplification. The category of literary texts is made up of those texts used in a characteristic way; when we are only concerned with the general usefulness of a particular text for this purpose, we are quite justified in making the simplified judgment (good or bad) which refers to that factor and to that factor alone. But this kind of crude judgment has been promoted to the status of the most important kind of judgment we make on literary texts, and this it cannot be. To compare two instances and to try and rank them with great precision relative to each other would be to ignore the fact that the category is one of a rough and ready kind to begin with. To compare two kings and to try to diagnose minute overall differences in their value on the scale of great kings would be unproductive, given that the factors involved may be entirely different for the two cases; and the same is true of the attempt to compare closely two works of art (I mean here any two, regardless of their differences) on a rank scale as if that scale were anything more than a very crude scale of utility. Only the need to act justifies that degree of concern with the general value judgment: if we are about to buy a ticket for this rather than that concert, or if a foundation is voting its money to support this rather than that artist, then a judgment is needed which will simplify a complex position down to the point where it translates into a decision one way or the other. Without this practical need, a series of more delicate statements is a much preferable analysis of the value of the works of literature concerned.

The most important point about general summary aesthetic judgments is not that they are meaningful or meaningless, but that they are crude and vague, and that we need not bother with them in their most general form unless a practical situation forces us to. Practical situations force us into all kinds of irrational acts; a weight limit on baggage may force us to choose between a tennis racket and a pair of binoculars. Yet it would be absurd to claim that anything about their real value had been said when one has decided that the one would be more important for the trip than the other. The category "good things to take on a vacation" is one we should not dwell upon outside the situation of packing; and though this scale may for its own purposes be a useful one, we should never fall victim to the temptation to rank everything on this single scale of usefulness in order to indicate its intrinsic[28] value. But it is just this gross kind of evaluative category that aesthetic theory seems to have become fixed upon; so that if anyone should want to analyze the category to the point where he abandons the general form of aesthetic value judgments, he is thought to have abandoned the notion of aesthetic value altogether—which is certainly not the case. On the contrary, it is to abandon a crude and uninteresting version of an aesthetic value judgment for more interesting and more analyzed statements.

When, in literary criticism, it is argued that X is better than Y, one might well ask what depends on the argument: Does the literature program syllabus only have room for one? Is reading time restricted so that only one can be chosen? Is the discussion over whether to reprint one but not the other of the authors concerned? Is it a

[28] In "Great Art. A Study in Meaning," p. 167, I argued that, "Strictly speaking, nothing has intrinsic value, if by this is meant value divorced from any situation. For an object to have value a relation with something other than itself is needed. Value must include valuer as well as thing valued. . . ." I then argued that precise assertions of value needed two terms, or the clear implication of two terms—those being the two things or aspects of situations between which a value relation was postulated. General value judgments contain only one, e.g., "this is good."

question of taking one or the other on a trip? If no such considerations can be found in the situation, the argument is pointless; it is a crude beginning to an investigation, which ought to be left immediately in favor of more useful statements. If we went into a shop and asked for a good radio set, it is likely that we should be asked what it was to be good for. What kind of price range? What kind of fidelity necessary? What kind of stations need it receive? And so on. Suppose now that we simply answered: "I want a good radio set." That kind of answer would be absurd; but it is this kind of obsession with the most unanalyzed form of evaluation that literary criticism, and aesthetic theory in general, has held to and refused to progress beyond. The vagueness and crudity of such judgments has led to their being celebrated as absolute and mysterious; and the simplification of a complex of factors has even been thought to produce a higher, rather than lower, form of statement.[29]

So far, I have been discussing the question of the value of literary texts from the standpoint of the critical analyst, whose function is to investigate literature, its meaning and value. But in a different sense every member of the community takes part in the process of evaluating literary texts. By his own actions, by his expressions of opinion, and by his effect on other members of the community,

---

[29] I mention here only the logical errors of absolutists in the matter of evaluation. There are probably psychological factors involved too; critics who are more than usually concerned with unanalyzed value judgments are often felt to be assertive and even bullying in personality, so that the imposition of their judgments on their readers appears as a stronger factor in the situation than constructive comment on literary texts.

everyone takes part in the formation of a consensus as to what is literature, and what is especially valuable as literature. The critic, too, is part of this process; but, though he may wield more influence than most, he is in this sense essentially a member of the community rather than an analyst of it and its literature. This will be especially true of journalist critics and of critics of contemporary literature; for them, a judgment of literary value functions to ensure the survival of a text as a literary text for the community. Here we are dealing with a matter of action, and the critic's work is directed to that end; general summary evaluations might in this context be entirely appropriate. As potential readers of the text, the readers of the critic are also part of the process of the text's becoming or not becoming literature. Recent philosophers[30] have emphasized the function of evaluations in appraising and persuading, all of which is to do with getting people to act in certain ways; once

---

[30] Cf. P. H. Nowell-Smith, *Ethics*, pp. 84–87. My argument in *Schiller's "Kalliasbriefe,"* p. 99, relied more heavily than I would now on the description of the contextual implications of aesthetic value judgments, i.e., the implication of the approval of the speaker, and of the prediction of approval by others, when one asserts that something is good. It is certainly true that these implications are there, and that they are part of the meaning of the judgment; but I should now think this all the more reason to view general value judgments as saying nothing very precise and to pursue the analysis of value in other directions. As I previously noted (e.g., "Great Art. A Study in Meaning," p. 168) any of the implications of general value judgments can be withdrawn, a fact that strikes at any attempt to construct a theory of value judgments of any one of them; Eichner's predictive theory of value judgments can easily be invalidated by noting such possible sentences as "This work is great but it will never be appreciated."

again, we find that general summary value judgments are practical in nature, and not instruments of analysis and knowledge.

I shall briefly summarize the results of this discussion. Assertions of value refer primarily not to the structural properties of texts, but to their performance as literary texts. This is a matter of conceptual analysis, not empirical research. The structural properties of highly valued texts may be many and various, and must be sought empirically, not speculated about. They are in no sense criteria of value.[31] Abandoning the notion that evaluations refer directly to properties of texts does not mean that the field is left to subjectivists; to talk descriptively of highly valued literary texts is to talk of their value.[32] An analytic investigation of structural properties is to be preferred to general evaluative judgments of the simple form, X is a great work; such judgments function only as crude incitements to action, and are the starting points for precise analysis rather than the end point to which analysis must lead. The illusion that such general judgments are the most important kind is born to some extent of their practical importance, and to some extent of their

[31] Even R. Wellek, in his review of F. R. Leavis's *Revaluation*, in *Scrutiny* 5 (1937), insisted that Leavis should have laid out his norms and criteria when he made evaluations. Cf. Leavis's reply in "Literary Criticism and Philosophy" in his *The Common Pursuit* (London, 1952), pp. 211–222.

[32] This is not the limited point made by W. Kayser ("Wertung und literarische Interpretation," in his *Die Vortragsreise*, Bern, 1954) that descriptive analysis can show up inconsistencies, and so lead to negative evaluations. It is the more important point that empirical investigation of the membership of an evaluative category (cf. my example of weeds) is an analysis of the factors causing the evaluation.

association with direct emotional responses to works of literature. Literary analysts who are unduly concerned with general value judgments are abandoning a productive, analytic role to become merely part of the scene (the consuming public and its literary texts) which it was their job to analyze.

5: The Relevant Context
of a Literary Text

THE QUESTION of the relevant context of a literary text
is an important one because it is the basis of the more
familiar question of what knowledge is necessary for the
understanding of a work of literature. It has often been
said that criticism should make the literary work more
understandable by recreating the original circumstances
of its composition: the historical situation in which the
author wrote, and the response of the contemporary
audience.[1] This view specifies the relevant context: it is
the original context of composition—biographical, social,
and historical. But in so doing it specifies also relevant information for the understanding of a literary text; we
need to know the facts of the original context to under-

[1] Wellek and Warren (*Theory of Literature*) have objected that
"If we should really be able to reconstruct the meaning which
Hamlet held for its contemporary audience, we would merely impoverish it" (p. 31). My logical analysis leads to a position that is
related to this insight, though developed in a different way. There
are a number of points in the argument of this chapter where I
am similarly indebted to the insights of other theorists, though my
analysis gives them a different kind of status and framework.

stand the work, and criticism should put us in possession of those facts.

A great difficulty of this area of literary theory, from the standpoint of logical analysis, is that it constitutes the most polemical territory of the whole field: logical analysis here becomes involved in the issues that make literary scholars accuse each other (on the one hand) of biographical reductionism, of irrelevant fact-grubbing, and of being unconcerned with literature for its literary value, and (on the other hand) of the fallacy of art for art's sake, of elementary ignorance of necessary background information, of lack of concern for the social importance of literature, and even of failure to read correctly. These series of accusations, we should observe, are two sides of an argument over how to treat literature —as social act or "merely" as literature. But the question of the way literary texts are treated is part of their definition; and for this reason the question of relevant context is much closer to that of the definition of literature than is generally supposed.

It does not take long to establish that, in practice, both sides of this argument can degenerate into something injurious to literature: the one side into critical snobbery and elitism that appear to claim that only the initiated (those with large amounts of highly specialized knowledge) can really understand literature, and the other into an insistence on the unique value of one's first response to a text, this response resisting modification in any way by knowledge or argument. But in between the caricatured extremes (which may of course represent some actual cases) the argument is not so easy, and this more difficult ground is generally avoided. Again and again, a curious structure occurs in these arguments: the adherent of one side of the dispute will complain bitterly at the way the other side caricatures his position, insisting that fair scholarly procedure must prevail in place of such blatant prejudice; and he then goes on to demolish the opposition by attacking a version of its argument that is patently just as caricatured.[2] This whole area of literary theory is evidently very controversial, and the analysis needs to take into account the fact that it causes so much inconclusive argument between rival reductionists. Yet "wise eclecticism" seems to thrive in this area, too, and for obvious reasons: it suspends the most unpleasant forms of these arguments and lets different people get on with doing what they want to do.

The simplest form of context to consider is that of biography; the most difficult is the general social context and its relevance to a text. I shall start with the easier of the two so that by the time I approach the more difficult, some principles will already have been established.

---

[2] I think here especially of the recent case of Crews, "Literature and Psychology," in *Relations of Literary Study*, who first declares that "Tempting as it is to dispose of a complex and disturbing subject by means of *ad hominem* ridicule, such a method of argument is unworthy of scholars" (p. 76), but then goes on a few pages later to say that "the 'Freudian reductionist' is used as a scarecrow to protect the scholar's private harvest of literary history or factual detail or didactic moralism" (p. 82). Mr. Crews's adversaries could well answer the second of these statements with the first. I am not here siding with one or the other position, but only drawing attention to the fact that no one seems to mind reductive arguments and *ad hominem* ridicule as long as he is not on the receiving end of it. Many other examples of this structure of argument can be found in the volume *Relations of Literary Study*.

The separation of the two is somewhat artificial, but for practical reasons it is useful in the early stage of this discussion.

When we concern ourselves with a piece of language, it is entirely normal to interpret it in the light of its context: indeed, in most cases not to do so leads to error. We find out what someone means not just from his actual words, but from his actions and the context he is in. The cry "over here!" may be interpreted as "what you are looking for is over here," or "bring that thing you are carrying over here," or "I am over here," depending on what the previous utterance was ("Where are you?" "Where do you want me to put this?" "Where have you put my coat?"). When the context does not make the speaker's meaning clear enough, then we ask, "What did you mean?" or "What did you have in mind?" For example, "Where shall I put this?" "Over here." "Do you mean on the floor or on the shelf?" We think of this as asking for the speaker's intent, for what he meant to say. This is often hard to distinguish from a demand that he simply say more, something else. In the case just discussed, "over here" may have been intended as a very general "in that area of the room," and when we ask "on the floor or on the shelf" we ask for something extra, something not originally intended. In a broad sense, then, notions such as "intent" or "what was meant" cover many things, for example, (a) what the speaker intended but did not make explicit, (b) further information over and above what had been thought out by the speaker, (c) a more precise and delimited version of what the speaker said and intended. A problem complicating the discussion here is the different senses of "mean." Think, for example, of a conversation in which a request for a cup of tea is followed two minutes later by the same speaker's saying, as he is given what he asked, "but you have given me tea." The reply is "but you asked for tea," which elicits the response "I meant coffee." In this example an error or slip of the tongue is corrected through reference to an intent. But the word "tea" does not mean (=signify, convey the same information as) "coffee," even if the speaker meant (intended to say) coffee. This example establishes that there is a radical difference between (a) statements describing the meaning (significance) of a piece of language, and (b) statements referring to a speaker's meaning or intent. The former is a question of the rules of language, the latter of much more diverse and uncontrollable factors; talk of "intent" may involve errors, omissions, lack of precision, or incompleteness in a piece of language when that language is compared to the function ("meaning" in the first sense) which either speaker or listener or both assume the piece of language ought to have.

This is the practical background to those situations where we talk of "intent" as giving us a better version of the thing to be communicated than does the actual piece of language itself. The question now arises, can we deal with literary texts in this way? That is, can we give an improved version of (correct, add to, delete from, make more specific, or whatever) their meaning by appeal to an intent? And can we infer this intent by knowledge of the biographical context of the author, including both any possible direct comments by him on the text, and his general situation as a man characteristically concerned with certain kinds of things and situations?

Literary scholarship had largely assumed an affirmative answer to this question until W. K. Wimsatt and M. C. Beardsley in a celebrated article[3] coined the term "Intentional Fallacy"; they held that the intent of the author is first of all not available to us (or perhaps even to him) and that even if it were it could not form an adequate basis for judging and interpreting his work. Since that time, the issues involved have been discussed many times,[4] but the discussion (whether pro or con that conclusion) has largely tended to go over the familiar ground gone over already by Wimsatt and Beardsley. In the

[3] W. K. Wimsatt and M. C. Beardsley, "The Intentional Fallacy," in *The Verbal Icon*, (originally 1946, *Sewanee Review* 54).

[4] E.g., in Wellek and Warren, chapter 4; H. M. Jones, "The Relevance of the Artist's Intentions," *British Journal of Aesthetics* 4 (1964); H. D. Aiken, "The Aesthetic Relevance of Artists' Intentions," *Journal of Philosophy* 52 (1955); E. D. Hirsch, *Validity in Interpretation* (New Haven, 1967); F. Cioffi, "Intention and Interpretation in Criticism," in C. Barrett (ed.), *Collected Papers in Aesthetics* (New York, 1966); W. K. Wimsatt, "Genesis: A Fallacy Revisited," in *The Disciplines of Criticism, Essays in Literary Theory and History*, eds. P. Demetz, T. Greene, L. Nelson, Jr. (New Haven, 1968); and P. D. Juhl, "Intention and Literary Interpretation." This is only a sample of the discussion of these issues. In practical terms, it is fair to say that the thesis of Wimsatt and Beardsley has never been accepted by more than a small proportion of critics; much labor has continued to be put into research into the author's viewpoint, and it is perhaps symptomatic that Edel, writing in the pamphlet *Relations of Literary Study* on the subject "Literature and Biography" can ignore the whole controversy, and simply state: "We can most truthfully study literature when we link the poem to the poet" (p. 66). By giving this unanalyzed statement the status of a truism, Edel avoids the entire theoretical basis of his subject. To talk of the "intent" of the poem, if this is an abstraction from the text which is justified by reference to the text, raises none of the problems of the intentional fallacy—except terminological confusion, for which reason the term is best avoided in this context.

following discussion, I, too, have no alternative but to go over some of this ground once more for the sake of the continuity of the argument; but I shall attempt to give the whole argument a new basis by assimilating it to my logical framework, and in particular to the preceding discussion of the definition of literature.

In the discussions to date of the intentional fallacy, the central questions have generally been: Can an author have a clear concept of what he has written? or Are poets generally better at composing poetry than they are at talking about what they have written? and so on. Now these questions are in themselves quite intelligible, and I shall return to them in a moment. But they are not the fundamental questions with which we must first of all be concerned; and to the extent that many anti-intentionalists have allowed them to become so central, they have become diverted from the focal point of the dispute. Even to talk of the adequacy or inadequacy of poets in formulating descriptions of their work, for example, is bound to raise the possibility of interpreting such statements on their part rather than merely accepting them; the intentionalist thus easily makes the question whether the poet's statements are always to be accepted as they stand a moot one from his point of view. This line of argument also leaves open the possibility that one can look at the overall circumstances of a poet's life and infer intent from his situation; in that case a statement of his intent in terms of his work's being a response by him to that situation would dispense entirely with the requirement that he be able to formulate it accurately himself.[5]

[5] J. Boyd, in his *Notes to Goethe's Poems* (Oxford, 1948), 1: 90, puts this kind of view with great simplicity; it is one that has long

To put the question in broader linguistic terms: it is quite natural, in everyday language, to infer the intent of an utterance by reference to its general context and in so doing not to be bound by the speaker's own possibly inadequate explanation of that intent. And that makes irrelevant the question whether poets in particular are to be trusted in their formulations of their intent; we are quite used to the idea of supplying part of the meaning of an utterance through its intent in a way that has no need whatever for any direct formulation of it by the speaker. From the standpoint of the analysis that follows, the traditional arguments against intentionalism have in a sense conceded the point at issue once they talk of the poet in relation to his poem in terms of speaker in relation to utterance at all.

From my discussion of the definition of literary texts, it will be remembered that the defining point for these texts is the use made of them, and the way in which they are treated; and further, that this use was centrally a matter of not taking them as part of the context of their origin in the way in which we normally treat pieces of language. Literary texts are not treated as part of the normal flow of speech, which has a purpose in its original context and is then discarded after that purpose is achieved, and they are not judged according to such limited purposes. These texts are defined as those that outgrow the original context of their utterance, and which

been assumed in the practice of literary critics: ". . . while a poem may adequately convey an emotional experience inspired by a particular 'occasion,' where prose would fail, a knowledge of the occasion cannot but contribute to its fuller effect." Boyd's comments on the poems make it their first duty to resurrect the "occasion" as fully as possible.

function in the community at large. They do not function in that original context, are not dependant on that context for meaning, and are not judged according to their appropriateness or success in achieving what was to be achieved there. Therefore, when we decide to treat a piece of language as literature, that decision is in itself a decision not to refer the text to its originator nor to treat it as a communication from him.[6] Literary texts can be converted into nonliterary texts quite simply: since the use made of the one is quite different from the use made of the other and, since it is this use (not properties of the texts) which is defining, we can make a poem not a poem by so treating it. We can treat a poem of Goethe as a letter from him to Friederike Brion. It may well have functioned that way in its context of origin; and there is nothing logically wrong in doing this. But we must be clear about our aim in doing so: it is not the aim of literary study. If our inquiry is to be a meaningful one, and not the wholly meaningless one of "statements about this text," we must think of these possible uses of the text as belonging to distinct activities, with their own very different rationales and criteria of relevance.

The one thing that is different about literary texts, then, is that they are not to be taken as part of the contexts of their origin; and to take them in this way is to annihilate exactly the thing that makes them literary texts. I am not making the point that this use is an inappropriate one, but the stronger point that the texts are actually made into something different by this use: they

[6] Cf. D. G. Mowatt, "Language, Literature, and Middle High German," *Seminar: A Journal of Germanic Studies* 1 (1965): 72, for a related point.

are not just literature misused, they are no longer literature at all. The process of a text becoming a literary text involves three stages: its originating in the context of its creator, its then being offered for use as literature, and its finally being accepted as such. In the final step, society makes the text into literature. The biographical approach returns the text to its former status, and reverses the process of its becoming a literary text.

This, it appears to me, is the most radical and accurate argument against intentionalism that can be made. Yet, so far, it is a theoretical argument, which shows that intentionalism is in theory injurious to literary texts. It may not seem to speak to all of those practical situations in which critics have information derived from the context of origin of a literary work, and have the psychological conviction that that knowledge has been helpful to them. For this reason I shall go beyond the general logical argument to discuss the various kinds of practical arguments for intentional knowledge in the light of both the logical problems peculiar to each one and of the general logical argument that I have already set out.

There is, first of all, a general claim that it can do no harm to know more about literary texts, but one answer to that will already, after my discussion of the aims of criticism, be clear enough: if something is irrelevant, it always deflects attention from what is relevant, and weakens the investigation in the process. But there is also in this case a more specific answer: when we examine carefully the way in which biographical or intentional information is used, it turns out to be the case that such information is directly harmful. Typical uses of such information interfere with and are even destructive of our relation to literary texts. Far from deepening that relation with the texts (as is frequently claimed), such statements tend to make it more superficial.

In being taken back to its original context, a poem is made more specific, and (as the arguments for and against this operation can both agree) something additional is brought to the poem. But that specificity is a loss, not a gain; what is taken away is the level of generality possessed by the text as a literary text. Let us assume, for example, that the process of a poet's composing his poem involved as a starting point a situation that he himself experienced; we can immediately see that it must have had much more detail than was eventually put into the text itself. To that extent, much of the original situation was left out. On the other hand, detail and emphasis may have been added which were not in the original situation. There is, then, both more and less in the text than in the original situation and the impact of the text is different from the original situation to the degree that those changes have occurred. To replace everything in the work that was there in the original situation is, in fact, to reverse the process of composition. The work became a work of literature after having been changed from the original situation, so that to put back all that the poet thought was irrelevant and therefore left out is to destroy the structure of the finished work by virtue of which it has its artistic impact and meaning; that meaning was created precisely by the selective operation that so many critics seem to be at pains to reverse and remove. This, then, is the sense in which knowing more, that is, putting back into the work what has been kept out of it, is to end up with less—with a work whose meaning has been made too local, whose controlled emphases have been removed, and which has been given a kind of specificity that it should not have. To do all this is to have forced the text to function in a limited situation in the life of one individual, instead of in the life of the community. This is all nothing less than the demolition of a literary structure.[7]

On occasion, the usefulness of biographical knowledge for literary criticism is argued in a way diametrically opposed to that which I have just considered: in seeking biographical information, the argument runs, we are not trying to reintroduce into the text the details that the poet chose to exclude in order to regard them, too, as part of the meaning of the text, but rather in order to see what choices were made for inclusion or exclusion of detail and emphasis, and thus to learn something about the meaning of the text by our increased awareness of the concerns demonstrated by the process of the literary text taking shape.[8] But this argument fails too; the study

---

[7] Edel, in "Literature and Biography," misconceives this kind of objection in his answers (p. 69) to the charge that biographical criticism is reductive. He replies that it may seem to reduce the mystery of works of literature, but replaces that with knowledge and insight. This is not what the objections to biographical criticism are about: they are generally about the introduction of irrelevant instead of relevant knowledge, and the reduction of the possible meanings of a literary text which occurs as a result.

[8] Colie, "Literature and History," in *Relations of Literary Study*, pp. 7–8, produces a revealing formulation: "Half the fun of reading works of this sort lies in our familiarity with the range of possible alternatives from which a given author may have chosen, in our ability to understand the author's professional situation. . . ." In admitting that it is "fun" to know the author's situation, and ignoring the crucial question of relevance, Colie tends to confirm that the motivation of this kind of literary criticism is less

of the creative process, in the sense of the development of a work in the hands of its author, contributes nothing whatsoever to our understanding of the meaning of the text; on the contrary, only an understanding of the meaning of the text makes the study of its genesis possible and intelligible (though still not useful from an interpretative standpoint).

Consider, for example, the comparison of variant readings, which is the tactic generally used in adducing the creative process as a means of understanding the poem.[9] It is in variants, which tell us of last-minute decisions by the poet, that his intent and concerns can be seen at work—so the argument generally runs. But, interestingly enough, the argument then takes two quite contradictory forms. One of them asserts that we can know more of what was in the author's mind from other versions, and so can confirm that a certain kind of idea is important in the work by noting that its expression was even clearer in a variant reading. This, in effect, imports emphases from variants into the final version. But there is an entirely opposite argument, namely, that special significance should be seen in the fact that an idea is deemphasized in the final version; that is, the final omission of the more explicit version of the rejected variant shows that the poet wished not to let that idea have such great impor-

---

a concern with an investigation having a clear purpose than the pursuit of a rather clubbish, in-group amusement for scholars.

[9] The treatment of this problem by Wellek and Warren (chapter 8) is clear and effective; my account follows theirs in part. For an entertaining account of the results of these critical misconceptions in the criticism of Goethe's poetry, cf. D. G. Mowatt, "In the Beginning was the First Version," *German Life and Letters*, n. s. 12 (1959).

tance in the work. Both arguments are commonly used and are equally invalid, as is indicated by the arbitrariness of using one rather than the other: in both cases, what is involved is an attempt to bolster a view of a degree of emphasis in a literary text which ought to be supported only by an examination and description of that emphasis as it appears in the final version; we have no reason to give that emphasis any other status than is assigned to it by the language that confronts us.

Of the two ways of using this kind of variant material, the first is more obviously erroneous, since it alters the text by deciding to reverse a choice that has been embodied in it. But the second is no less theoretically inadequate; it takes the text and redistributes its emphases, on the basis that those elements added latest are the most important. The concentration on what came last is quite arbitrary; why should we not consider the first elements the most important? The answer seems to be that there is no reason to do so, any more than to do the reverse. Eventually one must let all elements of a piece of language have the emphasis that they actually have in that language; if the author had really wanted something added late to have special emphasis, then the way to achieve that was precisely to give it special textual emphasis! If he did not give it that emphasis and we insist that such a special emphasis must exist, we have, without reason, redistributed the emphases of the text. It can, of course, always be fruitful to use variants, as well as closely related works of literature, to throw texts into sharp relief, and to aid us in thinking about their meaning; likewise, we can perform exercises such as: What would happen in this play if this short scene were omitted? These can all be categorized as ways of making very clear and sharp the function of parts of a text which are isolated for examination in this way. But the author's variants have no special status in this procedure; and the procedure is only one of helping us to think, not of deriving from other material information about the emphases of a text.[10]

Before we can see what it is that has occurred when a text has been changed from one version to another, we must look at the effect of the parts of the text concerned on the whole text; that is, we must interpret their function within both complete texts. And only after that can we form any judgment about the nature of the changes, which must be viewed not merely as the change of a few words that can be compared directly to each other, but as a change from a whole text meaning one thing to a whole text meaning another. For this reason I concluded elsewhere that ". . . the familiar thesis, that in order to understand the poem one must first know the genesis, really needs reversing: only by first understanding the poem can the genesis be understood."[11]

The logical relation between understanding the structure of a thing and understanding its history is an im-

---

[10] Cf. Wellek and Warren, p. 79.

[11] "Goethe's Revision of 'Willkommen und Abschied,'" *German Life and Letters*, n. s. 16 (1962): 21. This article and Mowatt's "In the Beginning was the First Version" discussed a further theoretical complication in the use of variant versions for interpretative purposes: each revision produces a different poem. In some cases an author has in effect picked up an early poem and created from it a new one with a sharply different meaning. In the case of Goethe's "Willkommen und Abschied," two very different poems must be recognized, not two versions, nor even two poems closely related in their meanings.

portant issue here, and that relation can be made clearer through pinpointing in a practical analogy the different kinds of understanding involved in the two cases.[12] Imagine, for example, a situation in which an automobile will not start, and its owner then says that he is unable to understand this. A mechanic arrives, does some tests, and arrives at the simple conclusion that there is no fuel in the tank. The owner of the car looks puzzled, and again says that he cannot understand it, for he filled the tank only the day before. Now in spite of the verbal similarity in his expressions of his lack of understanding at the two stages of this problem, there are two logically distinct issues involved. The first kind of understanding is structural: the owner's expression meant that he was unable to give an analysis of the automobile's failing to work. But the second is genetic: here, he had structural understanding, but wanted to know how that structural state of affairs had come about. On the one hand, then, there is the understanding of the structure of a thing or situation, and on the other hand, the understanding of how that structure originated. When the owner of the automobile has achieved enlightenment on the first score he is able to pursue the second: Was it that he only thought that he had filled the tank? Had someone siphoned his fuel out overnight? And so on. But the crucial point here is that the range of genetic questions that one can ask is controlled by the amount of structural knowledge one commands. Without knowing what is wrong structurally one cannot even begin to ask the right genetic questions: they cannot be known. What this means is that genetic questions depend on prior results of structural analysis,

[12] Cf. my *Schiller's "Kalliasbriefe,"* p. 31.

and therefore that the former are always dependant on the latter. Once one has some conception of what one is dealing with, one can ask how it came to be that way, but not before. Conversely, there is no valid inference from the genesis of a thing to its structure. Whatever structure one tries to create, the question of success or failure in achieving that structure can only be answered by looking at the structure and finding out what actually happened to the intent of its maker, and this is a question not of what he tried to do, but what he has, in fact, done.

There is always an unbridgeable gap between statements of intent to do something and statements of what has been done; this is not merely a question of efficiency in achieving one's aims. The practical consideration that most firmly separates statements of intent from what actually happens is that, right up to the last minute, intent may change or simply be modified in the actual process of the execution of what was intended. It is a normal and common experience that we have a general plan of a task or performance but change the plan as we come to terms with the problems of carrying it out, since only in that process do we really learn how sound or how complete our planning had been; large areas of the task may not have been thought out at all. As I write this book, it is emerging as something different from what I had "intended"; and my intent in the book as abstracted from my action as represented in its final shape takes precedence over any statement I may have made about my intent before it was written.

In the last analysis, arguments from genesis fall foul of a well-known dilemma: either the meaning and emphasis discerned through the genesis of the poem is actually in the poem, in which case it did not need to be sought elsewhere; or it is not in the poem, in which case it is simply not part of the poem at all. In the second case there can never be sufficient reason for writing into the poem something which is not there, in order to make it conform to a statement of intention or to an inferred intent, when in so doing we are going against the best evidence we have of the author's final intent, namely, the text that he finally produced.[13] Whatever his plans may have been, the text is the only evidence we can have of the modification that any previous intent underwent. Even if we grant the intentionalist thesis that the meaning of the poem is what the poet intended, it would still be true that the only reliable evidence of that intent is the poem, and from this it would follow that we should not prefer any other evidence to that of the poem in determining intent.

A milder version of the argument for knowledge of genesis and intention is one that suggests that such information draws our attention to facts about the text which we might otherwise not notice; this would make intentional and biographical statements helpful, even if not vital. But the argument for intentional statements as a pragmatic expedient rather than a necessary source of

[13] The more one allows the notion of unconscious intent to come into the discussion, the greater the general gap created between the author's statements and the work, and the more emphasis must be placed on the work as the evidence of that unconscious intent. Thus appeals to an "unconscious intent" to rescue intentionalism are self-defeating, since they push us toward the work and away from explicit statements of intent. Juhl overlooks this point, p. 4ff., and at the same time fails to seize the importance of the demonstration by Wimsatt and Beardsley of the ambiguity of the word "mean."

information is no less problematic. Since it is practical advantage that is appealed to, the point can be judged only from critical practice. And critical practice shows that biographical perspectives have not been used predominantly as a catalyst for thought about literary texts, but as a substitute for such thought. They have been a hindrance, rather than an aid, to interpretation, since, in practice, the detail and emphasis derived from biography have been preferred to those of the text; and so, whether from a practical or theoretical point of view, there is no reason not to approach the problems of textual emphasis directly.

The most fundamental logical error in biographical and intentional criticism, as I have already argued, is that of referring a literary text to the limited context of its origin, which by definition removes from it any literary status. But perhaps the most important logical weakness that leads critics in the direction of those kinds of statements in criticism lies in their often primitive notions of how to speak about a piece of language and its meaning. A simple example can be seen in one of the critical procedures that I have just discussed, namely, that of comparing variant readings to a final version of a literary text in order to gain an insight into what the text means through contrasting it with what it avoids. For a general fact about language is that it derives meaning by systematic contrasts; any expression derives its meaning from the choice of that expression rather than others which contrast with it in a variety of different ways. From a linguistic standpoint, then, to contrast a variant with a literary text is to limit the range of meaning of an expression by limiting the possible meaningful contrasts it involves, and to give one particular contrast a special status for which there is no conceivable justification: even the possible conscious choice in one area of meaning cannot justify giving special attention to that area, and ignoring the other contrasts that that expression depends on for its meaning. Instead of seeing one particular contrast as a clue to meaning, therefore, we must think of all possible contrasts as parts of the meaning of a piece of language.

Another example of how an inadequate account of language leads toward biographical criticism is provided by the common notion that words have denotative and connotative meanings.[14] We can easily see what words denote, the argument goes, but the question of connotation, of allusions and associations of words, is a much vaguer matter; while denotation is an easy matter to grasp, we can use some help in the form of information about what the poet really had in mind when it comes to the connotations of words. This whole argument depends on a referential view of language, since "denotation" is here the equivalent of "reference"; once again, the reference theory of meaning proves to be an important source of error in critical theory. I shall discuss more directly in the following chapter the validity of this theory of meaning and the inadequacy of its terminology for the analysis of literary texts. But even if we did not object to the theory and to its terms, it would still be invalid to use it to justify intentionalism.

The essential basis of this line of argument is the notion that much of a literary text is open and not completely determinate in its meaning. This feeling of a lack of

[14] Juhl relies a good deal on this kind of separation.

determinateness, of firmly graspable notions of the exact meaning of a word, is reflected in the kinds of areas of meaning that intentionalists pursue: these are typically not only connotations and allusions, but also ambiguities, private meanings of words not easily shared by readers, and so on. But this unwillingness to let a literary work remain at the degree of openness that it actually has is surely evidence of an insecurity on the part of the critic when faced with a complex and challenging text. If we assume that poets are men who have a gift for using language to produce structures of words that will say what they want to say, have implications that they wish to imply, and leave carefully open what they want to leave open—in short, if we assume that the inexplicitness is as controlled as the explicitness, and that ambiguity or allusiveness is something that the poet works with for his purposes, then there is no temptation to proceed as an intentionalist does. For what he does is to simplify what was made too complex for him to tolerate; he treats careful control both of connotation and denotation as error. He tries to seek out clear meanings that are delimited, (to use reference theory terminology) to reduce complex connotation to simple denotation, to remove ambiguity, and to supply simple answers from the poet's biography instead of from the more complex literary text. The implication in this procedure must surely be that the poet is an incompetent, a man who tries to communicate something simple and accidentally goes into unwanted complexities of language. This is most unlikely—though it might sometimes be the case. Yet even when it is the case, its implications must be faced; this or that text may be judged a failure. But to adopt this procedure and then act as if it were the norm for successful poems is very strange.

Instead of leaving the text in order to look into biographical sources for a determination of the character of the associations of a given word, or the emphasis of a given idea, it must be preferable to take the harder but more useful course of looking at the text and conceptualizing just what is implied there. Instead of seeking the irrelevantly specific information of biography, we should accept precisely the degree and kind of specificity offered us by the text, and respond accurately to it; instead of redistributing the emphases of the text for extraneous reasons, we should focus on the text's own emphases. Accurate response to these aspects of a text is not easy; but to say this is to say that responding to literature is not easy. Biographical criticism appears to be a simple means of avoiding the challenge. An extreme example of this is provided by criticism of Kafka: critics commonly become baffled by Kafka's bizarre and challenging work, and resort to his diaries in order to come up with the simplest possible biographical reductions of his work. All of which should make one ask: was that bizarre work only a very odd way of saying something so simple?[15]

Bizarreness, inexplicitness, allusiveness, ambiguity, and other kinds of puzzling features of literary texts

[15] See the evidence presented in my book *Narration in the German Novelle. Theory and Interpretation* (Cambridge, England, 1974), where I show that the type of statement "for Kafka, X means . . ." is as common now as ever it was.

will not be converted into something simple and thus
go away so easily.[16] Whenever intentionalism is used
as a device for simplifying a text, by the argument
that some features of a text are simply "there" but that
others, being less tangible, are not there in the same way,
it must be insisted that everything is there in the same
sense, if one is willing to respond to it.

Another important inadequacy in the linguistic theory
inherent in the position of many intentionalists is seen in
their view that, since particular authors use words in
their own special ways, these idiosyncratic usages need
elucidation with the help of information concerning that
author's individual usage. As I noted above, we commonly
use the notion of "intent" to supplement the meaning
of a text with material derived from its context, and in
so doing we are sometimes adding more specific meaning,
sometimes inserting what had been omitted, and sometimes even correcting errors. Intentionalists build on this
common occurrence to argue that we need know not only
the public meanings of words, but also the way in which
the poet is using them. I want next to show that the
phenomenon of special individual usage can indeed occur

---

[16] This common failure of literary scholarship is made worse
by the claim of many critics to be making things understandable
to lay readers, and so adopting the position of, e.g., "Kafka ex-
perts" in order to enlighten those less well prepared. In so doing,
they draw readers away from what Kafka wants them to experience. Joyce is another bizarre author whose critics commonly treat
this quality as something the reader must be helped to circumvent
—as though this were just an unfortunate accident about the
author; the reader is to be preserved, by giving him much biographical information, from the chaos Joyce so clearly wants to
get him into. Put simply, the critic's assistance to the reader
amounts to preventing him from experiencing the literary work.

in literary texts, but that this has nothing to do with intentionalism, and does nothing to justify the search for the poet's meaning in his private uses of words.

It is not necessary to claim that the meanings of words are clear in themselves to counter the intentionalist argument here; on the contrary, the correct reply lies in the other direction, and is precisely that the context of a word or sentence is indeed all important in determining its meaning. The paradox here is that the intentionalist's problems arise precisely because he does not take a word in its relevant context and let that context control what it can mean. Words in literary texts can and must be made more specific by referring them to their context; their associations must be no more nor less than those that the rest of the work selects and allows. To that extent, literary language works as ordinary language does. But there is one important difference: it is that literary texts have distinct boundaries, so that the extent of the context of a word is finite.[17] What does not get specified inside the text remains unspecified, and to specify anything beyond that degree of specificity raises again the problem of arbitrary importation into the text of an intent other than that embodied in the execution of the work. The issue here, then, is not one of whether to refer

[17] There is one complication in this argument, but not one that strikes at its basic logic: it is that the "boundaries of the text" can occasionally be variable. For example, a poem in a cycle of poems may be taken either as a text having its own boundaries, or as part of a text having larger ones; the same is true of the individual novels in Balzac's *Comédie Humaine*. The facts of these cases seem to show that the individual texts are commonly read in both ways, and there seems no reason to object to either way of reading them.

a word to its context but of which context is the relevant
one. Again, the definition of literature provides the answer: the context of the author's usage is part of the
limited context of origin and therefore not relevant.
From this point of view, the "special usage" of a particular poet[18] can only be a useful literary notion if it
originates from and is describable in terms of the literary
text. If we view the idiosyncratic usage of a poet only as
a matter of his use of a word with certain ideas in his
mind, with those ideas accessible only through knowledge of that mind, then all kinds of awkward questions
arise. For example: Why does the poet choose this very
inefficient way of communicating what he wants to say?
Can this be regarded as a very successful use of words?
Ought it not to be viewed as a misuse of words to use
them to mean something that they do not mean? But there
is no need to get into the kind of dilemma that such
questions create. For though poets often use words unusually, they are in this very process relying on normal
usage to create the unusual effect. Dylan Thomas, as is
well known, often juxtaposes words that cannot normally be juxtaposed at all. But that is not to say that he is
using private meanings for these words. On the contrary:
the clash of two words (and ideas) not normally seen together gives us his meaning. The use of the word is a
matter of the context in which it occurs; that use can indeed be strange, but its very strangeness depends on the
reader's awareness of the contrast with normal usage.
To think of this as "private" meaning is to avoid the

---

[18] I do not yet deal with the question of the author's language
as needing elucidation because it is that of his age rather than
his own individual usage. See below, pp. 144ff.

issue of just what the particular assemblage of words in the poem does, which is a quite public matter. Once again, a critic trying to play the role of the expert who must instruct the lay audience in what only the Dylan Thomas specialist knows from his privileged status merely succeeds in narrowing down the meaning of the poem and preventing the reader from coming to terms with the challenge of its striking language.[19]

My analysis so far has dealt with the fundamental issues of logical and linguistic theory which are involved in the question of the relevance of the biographical context to the work of literature. It remains to consider three ingenious attempts to rescue biographical and intentional criticism. The first begins by advocating an awareness of the psychological depths of a text. On the surface, it is argued, a literary text may seem self-sufficient; but below that surface there are stresses and strains that constitute its most important level of meaning. And since those stresses and strains are the products of the author's unconscious mind, we must focus our attention on the author's mind.[20] But the complications provided by this

[19] Again, this is nowhere more striking than in the case of criticism of Kafka. Critics still search the diaries for Kafka's private meanings and attempt to provide readers with a kind of translation from Kafka's language into theirs. Kafka's characteristic quality is thereby annihilated.

[20] Cf. Crews, in the two articles, "Literature and Psychology" and "Anaesthetic Criticism." Crews also advances the strange argument that ". . . the literary work which is completely free from its biographical determinants is not to be found . . ." ("Literature and Psychology," p. 81), from which one can only assume that he takes the opposition to his view to be making the impossible assertion that works are not determined by the poet's problems (instead of the view that it is irrelevant to their status as literature

argument are not sufficient to make the general logic of the situation that I have outlined change materially. If the deeper level of a text embodies strain and conflict, then that will be part of its effect, at that deeper level, on its readers. Conflict that did not find expression in the text will simply not get across to the reader, and to import it from an outside source raises once again the issue of arbitrary intervention into the action of an author. To make a distinction between the full-scale psychoanalysis of the author on the one hand, and the consideration of the implications of the text (at all levels) on the other, is not to allow us to opt for a superficial as opposed to a deep reading (by choosing to pursue the former but not the latter) but only to delimit the relevant area of depth from that which is irrelevant. If we concentrate on the . relevant context of literary texts—the context of their relation to the community—we can then analyze that relationship in all the depth that is desirable; there is no reason to argue that the exclusion of one specific neurosis from the picture (the actual neurosis of the author) commits us to ignoring the possible neurotic content of the text. The question, here as elsewhere, is how does this text speak to the community, for it is one of those texts that are singled out for its ability

───────────

that they are so determined). It is an odd feature of Crews's argument that he uses an essentially traditional biographical argument to support his self-consciously antitraditionalist Freudian approach; that there is no need to do so—in fact that Freudian interpretation need not fall foul of antibiographical arguments—was shown by B. A. Rowley, in his "Psychology and Literary Criticism," in *Psychoanalysis and the Social Sciences* (New York, 1958).

to do so. It is an odd thing to suggest that it really cannot do so until we have first had a clinical report on the poet, for the simple answer to this is that it has done so long before such a report was provided.

The second of these ingenious attempts to reinstate biographical criticism begins with an appeal to the privileged position of the author vis-à-vis his text; he must surely know more about it than anyone else, and therefore we should know what he said and thought about it. There would be no danger in this argument provided that the necessary distinctions were made, which they never are. In this view, the status of the author is essentially that of a very knowledgeable critic of his own work; that being so it is indeed likely that we can learn from his criticism of his work. However, it must be remembered that in formulating the matter in this way we have already decided that his opinion is not to be an authoritative one, but instead one that we shall treat as we treat that of any other critic: if what he says is illuminating, so much the better, and if not, then we shall feel free to disregard him. His statements are neither a key to interpretation, nor part of the complex to be interpreted. To view the question in this practical way is to subject the author's suggestions to the test of our own reason, and our own judgment of his work. And to judge from past experience it would seem to be the case that authors are sometimes very penetrating critics, sometimes not.

The last of the three asserts that we cannot judge the achievement of an author unless we know the circumstances of his life. But to this the answer is simple: to answer a biographical question, biographical evidence is certainly necessary.[21] The status of a text in the community is a question of literary value. The achievement of an author in being able to create that text is a matter to be judged according to how much he had to overcome to do it, and so on. But the hindrances that he faced, however great, do not determine the status of the text in the community—unless, of course, the work itself deals with them in some way.[22] The same argument holds when we deal with authorial originality;[23] no matter what evidence we may find of the extent of a particular author's intellectual and artistic debts, it is very unlikely that such factors will influence the judgment of his work in the community, though this may well influence our judgment of him as an artist.[24] In practice, a judgment

[21] Much of Juhl's argument (e.g., pp. 22–23) amounts to showing not that biographical evidence is necessary for literary interpretation, but that biographical evidence is necessary to answer biographical questions.

[22] Cf. my Schiller's "Kalliasbriefe," p. 29.

[23] The whole question of originality is usually much more complex than is allowed for by this kind of argument; if (as is commonly the case in, for example, medieval German epics) originality sometimes lies in a particularly subtle turn in what is largely handed to the poet by a predecessor or by a traditional story, a judgment of originality in terms of the extent of new material added by the later poet is of little value. Critics who concentrate on such factors as a poet's achievement and his place within a tradition tend to belong to that group which Crews attacks very effectively ("Anaesthetic Criticism," I) as proceeding on the assumption that "literature makes literature" and is "its own progenitor." I discuss this narrowly bookish view below, pp. 152–3.

[24] A small remaining issue here is that of textual criticism, i.e., the establishment of a "correct" text, which, according to many textual critics, involves the notion of getting at the readings that the author intended. See, for example, F. Bowers, "Textual Criticism," in *Aims and Methods*, ed. Thorpe. This position was discussed in an article "A Closer Look at 'Aims and Methods,'"

that a work is "derivative" usually amounts to the adverse criticism that that work is a poor imitation of something else, and so is lacking in imagination and force.

I now turn to the wider question of the relevance of the social and historical context of literary texts. Once more the guiding principle must be invoked that not everything that can be said about a text is relevant to a literary investigation, and that our grasp on what we are doing must not be weakened by the vague idea that the more we know the better,[25] whatever its character.

Modern Language Journal 50 (1966) by D. G. Mowatt, H. S. Robertson, and myself. Juhl (pp. 19–20) also thinks that this problem strengthens the case for knowing the "intent" of the poet. But this cannot be so. When there are several versions of a text, there are two possibilities: either all are by the poet himself, in which case, as I have argued, we may legitimately think of them as different but closely related texts, and choose between them only if circumstances force us to; or some versions have readings not originating from the poet, in which case as a practical and pragmatic matter we should tend to go back to the poet's own version (unless there is a quite powerful attraction in a version revised by another, as may be the case, for example, in Wagner's revision of Schumann's symphonies) simply on the grounds that it is much more likely that the creator of a structure of words that is known to be highly effective can do better than an editor who does not possess creative ability. For a penetrating discussion of "Interpretation and Emendation," see the chapter bearing that title in D. G. Mowatt's *Friedrich von Hüsen* (Cambridge, England, 1971), pp. 24–46. Mowatt demonstrates that editorial emendation is generally an attempt to make a poem fall more into line with the editor's often faulty understanding of it.

[25] An entirely different and legitimate use of "the more we know the better" refers to the general preparation of the reader of a literary text. The more he brings to a text in personal experience, including experience of diverse situations in his life and also experience of a variety of literary texts, the more he will be open to the experience that a literary text offers. This is, of course, nothing to do with the question under discussion, which concerns

We are here involved in one of the most difficult and persistent clashes of viewpoint in literary theory; it is on this ground that the case for *art engagé* as opposed to art for art's sake is argued out. One side may stress the time-lessness of art, the other its being a very direct social act at a particular time;[26] while the charge of "empty formal-ism" is countered with one of "historical reductionism."

The analysis of this issue begins in the same way as does that for the case of biographical context, though some complications will emerge at a later stage. The use of texts in such a way that they are not regarded as limited to and functioning within the original circum-stances of their origin is defining for literary texts; there-fore, to refer them back to that original context in order to treat them as functioning primarily in that context is to make them no longer literary texts. Literary historians commonly insist that knowledge of the original historical circumstances that gave rise to a work deepens our ap-preciation;[27] but the reverse is true. Concentration on such factors makes our understanding more localized, and hence more superficial; in taking this path we have again reversed the process of a text becoming literature. The same genetic arguments occur in this sphere as in that of biographical criticism, and with the same analysis; to speak of understanding the origin of a work of litera-ture is not the same thing as speaking of understanding

specific information about a particular text, not general receptivity to literary texts.

[26] It is perhaps at this point in their book that Wellek and War-ren seem most content to state the issues and leave them unre-solved. See, for example, their chapter 9.

[27] Colie ("Literature and History") argues this way, e.g., pp. 10 and 13.

its meaning, and only the confusion of the different uses of the word "understand" can make genetic explanation seem to be part of the statement of the meaning of the text. As before, it must be noted that an understanding of the meaning of the text is necessary before its genesis can be investigated, and that limitations in understanding the text will make one's ability to understand its genesis limited in exactly the same way.

Literary historians commonly use the trick of argument to which I referred at the beginning of this chapter—that of offering a choice between two views, one of which is their own, and the other an absurd alternative to it. But the alternatives offered reveal a good deal about their misconceptions concerning both their own views and the real nature of the objections to taking works of literature primarily in their historical context. For example, Spiller offers us the alternatives of either seeing the work in its historical dimension or reducing it to "a static and causeless existence"; Colie, that we either concern ourselves with the history of a work or commit ourselves to viewing it as existing only "an sich"; R. Hall, that we either take literature together with its cultural background and author's life history or take it to exist in a vacuum; and so on.[28] An even more common view is the simple one that to divorce a text from its historical context is to divorce literature from life.[29]

[28] Spiller, "Literary History," p. 51; Colie, "Literature and History," p. 1; R. A. Hall, Jr., *Cultural Symbolism in Literature* (Ithaca, 1963), p. 9. Cf. Ellis, Mowatt, and Robertson, "A Closer Look at 'Aims and Methods,'" for an analysis of Spiller's argument.

[29] E.g., Sutton, *Modern American Criticism*, chapter 9. See here the argument against Sutton by Adams (*The Interests of Criti-*

Clearly, no one would wish to divorce literature from life, to treat it in a vacuum, or to reduce it to something static. The question is this: Are these adequate characterizations of what a nonhistoricist criticism involves? My view is that they are, if anything, nearer to characterizing the historicist position itself than its opposite.

No activity that involves large numbers of people in the way that a concern with literary texts does can ever be thought of as cut off from life; likewise, there is no example of language activity that does not have some context and purpose. The critical question is one of what kind of relation to life, what context, and what purpose. The context of a work of literature is that of the whole society for which it is a literary text, and which has made it such; its purpose is precisely that use; and its relation to life is to the life of the whole community. If we insist on relating the text primarily to the context of its composition and to the life and social context of its author, we are cutting it off from that relation to life which is the relevant one, and substituting for it another that is greatly restricted. Far from stressing the social importance of literature, this approach undervalues the social importance of literature by construing its relation to society in too limited a way. The result is a simplification of the issues of the text down to those relevant to one particular social situation only;[30] but the literary value of the text resides

---

cism, p. 116) who rightly claims that Sutton does not argue the real issue raised by the New Critics, but treats them and their descendants as if they could be viewed as nineteenth-century aesthetes.

[30] This theoretical statement of the implications of historicist criticism is not at variance with the practical results of such criticism; historicist critics are in general very slow to respond to the

precisely in the fact that this limited social situation was outgrown. Such a view of literature might with some justice be described as a "static" one.

The opposed viewpoints of art for art's sake and *art engagé* represent a typical misconceived opposition, and it is one that has been extremely persistent; the latter view has often been identified with the historicist viewpoint, the former as antihistoricist. But the opposite of taking art in the author's immediate social context of his time is not to take it as pure enjoyment, any more than the opposite of treating art as art is to treat it as socially relevant.[31] It is when we treat art as relevant to the whole

---

human significance of a literary work, and tend to use the local historical situation upon which they dwell as a substitute for such a response to the text. And it seems also to be the case that literary historians, in spite of their professed desire to explain the causes of literature, never study the most relevant cause of a work becoming literature—its structure and meaning.

[31] See also Watson's espousal of the historicist viewpoint, and his description of the opposing views as anticognitive (*The Literary Critics*, p. 221); there is no reason whatever to oppose these two viewpoints, and so Watson's argument is also one of those that adduces support from an irrelevant and caricatured opposition. The name most often (and rightly) associated with the idea that the reader might come to terms with the challenge of the text without the safety of a limited historical context is that of I. A. Richards; see his *Practical Criticism* (London, 1929). The orthodox historicist reduction still flourishes even in work by contemporary linguists, e.g., M. Gregory and J. Spencer, "An Approach to the Study of Style," in *Linguistics and Style*, ed. J. Spencer (London, 1964). Only Firthian terminology, not Firth's sense of the different ways in which language could function, could be involved in the view that "A literary text may be said to have a context of situation in the sense in which it was understood by Firth" (p. 100). Gregory and Spencer make no distinction between literature and ordinary utterances as far as their relation to a context of origin is concerned.

society for which it is art that we treat it as art; when we do not do this we are neither treating it as art, nor are we dealing with its social relevance.

Satire is a case most often advanced to show the necessity of considering the original historical context of a literary text, and it will therefore be peculiarly appropriate to show how satire proves the reverse to be true. It is generally argued that without a knowledge of the local situation that was being satirized, we have only a vague apprehension of the humor and the issues involved; but when the shadowy figures who inhabit the text in an often two-dimensional form are identified as real people who once lived, and when they are given names and characteristics, then the whole situation becomes alive; the "satire cuts far deeper."[32] And so figures in the text are equated with real-life figures and the real-life situation is expounded and explained.

A kind of gain from this procedure is readily appreciated; but there has also been a loss. Suppose that we ask the question: What distinguishes the satire that has survived its original context from the satire that continually appears from time to time in newspapers and journals and is soon forgotten? The difference must lie in the fact that the former has something to say to people outside the original situation. Swift's *A Modest Proposal,* for example, survives and still plays a great role in the life of the English-speaking community. Now this does not happen because the contemporary Irish situation is still of interest to us from a historical point of view, or because Swift made some clever remarks about it; the social significance of his work is much wider than this, and to

[32] Colie, p. 13.

identify actual historical personages in his texts is to ignore the fact that they are not uniquely the people known to Swift—they are still with us. *A Modest Proposal* may well now make a great impact on a modern reader in the context of the war in Vietnam; it is a remarkable satire on the kind of technical solution to human problems that forgets about people, and of the insanity that bureaucratic talk can easily embody. And so even satire proves the point I have argued: to be concerned to find out the historical source is not to deepen, but to trivialize the meaning of the satire, to prevent ourselves from thinking about its relation to life in the deepest sense, to move from central issues to irrelevances. Even in a satire, those "scarcely concealed identities"[33] of actual historical figures are not the same as those of the figures in the text; and for the modern reader, his own experience is the important thing that he can bring to Swift's satire in order to grasp the depth of Swift's meaning.

The distinction between a kind of criticism that concerns itself with the original context of a literary text and one that does not is often spoken of as the difference between one that goes beyond the text and one that considers the text in itself. But this opposition, too, distorts the issue, and misses the most important aspect of the difference between the two positions. We might just as well put the matter the other way round, and think of the former as one that considers the original context in

[33] Again the practice of historicist scholarship confirms the theoretical point: the historical footnotes which are thought to be vital for a deeper understanding of satire remain historical footnotes and testify only to the historian's fascination with such footnotes.

itself, and the latter as one that goes beyond the original context. But the most important issue raised by this opposition of views is a linguistic one.

In the case of any piece of language, the question of meaning takes us outside the text: the text only exists by virtue of its being part of a linguistic system, and the meaning of the words used derives in every aspect (whether thought of as denotation and connotation, or in the terms of any other view of meaning) from that system. The notion of "the text and nothing but the text" is either right or wrong by definition, depending on how we understand the word "text." If we exclude everything but the signs on the paper, it is wrong and foolish; while if we include all that the text includes in whatever sense, we must be right, but at the cost of saying nothing. The question, then, still remains: What does the text imply, and what kind of evidence or material do we need to show it? Common to almost all critical positions is the use of information from outside the text to interpret the text, and the crucial question is that of the characterization of that information, not of whether we are entertaining any information at all—for clearly we are.

A better and more relevant distinction here is that between the shared meanings and associations of words in the linguistic community, on the one hand, and the local features of the original context of the composition of the text on the other. This distinction focuses the issue in a more useful way than does that between "textual" and "extratextual," and it allows us to see that ignoring what is "extratextual" (in the historicist's sense) is by no means to take the text in isolation; on the contrary, it is to refer it to a wider context, and even to use more information to interpret it.

The problem of allusion, for example, is much more easily dealt with in this framework; biblical allusions can be a meaningful part of a literary text only because the Bible is part of the shared experience of a given community, not because the author of that text in particular has read it.[34] Cultural allusions,[35] too, must be viewed as part of the stock of the linguistic community,[36] and so must allusions to historical situations that are sufficiently part of the consciousness of the community to present distinct images to its members. That is to say, the details of historical fact may not be relevant, but

[34] Juhl (p. 22) argues that to judge any part of one literary work as an allusion to another work, we must know that the author could have alluded to it. Even if we were to grant all its biographical premises, this argument would still be self-destructive; to demonstrate a negative of the order "Y never read nor heard of X" is virtually impossible. Since the most that could be shown is that there is no known evidence that Y read or heard of X, it must always be possible that the author could have alluded to the work in question; and so, Juhl's test creates no means of distinguishing one case from another.

[35] Linguists often try to exclude cultural allusion from their field of inquiry. But there can be no reason to restrict the field of linguistics in this way: the study of language should not be anything less than the whole system of communication of a linguistic community.

[36] It is probably best to view such phenomena as Goethe's references to his own work in this light; e.g., not as biographical information (reached by knowledge of Goethe's other work) but as the exploitation of the community's shared associations. His *Die Leiden des jungen Werthers* had become a cultural document by the time he referred directly to it in such poems as the "Trilogie der Leidenschaft" and the ode "Klein ist unter den Fürsten Germaniens. . . ."

any part of history that has become in a sense legendary will be part of the available stock of the community's shared ideas, and therefore part of its system of communication.

Literary criticism that proceeds by means of explanation of historical circumstances has the apparent advantage that it makes the work seem more accessible and more easily graspable to the reader from another age. But this advantage is indeed only apparent. Not only is this kind of assistance to the reader deceptive and dangerous in its substituting an acquaintance with some simple facts for the need to respond to the texts, but the degree of success of this procedure often has nothing to do with the historical localization at all. For the historical situations invoked most frequently are only graspable in terms of notions with which the reader is quite familiar from his own age, and which do not need the local historical situation to exemplify them. For example, the challenge to a rigid social system by a younger group which finds it restrictive, is a recurring situation in Western society, and a reader urged by a historical critic to feel his way back into a particular historical situation to understand a work that had this kind of situation as its original context has no need to do so; indeed, if he understands the historical situation at all, it is precisely in terms of his own experience. And so the historical critic's way of looking at this situation is the reverse of what is really happening; the reader is not understanding the work through knowledge of history, but understanding history by a knowledge from his own experience of the issues raised in the work. Shaw's blasphemy in *Pygmalion* will not be understood by any explanation of the social situation and the status of the word "bloody" at that time; it will be understood because the context of the work suggests that the word is tabu, and by the modern reader's understanding the concept of "tabu" words, even though nowadays different actual words or acts would exemplify it.

So far, I have been using the notion of a community within which literary texts function without going into the complexities of that notion; and it is a notion that presents some logical problems of its own. Of these, the most serious is that of defining the extent of the community and establishing its boundaries. The problem of defining the limits of a community is a familiar one in many fields. Take, for example, the problem of defining a linguistic community, a problem inherent in deciding whether a difference in two forms of speech is to be classed as the difference between two closely related languages, or between two dialects of the same language. If we have a series of forms of speech existing side by side over a geographical stretch, such that each is recognizable to its neighbor as a slightly different version of the adjacent tongue, but also such that the two outside edges of the geographic chain present forms of speech that are completely unintelligible to speakers of the other form, we have a classic problem of what a language is and of what forms of speech constitute dialects of others. We can scarcely say that we have here a series of slightly different languages, for each group will feel some sense of community (and enjoy perhaps almost total mutual intelligibility) with its adjacent groups, and even with those somewhat further away. The decision to classify the different forms as dialects is not, therefore, merely an

issue of our metalanguage, but describes appropriately
the intuition of the members of one group that others
exist who speak their language, but in a different way.
And yet, as we move along the chain of dialects, there
does come a point where, without any break in the continuity of the chain, the first group may no longer feel
anything in common with one that is several groups
away. It is clear that in this case the notion of an overall
language community has very ragged edges, and would
have to be defined as something like a relatively cohesive
group of dialects. This situation might well have been
the case in Europe for the Romance dialects, but for the
intervention of political factors; the political dominance
of two particular forms in the long chain has now become so great that instead of this difficult hypothetical
theoretical situation we now have "French" and "Italian,"
and we conceive of all forms of speech in the chain as
dialects of either French or Italian. But this sharp break
did not originally exist, and only the political impact of
the two forms now accepted as "standard" French and
Italian has made this easy way out possible.

In setting out this problem of the extent of a community, or of a language, I have been approaching an
analysis of a familiar issue in literary criticism, that of
the relevance for criticism of knowledge of an earlier
form of the English language (for example, seventeenth-
century English) or of another stage of English society
(for example, medieval England). The example I have
used involved gradual change throughout a geographical
spread, but the same kinds of issues of definition are involved in gradual change throughout temporal sequence
too. In the one case there is the mutual intelligibility of

physically adjacent language groups, in the other that of the mutual intelligibility of adjacent centuries of the same language group; and in both there is a feeling of overall sameness and cohesion combined with a feeling that there are noticeably different versions of that overall sameness. More important still, the same issue of encountering a foreign language (and therefore a foreign community) is raised as one jumps a long way along the chain.

Medieval literature is often taken as a critical example that requires a historicist criticism and even one that justifies historicist criticism in principle for all ages; from our time it is a long jump along the chain to medieval society and medieval language, and the result seems to be that we need much assistance in the form of explanations giving local information about the language and the historical times. But the example is deceptive, and careful distinctions are necessary in interpreting it in order to pin down just what kind of theoretical position it actually supports. The earliest stages of the language that recognizably became the distinct version of Low German that developed into modern English are indeed unintelligible to the modern English speaker. When, therefore, a critic cites the example of *Beowulf* in order to make the case for a kind of criticism that takes historical background to be all important, his case may seem impressive, since we do seem to lack the knowledge necessary to understand the work. And yet we can readily concede the need for knowledge of that community and its language without taking that fact to support the historicist's case. To learn the language of *Beowulf* is like learning a foreign language. To understand Goethe, I must learn German, with all that

that means: I must become conversant with the language
and conventions of the German speaking community. The
crucial theoretical point here is that this process must be
represented not as ascertaining the local circumstances
of the composition of the work, but as being initiated into
the community within which the literary text is literature.
Its paradigm is not learning what historical circumstances
gave rise to the composition of a work, but learning a
foreign language to be able to understand the literature of
that language. The relevant material that medieval scholars might urge us to learn in order to understand *Beowulf*
is not the facts of history, but social and linguistic conventions,[37] that is to say, how that society worked and
spoke; typically, however, they do not make this necessary distinction. The case of medieval literature, then,
does nothing to justify the view that literature should be
taken within the local circumstances of its origin.

Just as in the case of a group of dialects, the borderline
cases of mutual intelligibility give us most trouble: What
are the real borders of the community, and at what point
do we stop thinking of a remote century as the same
linguistic community as our own? This is a question that
does not allow a simple answer; there is a variable bound-
ary, and the decision to categorize something at its edge
one way or the other is going to be to some extent an arbitrary one. But the distinction between the two possibilities of categorization, and the attitudes that they will
entail, is clear enough; it will be the difference between

[37] To take a random example, Colie (p. 12) clearly does not
distinguish local historical facts from social conventions; she
treats "the assumptions of 'feudal' society" as on a par with the
characteristics of the historical audiences for whom Stendhal and
Balzac wrote.

viewing a literary text at that edge as something that needs to be understood in terms of a different community, the system of which must be learned, and viewing it as one that is part of our own community and its attitudes, albeit a remote version of this which is a challenge to our imagination.

Yet this last formulation raises several more complexities. There is first a matter of fact about literature which must weigh very heavily in the view we take of literary texts that are recognized as old, but still within our own culture. For in most societies, archaism and literature go together. Over and over again we meet the notion that the valued texts of a society are written in an older form of the language, so that an older form comes to have a function in the contemporary language of being the language of the sacred and venerable texts. In modern English, the speaker of the language must hold in his linguistic value system the notion of biblical and Shakespearean English to understand all that is said around him, and to respond correctly to it. The same phenomenon can be observed everywhere. In Russia there is Old Church Slavonic; in India there is Sanskrit; in Italy there is Latin; in Germany there is Luther's Bible; and in American Indian communities there are exactly analogous notions of the sacred old texts, literary and religious, in an archaic form of the language that gives the community a feeling of the continuity and venerable age of its culture. The same appears to be true of "primitive" cultures all over the world.

When we take this into account, the notion of past and present in literary texts becomes complex. The notions of "poetic" language and archaic language are related; "poetic language" is certainly a mode of the modern language, but there is also a feeling that it indicates age, and thus dignity and value, by being a form that is distinct from common speech, its content too rare and valuable for common speech. Of course, much literature is always being composed in the contemporary language, and on occasion is even aggressively thought of as being distinctively ordinary rather than "poetic"[38] in idiom. But it is destined to become, in a short time, a text in a slightly odd, and old, form of the language, and it is precisely in this guise that all literary works eventually exist and survive. A language can have many modes of speech for occasions and situations that are recognizable types: officialese, slang, and so on. Archaism must also be regarded as a mode of the modern language, reserved in most societies for religious and literary texts.

When we view the situation in this light, the historicist critic's view that we should put ourselves in the position of the author and his audience acquires yet one more problem to add to those that we have already discussed. It is that the contemporary audience's response to the contemporary text is not only a local one, but a fundamentally untypical one too; that is, untypical of what is to be the text's most normal and most literary situation, in which it is distinctively not a document in ordinary contemporary language. This is fundamentally the same error as that of urging that we use a contemporary translation of the Bible, a misunderstanding of the function of the older form of the language. For the twentieth-century audience, the sixteenth-century text can be nei-

[38] I mean "poetic language" here in its colloquial sense only, not as an equivalent to "the language of poetry."

ther a historian's sixteenth-century text,[39] nor simply a twentieth-century text, but is instead a twentieth-century archaic text. To try to reconstruct the sixteenth-century response to it is to remove the archaism, to return the text to an ordinary language status, and to remove from it the aspect of its language that marks it as being one of the society's revered texts.

So much for the general question of the overall archaic quality of a literary text; but the argument for reconstruction of the original historical circumstances of a text often appeals more specifically to changes that have taken place in the meanings of particular words over several hundred years.[40] Nevertheless, this problem is much easier to deal with than is generally supposed, and its solution, once more, does nothing to bolster historicism.

There are at least three possible ways in which the meaning of such usages becomes clear, but none of them involves reconstruction of the precise historical context. First, the context of the word in the literary text may give us its meaning. If it is of more than local importance in only one line of the text, the circumstances in which the word is used will convey the meaning required. The less often the word occurs, the less there is in the text to convey its special meaning, but the meaning of the word is then a matter of much less concern. The more

[39] Wellek and Warren argue (p. 31) that "It is simply not possible to stop being men of the twentieth-century while we engage in a judgment of the past"; this is a good point as far as it goes.

[40] For example, J. Thorpe, *Literary Scholarship* (Boston, 1964), p. 4: "When Milton says, 'I come to pluck your berries harsh and crude,' in the third line of 'Lycidas,' how is the student to know that 'crude' means 'unripe'—and certainly not 'unrefined' or 'unpolished'? Only by going outside the poem, presumably, to notes or to a dictionary or to someone who knows."

important the text makes the word, the more its meaning will be made evident by a series of contexts. Second,
there is a normal phenomenon, in our ordinary use of
language, of words being taken now in broader, now in
narrower senses; and the speaker of English is quite used
to the fact that a move from one context to another, from
one decade to another, or from one dialect of English to
another, produces new specializations of words. In most
cases the new senses do not need explanation; they are
obviously dependent on the same core area of meaning
that exists throughout the language, but have either
specialized or extended that core of meaning. My point
here is that dealing with situations that present new
specializations of existing words is something that all
speakers of a language have to be prepared to do.[41] Third,
there is the even simpler fact that any speaker of English
has to take into account in responding to words the possibility of archaic usage, and any good dictionary of the
modern language should contain significant archaic usages which are in an important sense part of the modern
language. Those occurring in the still current great literary texts should, of course, be included in the description of the range of possible usage in the modern
language; to know the modern English language fully involves knowing such archaisms too.

None of this is very problematic; all three possibilities present perfectly normal linguistic operations, which
involve "going outside the text" only in the same sense

[41] My argument here is fairly closely related to that of Mowatt
on the same topic in "Language, Literature, and Middle High German." An obvious example of this need to deal with new specializations is provided by the case of speakers of English, who quickly
learn to move freely between typical British and American dialects.

that any use of language is to be interpreted in the light of the shared linguistic system of the community. None of the three lends any weight to the view that to interpret a text we must specify a precise historical and personal context.

One more cause of the general tendency to think the modern reader's relation to a literary text in an idiom different from his own an unduly problematic one lies in the fact that the degree to which a text "mirrors" its historical context is generally much overestimated. The medieval knight in shining armor was a conventional image then, as now, and our interest in it now is only more obviously a matter of its value as an image. Similarly, Victorian melodrama evidently represented a convention, and it will always remain a possible convention, irrespective of what that society was in fact like. It is, no doubt, useful for historians to stress the differences between medieval man and modern man, and there are evidently differences; but the literary analyst is in a very different position. The continuity of a given culture must be the focus of his attention, and his analysis must always be turned toward questions of the shared experiences of members of that culture, and the meaning of its images of experience for any of its members, even though some of those images may have arisen in a particular historical or geographical part of the culture. The issues raised in the texts must be thought of as relevant throughout the community; that is why they are found in the community's literary texts. If they are thought of primarily as the experiences of another age, to which a modern reader is an onlooker, then by definition, the texts concerned are being treated not as the literary texts of his culture at all, but only as historical documents and the property of a culture foreign to him.

It is entirely possible, within the framework that I have outlined, to speak of "literary tradition" as being part of the source of meaning of a literary text, but only in the sense that a work can invoke the community's shared associations which reside in its literary texts. Yet this legitimate concern with literary tradition must be distinguished from the narrowly bookish view of those critics who see the modification of tradition almost as an end in itself. This kind of approach[42] sees the reason for literary works in terms of preceding literary works, and their meaning as being determined by their relation to those preceding works; at its most extreme, it views the writing of books as an activity that is above all about writing books. That kind of concern with literary tradition would, once more, remove literary texts from their relevant context. The dependence of literary texts upon all other literary texts is grossly exaggerated by adherents of such a view, which has evidently lost sight of the fact that literary texts relate primarily to the life of the community and not simply to that of literary scholars. Taking the literary text as functioning primarily in the limited

[42] This fallacy is frequent enough, and destructive enough, to warrant a name to make it comparable to the "Intentional Fallacy" and the "Affective Fallacy"; I propose the "Bookish Fallacy." A recent example is J. Fletcher, "The Criticism of Comparison: The Approach through Comparative Literature and Intellectual History," in *Contemporary Criticism*, eds. M. Bradbury and D. Palmer, Stratford-upon-Avon Studies 12 (New York, 1971). See, for example, p. 128: ". . . nothing springs *ex nihilo*, but from a corpus of books." Note, once more, the use of alternatives that are not in contrast with each other, and one of which is an absurdity, to force the right conclusion.

context of a small group of writers and students of writers is fully analogous to the more common reduction of the text's context to a local biographical and historical one; and the same trivialization occurs in both cases.

In this chapter, I have discussed common prevailing notions of the relevant context of a literary text, whether explicitly stated or simply implicit in common critical procedures. The general tendency to identify the relevant context as the context of origin, which the definition of literature shows to be a fundamental logical error, probably has much to do with a general psychological disposition deriving from the theory of language which we have found so often to be at the root of errors in literary theory; it has perhaps seemed tempting to see literary texts as referring to the situations and things that gave rise to them. But it seems to me that another factor in the psychology of critics cannot be underestimated here. Characteristically, literary critics have tended to see themselves as the providers of something essential to the reader's relationship to the literary texts of his society. Whether that thing has been seen in terms of biographical knowledge, historical knowledge, or knowledge of the literary tradition, this general tendency of critics has remained the same, and it embodies an important misconception about the function of critics. Their real importance lies not in their making possible the reader's relating to literary texts—he is perfectly able to do that for himself—but in the fact that critics at their best are good at talking about that relationship. For the reader who responds well to seeing that relationship treated with penetratingly accurate formulation, criticism may make it more interesting for him. But the result of insisting

that critics hold the key to entry into the relationship
has been destructive. By shaking the natural relationship,
and trying to substitute one based on knowledge of a
limited and irrelevant set of circumstances, critics have
made literature less interesting to readers, not more.

Since literary texts are inherently challenging and
often even puzzling, the critic's pose of supplying essential information and the key to the text has proved as
tempting to the reader as it has to the critic. It has given
him the illusion of understanding complex works with
minimum effort. Thus critics have often managed to place
a great wedge between readers and literary texts merely
by offering them an easy avoidance of the text's problems and complexities; instead of assisting and furthering
appreciation and understanding of literature, they have
generally had a destructive effect.

The first step in correcting this situation is for the
critic to see himself as an analyst of a situation rather than
as a priest who initiates another into an otherwise inaccessible situation. The special claims of the critic ("you
need to know this or that fact before you can appreciate
this work") have always amounted to seeking the role
of high priest. The special claims he might make in the
role of analyst would be of an altogether different and
more justifiable kind. If, for example, it were asserted
that one could not account for the appeal of a work
except through the analysis of the critic, the situation
would be very different. The critic-analyst would now
be seeking to understand what was happening when a
reader responded to a text—not to make it possible for
the response to happen. I turn to this question in my next
chapter.

6: The Analysis of
Literary Texts

THIS CHAPTER will be concerned with the whole question
of making statements about literary texts, both in terms
of their meaning and of their structure. I do not wish
the title of this chapter to prejudice in any way the possible outcome of the issues that it will treat. I might as
easily have announced this discussion with the words
"criticism" or "interpretation" replacing the word "analysis." My purpose would still be the same: an analysis
of all that these various terms can mean, and of the logical
relations between the various activities which they imply,
if indeed they are separable at all. In the preceding chapters, I have tried to show that the investigation of texts is
the same thing as the investigation of their value, and
that contextual information is only of relevance to literary
texts insofar as it is a question of the community's shared
meanings and associations in the language of the texts.
It is, therefore, a natural next step in my argument to
consider the logic of the investigation of these pieces of
language that are treated as literary texts.

Before entering this analysis, it is as well to get some
idea of the traditional questions and puzzles that have

been the recurring problems of this area of literary theory. There are two main groups. The first deals with the subject of concern of the analysis: Should the object of literary analysis be the philosophy of the work and its ideas, for example, or just the form of their presentation? Should we be concerned with the artistic composition and style of the work, or with its content (here "content" is commonly thought of as something that might exist outside the work of literature)? With its aesthetic value and structure, or its ideological or social value? There are many other versions of this kind of question, resting on the same basic opposition. The second group of questions concerns the nature of the procedures of analysis (or criticism, or interpretation). The traditional puzzles here are such queries as: Is criticism in any sense scientific, and are there any rules for criticism? Or, put more weakly: Is there any methodology of criticism, and can one talk of right and wrong ways to proceed? If no general statements of this kind are available, is criticism an illogical activity, one without any rules and standards that can be formulated? This group of related queries is evidently at the bottom of a question such as: How does analysis of a text relate to interpretation of it? Or: How do the "facts" of a text relate to interpretation? Can the interpretation itself conceivably be offered as a "fact" of the text?

The two complexes of problems of this chapter are evidently closely related. Both come together if we formulate the general problem of this discussion as follows: What are we looking for when we do an analysis (criticism, interpretation) of a literary text, how do we go about doing it, and what is the character of the results we achieve?

In the first of the two traditional groups of questions, a common feature running through the whole complex is easily discernible: it is a dualistic view of the properties of literary texts which separates something given (philosophy, plot, subject matter, ideas) from what is done to that given element (form, style, organization, artistic treatment). More importance or emphasis is often given to the second. It is easy to make a plausible case for this; for example, the theme of Romeo and Juliet is the subject of different literary works by William Shakespeare and by the Swiss writer Gottfried Keller. Here, the subject is the given, the treatment by each author the variable. Naturally, the variable would seem to be the focus of critical attention; it will constitute the real importance of the Shakespeare as opposed to the Keller text, the specific contribution of each great writer. But, in the course of the argument that follows, I shall try to show that this way of thinking of the analysis of literary texts is misleading and dangerous. I shall take a particular version of these dualistic notions as a paradigm: the notion of "style" as opposed to content or subject matter. Having investigated it in detail, I shall use it to draw conclusions that are valid for all the other versions of the dualism and which finally illuminate the basic question of what kind of thing analysis or criticism should aim to deal with in literary texts.

As in the previous chapter, we must note that some of this discussion takes place within a hotly disputed and polemical area of literary theory: here is the ground on which formalists and antiformalists have hurled insults at each other, the latter insisting that it is the "Weltanschauung" of a piece of literature that counts, while the former are concerned with (or at least are taken by their opponents to be concerned with) formal perfection and literary devices. Once more, we shall see that this dispute is ill-focused and unnecessary.

I choose "style" as a paradigm partly because this is the concept through which the expert knowledge and techniques of modern linguistics are usually brought to bear on the study of literature; and since modern linguistics claims to be "scientific," this in turn will serve to raise, in the later part of this chapter, the issue of the procedures and scientific status of criticism.

Linguists of all schools have approached the linguistic study of literary texts through the concept of style. In Britain, M. A. K. Halliday equates "stylistics" and "the linguistic study of literature,"[1] and the recent volume produced there dealing with the relation of linguistics and literature was entitled Essays on Style and Language.[2] In America, the volume Style in Language[3] has been the most weighty document in the linguistic study of literature, while writers not represented in that compendium have also assumed the notions of style and stylistics to be their starting points.[4] Whether one takes linguists

[1] "Categories of the Theory of Grammar," Word 17 (1961): 242. Part of this sixth chapter follows the argument of my article "Linguistics, Literature, and the Concept of Style," Word 26 (1970).

[2] R. Fowler, ed., (London, 1966). Cf. also Linguistics and Style, ed. J. Spencer.

[3] T. A. Sebeok, ed. (Cambridge, Mass., 1960). Cf. also Linguistics and Literary Style, ed. D. Freeman; and Literary Style: A Symposium, ed. S. Chatman (London, 1971).

[4] Notably M. Riffaterre, "Criteria for Style Analysis," Word 15

writing in the framework of Chomsky, like Richard Ohmann ("Generative Grammars and the Concept of Literary Style")[5] or more orthodox structuralists like Archibald Hill,[6] the terms "style" and "stylistics" are central.

The common assumption with regard to the starting
point of the inquiry has not been matched by much
else in the way of common ground, and no theory of
style (whether linguistic or literary) has seemed to be
promising to any large body of opinion; critical comment on most of the contributions to *Style in Language*,
for example, has not been enthusiastic.[7] Ohmann, writing very recently, finds stylistics "in a state of disorgani-
zation," the subject "remarkably unencumbered by theoretical insights," and the concept of style itself, even after
his own attempt to explicate it, "elusive."[8] It would be
difficult to disagree with these judgments, in spite of the
amount of work that has recently been devoted to the
subject.

Most linguistic stylisticians believe, Riffaterre claimed

(1959): 154–174, and "Stylistic Context," *Word* 16 (1960): 207–
218.

[5] *Word* 20 (1964): 423–439.

[6] Cf. his "Poetry and Stylistics." Address given at the University
of Virginia on September 21, 1956, in the Peter Rushton Seminars
in Contemporary Prose and Poetry, and circulated privately.

[7] R. Jakobson's closing statement, however, ("Closing Statement: Linguistics and Poetics") is a brilliant essay. Jacobson
avoids the term "stylistics," preferring instead "poetics."

[8] Ohmann, pp. 423, 425, and 439. The same judgment is made
by Gregory and Spencer in their essay "An Approach to the
Study of Style," in *Linguistics and Style*; style is "recognizable
but elusive" (p. 59). R. A. Sayce also finds the term in a state of
confusion in the opening remarks of his "The Definition of the
Term 'Style,'" *Proceedings of the International Comparative Literature Association*, 3rd Congress (1962), pp. 156–166.

with some justice in 1959, that a stylistic device consists in a deviation from the linguistic norm.[9] That is to say, in our ordinary use of language we have all kinds of normal expectations, and the grammar of a language is a codification of such expectations; but stylistic devices are felt to be deviations from what we normally expect. The limitations of this view are easily exposed by Riffaterre, Wellek,[10] and others; to take only the most simple and immediate argument against it, not all such deviation is felt to be style, and not all style consists in a deviation from the norm. Quite commonly, a piece of language that works well within the norms of ordinary usage is still said to have a certain kind of style. Riffaterre,[11] after his rejection of the deviation model of style, advances a view that is not entirely dissimilar to it, and is subject to some of the same criticisms: for him, stylistic devices deviate from the norm established in the particular context. From the point of view of literary analysis, this is an improvement in that it attempts to deal with the expectations established within a text, but it will not work as a theory of style; it cannot deal with those cases where style strikes us as residing in the use of exactly the right word for

[9] Riffaterre, "Criteria," p. 167.

[10] See Wellek's "Closing Statement" in *Style in Language*, ed. Sebeok. S. R. Levin ("Deviation—Statistical and Determinate—in Poetic Language," *Lingua* 12, 1963: 276–290), in his reply to Wellek's attack on the deviation model, misses the point. Wellek's objection is not that the deviation model leads us beyond grammar, but that such a treatment is illegitimately atomistic. J. P. Thorne has recently produced a new version of the "deviation" theory in his "Poetry, Stylistics, and Imaginary Grammars." For its details, see above, chapter 4, n. 22. It is subject to the same criticisms as other versions of this theory.

[11] Riffaterre, "Criteria," p. 169.

the context, or where it is the product of a stylistically homogeneous text. Such cases show that the style of a text cannot always be discussed in terms of individual devices that are isolable and segmentable,[12] and that it cannot always be thought of as something unusual, surprising, or unpredictable.

Linguists have evidently not been very successful in their attempts to deal with the concept of style; and by now there is a widespread feeling among critics of literature that "stylistics" brandishes a formidable apparatus of linguistic terminology, some taken over from general linguistics, some coined for the occasion, but that little of value has so far been contributed by it to the study of literature. The reason for this state of affairs is to be traced to the concept used as the basis of the discussion.

Though the concept of style is continually being subjected to more and more complex definitions, we should not forget that its origin is in ordinary, unreflective language. Its meaning in ordinary language can be found in any dictionary. Common to all such dictionary statements is an explanation that it refers to a way, manner, or form of doing or saying something.[13] It is thus in ordi-

[12] An unusually direct statement that style can be segmented is by W. A. Koch, "On the Principles of Stylistics," *Lingua* 12 (1963): 416: "Any text whatever may be subjected to a stylistic segmentation."

[13] I do not here ignore the very great efforts which have been devoted to the definition and redefinition of style, and the multiplicity of meaning found in discussions of it. See, for example, N. E. Enkvist's essay "On Defining Style" in *Linguistics and Style*, ed. Spencer. Such discussions have resulted in great numbers of competing "definitions" of style, and numerous laments such as that "style has proved notoriously hard of stringent definition" (Enkvist, p. 54). I shall argue below that these efforts have been

nary usage primarily a dualistic concept which distinguishes two elements in a piece of language: one of them a constant, the other a variable. Ohmann[14] concludes from this that ". . . the theorist of style is confronted by a kind of task that is commonplace enough in most fields: the task of explicating and toughening up for rigorous use a notion already familiar to the layman." But in saying this he has jumped a step: there is a stage in an investigation where we must decide either that an ordinary language concept can be tightened up, defined rigorously, and made useful for a precise investigation, or that it is too misleading and confused to be useful. There is no *a priori* guarantee what the answer will be; it depends on the particular concept. An example of an ordinary language term which, like "style," seemed to have a clear field of reference, but which has been abandoned by specialists, is "madness"; this has been replaced by the term "mental illness." The second term has then gradually invaded ordinary language, and there, too, may replace the first. A difference in extent of a field of reference cannot be the issue here: it is the same or very nearly the same for both terms. The change in terms involves a different attitude on the part of the speaker, a different classification of the phenomenon concerned, and, indeed, a different theory of its basis and of ways of dealing with it. The ordinary language term was part of an ordinary language and common-sense theory of certain phenomena. The theory needed replacing; the word therefore also needed replacing.

---

misguided and that the laments are the result of a mistaken notion of definition.

[14] Ohmann, p. 423. The same kind of argument is found in Spencer and Gregory, p. 59.

This choice that we have when dealing with an ordinary language concept has been largely ignored by both linguists and critics. "A style is a way of writing—that is what the word means," writes Ohmann,[15] as if one simply had to accept the concept and go on from there. Riffaterre offers a rigorous definition, and thus wholeheartedly takes the first of the alternatives that I mentioned above, though again without considering that a choice was available: "*Style* is understood as an emphasis (expressive, affective, or aesthetic) added to the information conveyed by the linguistic structure, without alteration of meaning. Which is to say that language expresses and that style stresses. . . ."[16] This is certainly a rigorous and uncompromising definition, but could not be said to be a violation of the ordinary language use of "style." And yet, for critics of literature, it would seem like a *reductio ad absurdum* of the concept of style. For, as Ohmann also notes:[17]

. . . the relevant division between fixed and variable components in literature is by no means so obvious. What *is* content, and what is form, or style? The attack on a dichotomy of form and content has been persistent in modern criticism; to change so much as a word, the argument runs, is to change the meaning as well. This austere doctrine has a certain theoretical appeal given the supposed impossibility of finding exact synonyms, and the ontological queerness of disembodied content—propositions, for instance—divorced from any verbal expression. Yet at the same time this doctrine leads to the altogether counter-intuitive conclusion that there can be no such thing as style, or that style is simply a part of content.

[15] Ohmann, p. 423. Koch's ("On the Principles of Stylistics") beginning shows a similar reliance on the concept of style as an irremovable one.

[16] Riffaterre, "Criteria," p. 155.

[17] Ohmann, p. 427.

Here, it seems to me, Ohmann has stated an important reason for the critics' reluctance to consider the possibility of abandoning the concept of style, but he has not advanced a valid argument to support this reluctance. For if I were to translate Ohmann's comment into the context of the analogy I have already used, I should end up with a statement like this: "Doctors have consistently attacked the dichotomy of madness and illness. To be mad, they say, is to be sick, and subject to treatment. This austere argument has a certain theoretical appeal. But it leads to the counter-intuitive conclusion that there is no such thing as madness, or that madness is simply part of sickness."

The obvious lack of logical consequence in this adaptation of Ohmann shows the methodological error. It is not unusual for research to make assumptions that are counter-intuitive, in the sense that they run counter to our normal assumptions, for it is precisely those assumptions that research may need to change. But, in any case, the critics' line of argument does not lead to the conclusion that Ohmann draws from it, any more than it follows from my adapted version that madness does not exist. The phenomena thought of as "madness" and "style" continue to exist and to exist distinctively; what is questioned in both cases is the usefulness of the popular concepts concerned for the purposes of an investigation. There is, however, a fundamental difference in the two situations. Doctors have rejected the concept of madness because they rejected the theory that it entailed, but the critics to whom Ohmann refers have by contrast done something very strange: they have attempted to keep the concept, and at the same time to reject the theory that is inseparable from it. And if they have done this it is surely because they, too, have made a central mistake: they have thought that to abolish the concept would be to abolish the phenomenon.

I want now to turn to some reasons for the rejection of the theory inherent in the very word "style," and therefore inherent in its retention in any form. Unless it can be shown that an ordinary language concept can usefully be adapted for the purposes of a precise investigation, there is, I have argued, no obligation to keep it as far as the investigator is concerned. The question then arises: Can it be so adapted? Basic to the concept of style in language is a dualistic model; one aspect of language is distinguished from another. If the concept of style is to be useful, then, we must be able to make and sustain a distinction between two aspects of language which is either the same as that found in the ordinary language usage of the word (that is, the distinction between meaning and style), or reasonably closely related to it; for example, the word could be useful if we were able to distinguish two distinct types of meaning in language and that distinction had some relation to the popular distinction between style and meaning.[18] I shall first try to show that the popular distinction is impossible, and then that no related distinction of two kinds of meaning is possible.

A set of words that would very clearly involve the ordinary language notion of style would be "start," "begin," and "commence." These three, we might ordinarily say, mean the same thing, but differ stylistically: they belong to different stylistic levels. Yet a more accurate descrip-

[18] Koch attempts to do this; see, for example, his p. 412.

tion of the three words would distinguish them in terms of their different meanings. It is true, in a superficial way that suits ordinary discourse, that the "same thing" is involved with all three; but not exactly the same thing. Though there is some overlap, we generally separate the usages of these words so that proceedings commence, races start, while children begin to play. In one respect the same thing happens. But in other respects, different things happen. A law court is not a horse race. We can speak of a "formal level of language," only because there are formal things and situations such as law courts. Even if we use the terms of the reference theory of meaning, we can say that the "reference" of that formal level of language is to a certain kind of situation, just as surely as the common "reference" of all of the three words (start, begin, commence) is to a certain kind of event. The use of one of the terms rather than the other means that the speaker has classified the event concerned in a particular way and has thus seen in it a distinctively different thing from what would have been the case had he used another of the trio of words. And so, *what* he has said (not *how* he has said it) means something that is distinctively different from what he might otherwise have said. The use of the word "commence" in relation to a dance, for example, may well give enough information about that event to dissuade devotees of certain types of dancing from attending it. To speak strictly, therefore, these three words ought not to be called three ways of saying the same thing: they are three closely related but different words, and three closely related but different ideas. They have an overlap of meaning that is considerable, but also an area of meaning that is distinct.

Suppose that we had a common word in our language, which was neutral with regard to all except the common area of the three, and that the word were "inception." Then "commence" would be equivalent to "inception of a formal event or situation." The relation of these two terms ("commence" and "inception") would be that of species to genus, such as that of "elm" to "tree." It is obvious that the relation of "oak" to "elm" would still involve common and different elements of meaning even if we had no word "tree": we could not describe this as meaning plus style, however large the common element. The same is the case with "begin," "start," and "commence," and with all other such systems of related words. The difference between the two sets of words (trees and inceptions) is not a matter of factual as opposed to stylistic variations between the words in each set, for both sets have factual variations within them. The difference is simply that, in the case of "inceptions," the factual variations involved are found in many other related sets of words where "formal" and "informal" are distinguished. It is the fact that this distinction is widespread and operates systematically in many sets of words that allows us to use the notion of a formal "style."

The difference between "very big" and "enormous" might well be termed one of emphasis; but that is just as much a change of meaning as the change between "big" and "very big." It is a curious fact that when an extra word is used to differentiate two expressions we tend in ordinary discourse to say that meaning has been added, yet when one expression is replaced by another perhaps more differentiated expression, an entirely parallel change of meaning may tend to be called "style." The word "formal" is one that has a recognizable and factual meaning; but when its area of meaning is absorbed into another word (for example, "commence"), and is used to differentiate that word from another that is closely related to it ("start"), the differentiation is commonly termed "stylistic." Yet there seems to be no theoretical reason for the different descriptions of this case and that of "big" and "very big." Similarly, a difference of stress is surely a difference of meaning. The semantic difference between "was it very big?" and "was it *very* big?"[19] is clear. Whether stress resides in intonation (where it is obviously part of meaning) or in any other linguistic feature, the result is the same.

Rather than go on to discuss more examples—a procedure that can never rule out the possibility of further ones that may be intractable—I can perhaps here offer a dilemma: either the use of two expressions is indistinguishable, in which case they are genuinely freely variant in every sense; or their usage is distinguishable, in which case their meaning is different. The concept of "free variation" can, of course, never be more than a hypothesis: we cannot rule out the possibility of hitting on a distinguishing feature, however slight, in the usage of two expressions, even though they may for the moment seem to us to be in all contexts interchangeable.[20]

So far, I have argued that what are termed in ordinary language "stylistic" variations are differences of meaning,

[19] The first merely asks for information concerning size; the second grants that the object is big, but asks for more precise information. These are two different questions, not the same question with a different stress.

[20] I doubt the existence of completely freely varying expressions; but this doubt has no bearing on my argument.

and that, therefore, "style" is meaning. It remains to be shown that a dichotomy of two distinguishable types of meaning cannot replace the dichotomy of style and meaning; a strict dualist might still argue here that his use of "meaning" was different from my own, that I had merely shown that it was possible to use the word "meaning" to refer to both sides of the dualism, and that no change of substance was necessary in his theory if one replaced the terminology of "meaning" and "emphasis" by speaking instead of two aspects of meaning.

W. A. Koch[21] advances a view of this kind, and calls stylistics "split semantics." He contrasts two words that differ stylistically, and concludes that they have a common area of meaning and in addition one that is not common, a "semantic differential." His diagrammatic representation of this is two oblongs, each representing one of the words: a large unshaded portion of each represents the common meaning, a small shaded area the semantic differential. This sounds a plausible enough gloss on our ordinary use of the notion of style, but as a theory it has a fatal weakness. For two distinguishable types of meaning to be involved, the split in the semantics of a given word would have to be made in the same way in all its uses, and that is clearly not the case. The "semantic differential" between two words is, in fact, the result of the particular opposition of those two words; the same words contrasted to others would show different areas of similar and dissimilar meaning. The separation of two elements of the meaning of a word achieved by Koch is therefore not a typological distinction, but only a temporary and local one produced by an arbitrary juxtaposition

---

[21] Koch, "On the Principles of Stylistics."

of one word and another. And so, the attempt to separate out part of the meaning of a word as its "stylistic" meaning in this way fails.

If, then, all "stylistic variations" are simply changes of meaning, and if no distinct type of meaning is to be found in them, then "style" cannot be a theoretically useful concept. But if this is so, some explanation must be given of the fact that the concept of style does persist, often seems useful, and is defined and redefined endlessly. The explanation of this fact must be given in two parts, the first in relation to popular, the second to scholarly usage.

The ordinary language use of the concept of style is dependent on a local purpose in a given context. We can indeed say in ordinary language that there are a dozen ways of "saying the same thing," but this is because we wish to achieve a quite delimitable purpose, and can seem to treat everything except that purpose as subordinate to it. If I am in command of a squad of soldiers and wish them to put some bullets into a particular target, then it makes no difference *for this purpose* whether I say "commence firing" or "begin firing." But the particular phrase I use does other things than merely serve that purpose; the whole situation has changed, slightly but noticeably. Similarly, the phrases "you can go now" and "get out" can be ways of "saying the same thing"; that is, they can achieve the same limited purpose of removing a physical presence. That more and different things have been achieved, with the second particularly, will become apparent on the next meeting of speaker and addressee. In ordinary language, then, given a vast number of expressions in a language, all with their own unique set of rules of use yet all having areas of overlap with others, I can, in a given situation, choose from a number to achieve a particular local purpose, and I may think of this operation as choosing between ways of saying the same thing. But these expressions only exist as alternatives to one another within the unique context of my local purpose; they are not alternatives in the sense of having identical meanings. I am able to treat the difference in meaning between them as "style," because they are not central to my limited purpose.[22] Our use of "style" in ordinary language is usually a way of avoiding those areas of the meaning of a word that are not considered essential to the speaker's present dominant purpose. To return to Koch's theory of "split semantics": the split he diagnoses between a core of meaning and a "semantic differential" (style) is not a theoretical or a typological distinction, but only the local product of a particular purpose.

This account of the popular usage of the concept of style should indicate its inappropriateness as a concept in the theory of language. Several expressions may be able to fulfill a function which is the dominant one for a speaker in a given situation. But that fact cannot make the linguist ignore the additional differences in function between the expressions. A speaker in saying "commence firing" may not be worried about what it is that has been achieved apart from producing fire; but the student of

---

[22] Though the dualistic model has a useful function in ordinary discourse, it can of course be dangerous here too; to think of a choice between expressions as a choice among closely related meanings rather than among stylistic alternatives meaning the same thing (ways of saying the same thing), would make a speaker more aware that he was doing other things than merely achieving his present limited purpose—and those other things may turn out to be important for purposes that may matter to him outside the present context of his speech.

language must be. He cannot avoid noting the speaker's classification and in a sense alteration of the situation, and his giving of information about himself.[23]

The ordinary language use of the concept of style, therefore, relies on the existence of a dominant purpose for a particular utterance which seems to permit us to focus on a particular aspect of the meaning of an expression, so simplifying it to the point where it can be thought of as having alternatives. These circumstances, which create the possibility of the use of the concept of style in ordinary discourse, can scarcely occur in literary texts; there we are not dealing with speech situations that we can simplify in this way, and we cannot judge language in literary texts according to whether it achieves limited purposes. Literature makes maximal use of the patterns of meaning of expressions, and does not generally simplify and subordinate them to a simple purpose. These texts are contemplated until their details are absorbed and become important, while it is such details that are made to seem unimportant in ordinary language by dualistic concepts such as "style." Literary texts are not limited speech acts with a single predominant purpose, and seldom can one ascribe to them any simple statement of purpose at all. Choosing a precise meaning between close alternatives may be crucially important in these texts, where such precision might be ignored for practical purposes in ordinary language. The concept of style becomes more and more inappropriate as we move from ordinary discourse to the study of language and finally to the

[23] That this last type of information is that most commonly written off by a dualistic model of essentials or extras is seen in the phrase "le style c'est l'homme."

study of literature; and it is precisely an account of its use in ordinary discourse which demonstrates its complete inappropriateness in literary study.

From this point of view, the persistence of the concept of style, and especially its elaboration and cultivation, might seem difficult to account for. The mere retention is explained by the point made earlier: the kinds of effect thought of as "style" (for example, precise choices between closely related expressions) are important for literary study, and to reject the concept "style" may have seemed like rejecting these effects. It is certainly paradoxical that, as a result, a concept that originates in ordinary language as a means of downgrading certain elements in the meaning of an expression in order that others may be concentrated on, should then be preserved precisely because those elements have had restored to them the importance that the concept of style denied them.

The elaboration of the definition of the concept follows from this contradictory position. A primitive term from ordinary language has been accepted into the conceptual vocabulary of a study while the theory that it implies is felt to be inadequate. In the puzzlement that results, the source of the trouble is attributed to the complexity of the concept, so that to solve the problem its meaning is elaborated. The "real" meaning of an elusive and obscure word is then the subject of the investigation,[24] and

[24] Cf. the discussion by D. G. Mowatt and myself of some concepts in Staiger's poetics: "Language, Metaphysics, and Staiger's Critical Categories," *Seminar: A Journal of Germanic Studies* 1 (1965). The process of compensating for the shortcomings of primitive terms by treating them as elusive, mysterious concepts is fairly common in literary study; the concept of "Realism" is a good example of this.

the primitive term has by this time had its appearance quite changed by sophisticated confusion. But the term itself can never by this process be made anything other than a theoretically primitive one. The general confusion over the definition of "style" is further aggravated by a confusion between those sentences beginning "style is . . ." which are properly definitions (that is, attempts to give the meaning of the term) and those that are statements of fact. "Style is a way of saying something" is a definition; "Style is a product of structure"[25] is a statement taking for granted the meaning of "style," (in one sense what style is) and attempting to give us information about its basis, to tell us facts about it. Enkvist, for example, is evidently confusing the two different kinds of statements when he offers a "brief definition" of style in these terms: "The style of a text is the aggregate of the contextual probabilities of its linguistic items."[26] This confusion of radically different functions of "is"[27] allows the already confused problem of linguis-

[25] I take this statement from D. G. Mowatt and P. Dembowski "Literary Study and Linguistics," *Canadian Journal of Linguistics* 11 (1965): 44. I have given a fuller explanation of the distinction between the two uses of "is" (definition as opposed to information) in my discussion of the definition of literature; see above, pp. 31–33.

[26] "On Defining Style," p. 28. Only on the basis of this methodological mistake could Enkvist make the further statement: "Thus stylistic selection should not be defined as 'the choice between items that mean more or less the same'" (p. 54). He is wrongly treating as alternatives a statement about style and a definition of style, and assuming that to accept the former means rejecting the latter. His long treatment of the many "definitions" of style is vitiated by this mistake, and so are the definitions that he reports.

[27] The two functions are shown most simply and clearly in the

tic usage (the investigation of the meaning of the term) to be infinitely more confused by bringing into the definition the results of research into the phenomena concerned.

If my argument has been correct, then we should not talk of the stylistic function of a linguistic item, but instead of its *precise* function; nor of the style of a piece of language, but instead of *precisely* what it means and says. For what we are in fact doing in these cases is *looking more closely at what the language does*, not looking for a different kind of thing at all. To return to my example of the Romeo and Juliet theme and its different treatment by Shakespeare and Keller: the appropriate way of speaking of this phenomenon is not in terms of a

---

following pair of sentences: "a ball is round" and "a ball is red." The first explains the meaning of the term "ball"; the second could be used by someone explaining a game, and is nothing to do with the definition of the term "ball." Still further complications are raised by the confusion of stipulative definitions (terms introduced into an investigation with a stipulated meaning and no other) and reportative definitions (reports of the normal usage of a term already existing in language). For example, Sayce ("The Definition of the Term 'Style'") begins by saying that words have the meaning their user chooses (true of stipulative, not true of reportative definitions) and then goes on from this to consider the definition of "style," a term that is already used popularly and in scholarship, and which therefore must have a reportative definition. His proposed definition, "the use of language in a work of art" (p. 157), is of interest not as a newly introduced concept with a stipulated definition, but only because it is an attempt to do something with a concept already established in literary study. If taken seriously, this stipulation abolishes the concept of style, though it proposes to go on using the word in an almost empty sense—an unnecessarily confusing procedure; that the word "style" is used at all is evidence that the ordinary language meaning is still being exploited, however.

different form with same content, but simply in terms of a *partial identity* of content. There is the basic theme and much more besides in each case; and the different meaning is a product of the different wholes.

The concept of style is the most common dualistic concept invoked in criticism of literary texts. What I have tried to show is that dualistic thinking in formulating the concerns of criticism is an error. We cannot think of those concerns in terms of an investigation of any specifically literary quality of a literary text, or of a literary presentation of what is said in it. Our concern must be quite simply with what the text says—precisely and in detail. This conclusion not only reinforces the findings of my earlier chapters; it is demanded by them. My investigation of the definition of literature, for example, came to the conclusion that there were no defining "literary" features common to literary texts, but that these texts were categorized as literature because of their use. The discussion in this chapter has confirmed, from a different direction, that literary texts do not have a separable formal, stylistic, or aesthetic property, to discover and isolate which might then be the aim of literary criticism. My discussion of aesthetic value, again as a result of a different kind of argument, concluded that there were no isolable criteria for literary value. In that area of theory I diagnosed an error similar to that commonly encountered in "stylistic" investigations. When evaluations are made in terms of criteria, what, in fact, happens is that partial evaluations of the text are mistakenly taken to be the touchstones of total evaluations of the text. The analogous error in the theory that concentrates on the "style" of a text as its important feature lies in the attempt to isolate a part of the meaning of the text which ought instead to be taken as one element among the many, the interaction of which creates the whole meaning. In both cases, some of the elements are promoted to a position of being indicative of the value of the text, instead of the meaning and value of the text being sought in the particular interrelation established between all its elements. By itself, to state that the meaning and value of a text must be sought in all of what it says might seem trite indeed. But the contrast of this statement with prevailing beliefs in critical theory is what gives it its meaning: it contrasts sharply with all criterion theories, all "style" theories, and theories that distinguish content from the aesthetic elements in a text. And from this statement follows the important point that to speak of the "aesthetic aspect" of a text is not to speak of its structure, but instead of its use.

The analysis that I have developed has an important bearing on the traditional dispute between formalists and ideologists. This controversy has never been well focused, since the two sides have consistently stated the opposition between them in terms that do not achieve a clearly delineated contrast of positions that exclude each other; two different and separable issues were usually being discussed at the same time and so confused: the textual issue of form and content on the one hand, and the issue of the relevant context of the literary text on the other.[28] A po-

---

[28] A simple version of this opposition of positions which are not in contrast with each other is provided by Hermand, *Synthetisches Interpretieren*, p. 182, who insists that we need not ". . . eine bloss formalästhetische Wertskala, sondern ein Geschichtsbewusstsein." This opposition is so common that Hermand feels no need to explain how the acceptance of one side necessarily involves the negation of the other. The necessary analysis

sition on one of the issues has been taken to imply an automatic position on the other; "formalists" are usually said not to be concerned with context, but only with the literariness of the text, while ideologists or historical and biographical contextualists are said to be concerned with the content of the text.

In a certain clear and elementary sense, there is no doubt that a formalist position is incorrect if formalism is taken to deny that we are concerned with what the literary text says in the way that we are concerned with what any other piece of language says. So far, the ideologists are right, and (certain kinds of) formalists wrong: we must be concerned above all with the content of the literary text. But in practice the case is reversed: "formalist" critics have usually been more closely concerned with the content of a text than the ideologists. And this is because even when mistakenly talking of "form," "style," or other literary devices, the formalist critic has often been doing something that antiformalists seldom do: he has been looking very closely at precisely what the text says in all its details. The antiformalist has usually been satisfied to abstract a fairly superficial "content" or ideology and then to limit the meaning of the text even more by referring it to the context of its origin. This procedure relates to the misstated contrast to which I have referred; the denial of "formalism" or of an "aesthetic" approach has been thought to lead automatically to a historicist criticism. But there is no logical contrast between these positions,[29] and the antiformalist position

---

of the content and human significance of a literary work would contrast equally with both sides of Hermand's unreal opposition.

[29] See, once more, that opposition accepted in Scott's discus-

that I reach in the argument of this chapter is entirely consistent with an antihistoricist view of the context of a literary work. A reasonable judgment of the traditional dispute between formalists and antiformalists might be that while formalists have been theoretically in error in their view of the status of form or style, in practical terms they have been more useful as critics than antiformalists, since they have generally looked more carefully at aspects of literary texts which were subtle and yet centrally important for the whole. It has, of course, been possible for literary "formalists" to degenerate into mechanical hunters of isolated literary effects, and not to relate them to the human significance of the text; but the fact remains that the techniques that have led to a more subtle and interesting analysis of the meaning and content of literary texts were developed by such critics. Antiformalists were in theory right to insist that literary texts be related to life, but in practice did less to relate literature to life than their opponents, because they chose to relate them not to the life of the community but only to the limited context of life in which the texts originated. To be sure, they expressed immediate concern with the human significance of literary texts (in so doing contrasting themselves with formalists) but achieved much less in their accounts of this significance. They usually abstracted from texts problems of some generality (for example, "protest against society," "decadence," "honor," and so on) that could be abstracted with ease from a dozen very different works of literature. The avoidance of textual detail that yielded the particular meaning of a text was

---

sion, "The Formalistic Approach," *Five Approaches of Literary Criticism*, p. 179.

compensated for by introducing the detail of the life and times of the author in an attempt to overcome the triteness of an initial over-general abstraction. In that formalists looked more closely at texts, they were bound to see more meaning in them, and so more of what made them relevant to the life of the community.[30]

The logical weakness of formalist theories does not necessarily mean that statements about the "form" of literary works are not useful. All that is at issue here is the reinterpretation of such statements as statements that are about the meaning of the texts; to say something about the form of a literary work is simply to say something about what it says. To state that a drama is in the classical five-act form, for example, is to point to five divisions in what the text says, and to raise the question of the relations existing between these divisions; something has been said which has these five parts to it, and that fact is a fact about what has been said. The point here is that all meaning in language arises from formal contrasts of one expression with another, so that two pieces of language containing the same words can easily mean different things merely through a contrast between them consisting in a different set of relations between those identical words. One such distinctive set of relations could simply consist in the form of a five-act drama. Compare, for example, the seemingly identical statements, "he is brilliant, but troublesome," and "he is troublesome, but brilliant." In actual usage, the first,

---

[30] Rodway's ("What the Critics Really Need") separation of formal literary evaluation from evaluation by reference to the wider relevance of what is said is, therefore, impossible to sustain; the judgment of the literary value of a text is the same judgment as that of its relevance to the community.

but not the second, represents a conclusion that the individual's weaknesses outweigh his talents; and in so far, the different arrangement of words says something different. We can talk of the formal difference between the two sentences, but that is another (and legitimate) means of referring to a set of meaningful contrasts.

Similarly, statements about the organization of literary texts are best reinterpreted as part of a description of what has been said, not of how it has been said. It is often said that literary texts show a greater degree of organization than other texts. There will be various ways of interpreting this, depending on how "this text is well organized" is understood in a particular context. If it is understood to imply that the text focuses on its theme without digression or irrelevance, then it can easily be analyzed in terms of what is said: that is, what is said is sharply restricted to a particular subject or theme. If it is understood to imply that the text presents its central concern in an effective manner, then that, too, is analyzable in terms of what is said. It is only necessary here to see that what is frequently an adverbial can just as easily be made an adjectival; for example, we can talk of something being said in a subtle, effective, or dramatic manner, but we could equally well say that something subtle, effective, or dramatic had been said. Finally, if statements about the often high degree of organization of literary texts are interpreted to mean that literary texts often make maximal use of the possibilities of language to say a great deal in a short space (for example, a sonnet means more than any ordinary fourteen lines of English because of a greater control and organization) then this, more even than the first two cases, can be seen as a direct statement about what is said; more is said, because there is greater and more systematic use of linguistic forms.

It follows that the aims of criticism should never be spoken of in formalist terms; that is to say, the aims of criticism are not the investigation of literary symbolism, or of metaphor, or of any other feature thought of as literary in nature, even though this may well be an important aspect of criticism in a number of cases. These features of literary texts must be thought of as part of a stock of extra expressive devices common in literature (along with verse, dramatic form, and other aspects of poetic license). But they are not defining, they are not necessary, and they are not the focal point of criticism.

In my discussion of value I concluded that an investigation of the actual texts and what they contained was in itself an investigation of their value. It is now clear that this may be extended: an investigation of what literary texts actually say is an investigation of their value. And, again, only a basically referential attitude to their meaning which made too quick and too incomplete an abstraction of "content," and ignored those aspects of meaning that are hard to deal with in referential terms—only such an attitude to meaning could have made the situation seem otherwise; for the things referred to as "style," "emphasis," or "connotations," are essentially the casualties of the reference theory of meaning. From a reference theory of meaning standpoint, to think of criticism as dealing primarily with the (referential) content of the text would indeed seem to omit all the subtlety of a literary text, and all that made the text seem valuable as literature.

To sum up the first half of the argument of this chapter: any formal element in a text is an aspect of its meaningfulness that is fully comparable on equal terms to any other aspect, notwithstanding the fact that it may on occasion loosely be described in local terms as emphasis, form, or style. Such terms do not indicate a different kind of meaning, and likewise the attempted distinction between "what is said" and "how it is said"[31] when analyzed turns out to be no more than a distinction between "gross surface meaning" and "more differentiated and investigated meaning." It is, therefore, an error to take this as a theoretical distinction, and this error is basic to the work of most linguists[32] when they attempt to deal with literature. To take this antiformalist position, however, must not lead us to accept the position popularly thought to be the necessary alternative to aesthetic or formal criticism, namely a historicist or ideological criticism; the two positions do not contrast, and are equally erroneous.

I turn now to the question of the procedures of criticism. It must follow from my argument so far that analysis of a text and interpretation of it cannot in principle be different activities.[33] Both are concerned with the

[31] Goethe's "Das was bedenke, mehr bedenke wie" might appear, on its face, bad theory; but the appearance here is contradicted by a closer acquaintance with Goethe's theory. See, for example, two relevant articles by E. M. Wilkinson, " 'Form' and 'Content' in the Aesthetics of German Classicism," in *Stil- und Formprobleme in der Literatur*, ed. P. Böckmann (Heidelberg, 1959), and "Goethe's Conception of Form," *Proceedings of the British Academy* 38 (1951).

[32] E.g., Moulton's article "Linguistics" in the MLA pamphlet *Aims and Methods*, p. 18, provides a simple statement that we need to judge the literary work from two points of view, "(1) What the author says, (2) how he says it."

[33] Yet even Weitz (*Hamlet and the Philosophy of Literary*

investigation of the meaning of a text. This is easy to see in the case of the word "interpretation"; but if "analysis" is taken to be concerned with the most general principles of organization of a certain set of linguistic elements, it must also be an interpretation of the ways in which they relate to each other and so of the resultant meaning of the whole. All "formal" statements about texts are therefore part of an interpretation of the text, while all interpretations must be justified by the results of analysis.

The basis of all interpretative statements is that they are, in a sense that I shall now explain (and which has many important consequences), combinative. I have said that the investigation of the "stylistic" function of an aspect of a piece of language is an investigation of its precise function. But what, in turn, can that consist in? It can only be a question of the relation of one particular element to all the other elements that make up the text. When we ask, What in this work is the function of X? we are asking for the relation of X to the rest of the work, and the way in which it combines with all the other features of the work to give its total meaning. Interpretation and analysis are, therefore, essentially investigations of the combinations of linguistic features in particular texts into a single whole. This proposition, like other conclusions that I have reached, appears neither complex nor startling; but its force can be appreciated when it is set in contrast to well-established theories and practices. Almost all linguists, for example, have an isolative rather than a combinative approach to the analysis of literary texts: they attempt to "isolate" style, to point to specific

Criticism), though seeking to write from a Wittgensteinian perspective, continues to treat them as separable.

isolable features of "literary" language, and so on. This must be self-defeating; the point is that those effects that they seek to isolate in specific features of a text arise precisely from the combination of all the features of a text.

This consideration leads to an instructive distinction between the linguistic analysis of a language, and the linguistic analysis of a literary text;[34] it will be seen that most linguists approach literary texts without having made the transition from the former to the latter, in that they still behave as though they were doing a kind of analysis similar to that which they more normally perform in analyzing the structure of languages.

When a language is analyzed, the results of the analysis are the possible patterns and structures of the language, codified in grammars and dictionaries. But the analysis of a particular text is concerned with the synthesis of those possible linguistic structures to form an individual text. Both exercises involve analysis; but in the first, analysis is an end in itself, while in the second, the end is the investigation of the combination and interaction of structures found by analysis. Both are concerned with meaning and structure: the first, with the inventory of structures within a given language, and their functions in general; the second, with the interaction of a given set of structures, and with the resulting structure and meaning of the whole text. Put another way, the first generalizes about the possibilities of the language, and classifies

[34] This part of my argument owes something to de Saussure's related (though not identical) distinction between "langue" and "parole"; but in the particular use made of the distinction here I owe rather more to conversations with D. G. Mowatt.

them; the second particularizes about the relation in a
text of a given combination of them.

An analogy can be made between the relation of these
two kinds of study of language and the relation of physics
to engineering. A physicist attempts to isolate the mech-
anisms of the physical world. An engineer, on the other
hand, instead of analyzing the basic patterns of the physical world, is concerned with the functioning together of
these isolated patterns in a unique given structure. He is
concerned with its equilibrium, with how each element
contributes to the stability of the structure, and how
general physical laws interact in the finished structure.
A similar distinction can be seen in the study, on the one
hand, of the principles of genetics and ecology and, on the
other, of a particular ecosystem: there, too, the emphasis
will be on combination and equilibrium of the general
principles in a particular case. In the same way, critics
of literature are concerned with the interaction of general
possibilities of a language to form a unique structure.

The "combinative" study of language texts is not confined to literary study, though literary texts understandably loom large as material for consideration since they
present especially interesting combinations of the structures of a language. There are, however, many other
types of texts that may be worth such combinative study;
political speeches might be one example. There is no reason to suppose that the study of language should not include both generalizing and particularizing, even though
the overwhelming majority of linguists are concerned
exclusively with the isolation of the general possibilities
of a given language.[35] The question of whether the study

[35] I thus agree with Jakobson ("Closing Statement," p. 350):

of literature should therefore be regarded as part of the study of language, is one I shall return to in a later chapter. For the moment, I want to point to a practical consequence of the tendency to restrict "linguistics" to the activity that describes the general possibilities of languages: it is that any study of literary texts that was consciously "linguistic" in orientation has proceeded on isolative and classificatory lines;[36] that is to say, instead of investigating the particular combination of linguistic elements found in a text, it has stopped at identifying and exemplifying individual features of the language. The "deviation" model of style, for example, has been the result and the implement of pursuing the questions

---

"Since linguistics is the global science of verbal structure, poetics may be regarded as an integral part of linguistics." And my distinction of two types of linguistic study is not entirely inconsistent with his dictum (p. 358): *"The poetic function projects the principle of equivalence from the axis of selection into the axis of combination."*

[36] An interesting sign of a move away from isolative investigations on the part of a linguist is found in M.A.K. Halliday, "The Linguistic Study of Literary Texts," *Proceedings of the IXth International Congress of Linguists*, (The Hague, 1964), p. 303: "While insisting that stylistic studies use the same methods and categories as non-literary descriptions, we must make the proviso that such studies may require new alignments or groupings of descriptive categories, through which the special properties of a text may be recognized. This may include the bringing together of categories and items described at different levels as well as those scattered throughout the description of any one level. An example of such a grouping, in which various grammatical and lexical features are brought together, is 'cohesion.' " The study of the combination of linguistic structures at various levels is, then, according to Halliday, formal and linguistic. But "cohesion" should be regarded in a more general way—not as a limited abstraction from particular texts, but as the general framework for the investigation of any text.

of an isolative general linguistics; it attempted typically to treat style as a single isolable device and to isolate its distinctive features in order to describe it as a deviance from the grammar of a language.[37]

I want now to turn to the question of how a combinative kind of study of a text must proceed and how its methods are to be conceived. We confront here questions as to the methodological status of criticism: Are its methods in any sense analogous to those of the sciences? Can critical procedures be described at all—or is the attempt to think in general terms about critical procedures fruitless in principle? Must we be content with viewing the whole field as one in which individual judgment follows no rules, and thus to which notions of sound procedure are inapplicable?

A widely held view (or rather attitude, since it is in the main unformulated) makes a distinction between elementary factual observations and subsequent interpretation that goes beyond them; the former are subject to methodological controls, the latter is an act of judgment of a different order, and no rules or procedures relate to it. The most explicit version of this view is that which

[37] Riffaterre goes even further and separates language from style: we must avoid, he says, "the confusion between style and language" ("Criteria," p. 154). Riffaterre is misled partly by his rigid dualism (language is for him the "vehicle" of style) but also by the absence of a distinction between isolative and combinative investigations: "*stylistic facts . . . must have a specific character, since otherwise they could not be distinguished from linguistic facts.*" Here "linguistic facts" is evidently the equivalent of "isolated linguistic facts," but the logic of the argument breaks down if we substitute this expanded phrase. The "specific character" sought lies in the combinations of isolable linguistic facts; that is, it is still linguistic.

commonly arises when the relation of linguistic analysis to literary criticism is discussed. Here the split between two methodologically different activities becomes a division of labor between critic and linguist. The latter scrutinizes the text, comes up with scientifically controlled and verifiable facts, and passes them on to the critic, who will provide a literary interpretation of them.[38] Thus anything precise and controlled is precritical; while anything that is critical is not scientific. The gap between the two seems unbridgeable; the linguist's facts are true and precise, but seem trivial; the critic's judgments are weighty, but unproven and unprovable. Depending on the cast of mind of the individual concerned, the critic's results are seen as either gloriously beyond science and control, penetrating into the sphere where genius exists, or they are seen as mere subjectivism, beneath the dignity and certainty of science. This common notion of the methodological status of criticism is, if I am correct, completely mistaken; but its mistake is instructive and central, and it will serve well to introduce the view of critical method that I want to propose.

[38] See, for example, D. Freeman's review of a collection of essays devoted to linguistic analysis of literature, which he welcomes because it works with the theory under discussion in my text (*Journal of Linguistics* 4, 1968: 109–115, review of R. Fowler, ed., *Essays on Style and Language*). Freeman thinks that linguistic analysis of literary texts is ". . . a precritical, rather than a critical, activity, although a critical intelligence must inform it. The linguist attempts to isolate the distinctive, idiosyncratic features of one particular act (or series of acts) of language: a literary text." It is ". . . an activity prior to and distinct from, but not irrelevant to, the act of criticism itself." Here the connection can clearly be seen between the "isolative" view of linguistic analysis of literature and the popular view of the methodological status of criticism.

In comparisons of literary criticism and scientific method which run on these lines, it is important to examine carefully the notion of science on which the comparison rests. In the popular view of science, progress is linear. We learn more, and add it to what we already know. This is in essence the Cartesian view of science; as we increase scientific knowledge we progress from the known to the unknown. Knowledge is stored like bricks: one gets more and more of them, and piles one on top of the other. The Cartesian view is still the basis of common-sense attitudes to scientific progress; it thinks of procedure as mainly deductive, and sees little scope for imaginative leaps—hence the feeling that criticism, which makes such leaps, is unscientific. Although precise observation provides a few building blocks for the critic to stand on, he still, it seems, leaps off into the void when he makes an interpretation—unlike the scientist, who keeps adding to his pile of bricks. Once again, we may legitimately think of this attitude to science as part of the habits of mind engendered by the reference theory of meaning: each scientific proposition is a linguistic representation of a fact about the world and a simple reference to it which will not need revision or reformulation, since it is a copy of something that is there to be referred to. But the popular view of science turns out to be an inadequate one; and when criticism is compared to a more reasonable view of scientific method, the large distinction between the two, which results from the popular view, completely disappears.

The Cartesian view of scientific method has, of course, been subjected to much criticism by philosophers of science, and only survives as a feature of "common sense" unreflective views of science, which unfortunately include the view of science typically held by literary critics. Long ago, Goethe's admonition "dass alles Faktische schon Theorie ist," questioned the separability of facts from the theories within which they had been developed; C. S. Peirce wrote a brilliant and devastating attack on the Cartesian notion that science proceeded deductively from the known to the unknown;[39] and popularizations have begun to appear of Peirce's argument, such as the recent book by Kuhn, *The Structure of Scientific Revolutions*.[40] I shall present a simplified version of this argument in order to show how the Cartesian view has helped to misrepresent the nature of criticism.

The basic error of Cartesian science is the view that there are "known facts" that can simply be logged and used as springboards to the next, as yet unknown, fact; for new knowledge may profoundly affect the character of what we thought we already knew, and cause us to rethink our conception of the "already known." This is because, as Goethe saw, the facts we think we know are part of some general theory that we hold, and new experiences may force us to modify that general theory. We do not passively accept true facts from the world, as the reference theory of meaning seems to allow; we process and abstract from all that we experience, and our statements of particular facts are always in terms of our best current abstraction from (or theory of) the general area of experience to which those facts belong.

[39] See the analysis of Peirce's criticisms of Descartes in W. B. Gallie, *Peirce and Pragmatism* (Harmondsworth, Middlesex, 1952).

[40] T. S. Kuhn, *The Structure of Scientific Revolutions* (Chicago, 1962). Kuhn does not display the sources of the basic ideas of his argument as clearly as might be wished.

Our very statements of the "facts," then, embody interpretations and constructions that we have placed upon them. If this often seems not to be the case, and if, in practice, we seem to be able to make a distinction between the facts and our search for an interpretation of them, this is because we are working already with a preliminary general interpretation which we so take for granted that it seems to be unquestionable, and which provides the basis for our formulation of the facts. In such a case, then, what we are actually doing is not seeking an interpretation of uninterpreted facts, but instead seeking an extension of the basic interpretation embodied both in their formulation and in the fact of these (rather than some others) being the subject of attention at all. An impasse in inquiry is often reached when such an extension is not forthcoming because the assumed basic interpretation itself is defective. At this point, our whole understanding which is basic to the formulation and selection of facts is inadequate, and a complete new theory (not an extension of the old one) will have to emerge if we are to make progress. And that will mean that all the facts we thought we knew are thrown up into the air: far from being unquestionable building blocks for future advances, they must, in any major advance in knowledge, be destroyed and reformed.

The view of scientific method which must replace the Cartesian one, therefore, is as follows: all knowledge is in the nature of a theory or hypothesis that organizes as best we can all the experiences we have to account for. What we experience influences our general view, but our general view at any one time also influences what we look for. This statement can be reformulated in the strict terms of hypothesis and experiment: our hypothesis suggests experiments, but the results of experiments modify hypotheses and suggest new ones, which in turn suggest new experiments that will be critical for the new hypotheses. It is important to see that this technical language is only a restatement of a normal, everyday procedure: we approach all new situations in the light of our existing views (themselves abstractions from situations we have already experienced) and tend to notice what is important in the light of those preexisting views. But what we notice affects the character of our existing views, since it is never quite what we expected, and these changes in our general views then suggest to us new kinds of things that we should now be on the lookout for. It is in just this way, for example, that we experience and develop our view of another person; we do not simply add up experiences to a general view of him, but continually move between a general attitude and particular experiences, with both modifying the other, as developing understanding modifies the formulation of what had seemed "facts" about him. Hypothesis and experiment, therefore, is not merely a scientific and technical process; it is a refined statement of how knowledge and understanding progress in any sphere, even everyday affairs. There is no sphere in which the view of knowledge as the continual acquisition of unalterable building blocks is tenable. In all spheres, we investigate by means of assumptions we have made, consciously or unconsciously search out what bears on these assumptions, and have to abandon them in favor of others when the pressure of experience goes too much against them. There is no way of observing neutral facts neutrally. We must decide where to look and how to abstract from what we find, and both these decisions are results of the vantage point from which we begin. To say that facts suggest interpretations is just as true as saying that interpretations suggest facts.

The process of knowledge is not, then, a linear progression that assembles facts the interpretation of which follows from their piling up; it is a circular process of continual refinement, in which an interpretation is held up to scrutiny in the light of observations, and observations are scrutinized in the light of an interpretation. Any new observation may change our general view of all previous ones, while each change in general view will generate new observations and "facts." We swing from general to particular and back again, each swing making the interpretative hypothesis more complex and inclusive. Evidently, such a procedure is not uncontrolled, and is not mere judgment without some sort of objective check, for it is the procedure of the most "objective" sciences. But neither does it produce absolute certainty or dispense with the need for imagination, guesswork, and hunches.[41]

[41] A typical argument which misdescribes scientific method in order to achieve a spurious contrast with literary criticism is that by Rodway, "What the Critics Really Need"; see my criticism of his argument in *Twentieth Century* 172 (1963). Having ruled out scientific method as a model for criticism, he suggests the model of the law court, where persuasiveness is the essence of the procedure, i.e., the "truthful, lying, passionate pleading of humanity." But this (one would hope!) is just as much a misdescription of law courts; verifiable facts are surely the subject of the inquiry in a court, and the formalized system of evidence-taking is designed precisely to sort out lying, pleading, and persuasiveness from the establishment of the facts. Would even Rodway be happy to be judged in the kind of law court he describes? H. Levin's *Why Literary Criticism is not an Exact Science* (Cambridge, Mass., 1967) is another example of the standard contrast between criticism and scientific method based on a restricted view of science.

Here, it is all a question of which particular stage in investigation we are thinking of. The process of observation and experiment requires great control, precision, and "objectivity." The stage of experimentation also calls for deductive reasoning; if our hypothesis is true, then it can be deduced from it that a particular observation should turn up a particular fact. But the other stage in the cycle of investigation requires a different mental operation; for when observed facts are not consistent with the initial hypothesis, an imaginative reconstruction of all the known facts into another shape is necessary— that is, a new hypothesis. There are no "rules" for this, and "inspired guesswork" and "intuition" can legitimately have a role at this stage.

It will readily be seen that the typical version of the contrast between science and literary criticism creates a gulf between the two by dwelling on the precise, observational stage in the one case and the interpretative stage in the other; this results in a contrast between the certainty of science on the one hand, and the judgmental character of criticism on the other. This contrast is quite false; in both cases, we find the two stages of observation-making and hypothesis-development.[42] The stan-

[42] D. G. Mowatt and I first suggested that interpretations of poems were procedurally analogous to scientific hypotheses in a lecture to the "Linguistics and Literature" section of the British Linguistics Association conference at Hull, in 1961. The idea seems to have taken root and become general there; two other members of the group (M. Gregory and J. Spencer) include it in their essay "An Approach to the Study of Style," p. 61. The implications of the idea are not thought through in this essay, however; five pages later the authors contradict it by introducing and advocating substantially the same division of labor between linguists and critics described in my text—one that implies a

dard view of the split between science and criticism thus relies on a contrast between two stages of a cycle where the whole cycle is common to both fields; the contrast of interpretative judgment to precise observation is a contrast found within both fields, not between the two fields. This situation is not without some irony, for on occasion a critic has pronounced the essence of criticism to be cyclic—a progression from general interpretation to the particulars of a text, which then leads to a modification of the interpretation, followed by a new look at the particulars of the text, and so on; all of which is perfectly true. Spitzer, for example, advanced such a view. In advancing it, he thought he had distinguished criticism from science; but in reality he was only documenting his own progress to a non-Cartesian view of criticism while retaining a Cartesian view of science.[43]

If, then, we compare comparable stages of the inquiry, no real contrast is achieved between the descriptions of scientific method and literary interpretation by such assertions as that judgment is necessary in the latter case, or that precision is achieved in the former. I am not saying that science is in all ways like criticism; the sciences are evidently more advanced both in the complexities of their interpretative theory and in the sophistication of

---

"building-blocks" view of critical procedure, not one of hypothesis and observation.

[43] L. Spitzer, *Linguistics and Literary History* (Princeton, 1948). Spitzer calls the procedure of criticism the "philological circle"; it is, of course, the circle of inquiry in general. Spitzer's view is not very far removed from that of W. Dilthey, who in his *Einleitung in die Geisteswissenschaften* (Berlin, 1883) also distinguished the methods of the sciences from those of the humanities. Similar results are there achieved by a similarly restrictive view of science.

their observational techniques. My point is simply that a distinction cannot be made between the two in terms of a different kind of procedural logic.

I want now to show how the misdescription of criticism that is embodied in the standard account of the differences between science and criticism severely hampers actual criticism. The first loss to criticism resulting from this kind of attitude lies in the impoverishment of the whole notion of investigative method. "Judgment" and "interpretation" become leaps into the void, instead of part of a systematic sequence of thoughts, while any precise aspects of investigating literature are thought of as "mechanical," instead of as the instruments through which judgments operate. In effect, both parts of the cycle are devalued, and the critic is set free to say whatever he wants to say. The standard view seems to set a high value on judgment as an imaginative act, but in fact it does so in a way that makes the imagination sterile, for in operating outside the interpretative cycle it becomes a dead end; it acts once only and then stops. Once we have used interpretative judgment and imagination, we are done with them, and thus they do not function to renew the interpretative cycle and to provide material that will make the next round of observing fruitful and conducive to further acts of imaginative interpretation. In such a situation judgment cannot develop because it is not subject to scrutiny through re-observation: it is commonly thought of as an "individual"[44] act (which

[44] Thorne, "Poetry, Stylistics, and Imaginary Grammars," p. 150. Thorne operates here with the standard gap between linguistic description and interpretation: "I do not see how it is possible to establish such a connexion."

seems to imply that it is not an investigator's act at all), a nonscientific act,[45] but at all events it is a final act and an unanalyzable one. Paradoxically, critics seem to be offering a view of judgment and imagination that lets them operate without restriction, but are in fact restricting their operation in very important ways; for imagination must instead be made to work in criticism not in one grandiose act but over and over again. A first impression of a work is necessarily intuitive, but when more detail of the work is contemplated and found not to be consistent with that first impression, a new imaginative act is necessary to transform it into something that takes more textual detail into account; and the new imaginative reconstruction again becomes a tool for further thought about individual passages, the results of which again lead to further redefinition of our general account. This progressive increasing of complexity is abruptly stopped in the limited view of judgment and imagination that is used to contrast with a "mechanical" science.

In similar fashion, the notion of precise observation is devalued by the standard contrast between criticism and science; it is thought of as "mechanical" (or perhaps just "scientific") and beneath the intellectual level of criticism. It is, of course, true that there are no mechanical procedures for criticism[46]—but there are none in scien-

----

[45] E.g., Rodway, p. 157, and Spiller ("Literary History") p. 45.

[46] There are some procedures in scientific fields which can be mechanically described—but they are not procedures for the discovering of new knowledge. Writing a sonnet, too, involves certain mechanical rules, but that is characteristic as a whole neither of sonnet-writing nor of criticism. This example shows again how one easily obtains a spurious contrast between criticism and science. One simply forgets that literature involves some mechani-

tific discovery either. Since precise observation is not seen as an instrument of the imagination, it, too, degenerates and then seems to deserve its image as a mechanical activity. The fruitful cycle of investigation has been stopped: imagination does not guide observation, nor does observation present new material for imaginative interpretation. Methodical observation ought to be generated by an act of imagination, and then work backwards upon that act—none of which is mechanical. The comparison of the certainties of science with the uncertainties of criticism again functions to limit critical method, in that the certainty of one side is exaggerated and the other diminished in order to achieve a false contrast; the appropriate comparison would be between the uncertainties involved in framing new scientific hypotheses and those involved in critical interpretation, and they are indeed comparable.

It will by now be clear that the theory of the division of labor between critics and linguists, which I have outlined above, is based on the standard misconception about the relation of science and criticism. According to that theory, linguists observe facts about texts, then hand them to the critic for interpretation. But this is a case of the right hand not knowing what the left hand is doing with a vengeance; for anyone who sets out to make observations must be looking for something, and in so doing cannot fail to be acting on some hypothesis (whether formulated or assumed) as to what to look for. He does

---

cal rules; and then one takes as typical of science some mechanical laboratory procedures and forgets that anything else is involved in the scientific enterprise—and the contrast that is wished has been made.

not, and cannot, gather neutral facts and pass them on to the critic for interpretation. There are many different places to look for "facts," and many ways of formulating them. To pass on a particular selection, formulated and grouped in a certain way, is to have acted on a view of the text that is an interpretative hypothesis about it. In observing and analyzing, therefore, the "linguist" is an interpreter.[47] If he does pass on his results to a critic in the division of labor recommended by this view, what then happens? Possibly, the "critic" can interpret the facts as the "linguist" did—that is, the implied hypothesis of the latter transmits itself to the former, who makes it explicit. But that is a strange procedure—the interpretation belongs to the initiator of the observations, not to their recipient. Perhaps the "critic" may go beyond them, or may perceive in them a contradiction, which would mean that the "linguist's" hypothesis was not adequate, and had been shown to be so by the contradictory nature of the results. In this case, he would need to reformulate or change the original hypothesis, and do more observing of the details of the text in the light of the newer and

[47] It is sometimes said that the linguist does a complete analysis of a text, only then presenting to the critic what turns out to be significant. Since the analysis is complete, the argument then runs, interpretation was not involved in it. But this, too, is theoretically untenable, and for several reasons. First, the judgment of what is significant can never be mechanical, but must be an interpretative judgment; second, a complete analysis is an impossible notion in itself; and third, it is, in principle, pointless to do a "complete" (as exhaustive as current theory allows?) analysis of a text, unless one's aim is simply an exemplification of, e.g., English grammar, for which any text could suffice. There is, then, no way that a linguist can claim not to be making interpretative judgments in presenting (to the world or just to critics) significant facts about a literary text.

more developed interpretation. But, presumably, he must, on the division of labor theory, hand the observing back to the linguist to let him do it. This never in fact happens; to act in this way would be to expose the absurdity of the whole procedure, for no one observes without an interpretative hypothesis, and no one forms such an hypothesis without being prepared to observe for himself. The practical results of this kind of view are extremely serious, and explain the undeveloped nature of most attempts at literary analysis. It produces, first of all, a strange helplessness in the face of "facts." Facts are not thought of as part of the cycle of investigation in which we go from facts to interpretation and back to facts again, each time reorienting the one according to the other. They are not reworked, but are treated as immutable and unchangeable; the step from facts to interpretations and the use of judgment is again a leap into the void. There is some irony in a situation where critics first create a gap between facts and interpretations, and then complain of that gap and of how facts do not help them.

The division of labor must conversely produce the same helplessness in handling interpretations. Interpretations are generally concealed and not formulated by linguists studying literature, and yet linguists who claim to have observed scientifically a certain kind of clause structure in a certain poem must have worked on the interpretative assumption that this is an important feature of the poem. But if they refuse to state and admit to that interpretation, they cannot refine and develop it in light of their subsequent observations. And the cycle of investigation comes to a dead halt; interpretation cannot progress. The division of labor theory therefore effectively prevents the continual move from the facts (linguistic or otherwise) of the text to interpretation, to new views of the facts, to more refined interpretation.

An interpretation, then, is a hypothesis about the most general organization and coherence of all the elements that form a literary text. The most satisfying interpretation will be that which is the most inclusive. The procedure of investigation will be that of any inquiry: a continual move between general notions of the coherence of the text, and consideration of the function within the whole of particular parts of it. General conceptions will change in the light of particular observations, and new particular observations will then become necessary in the light of the changed conceptions. The main reason why interpretations usually seem not to be entailed by the facts of the literary text[48] lies precisely in the fact that a continued process of this kind is not generally seen to be the essential method of criticism.

A corollary of this argument can easily be seen: if precise linguistic descriptions of texts are relevant to interpretations, then critics must be able to make them themselves; in that sense they must be linguists, and know how the material that they are investigating works. Critics of literature must command all stages of the cycle of investigation just as is necessary in any other kind of field. Scientists cannot hypothesize without knowing the nature of their data; and conversely, no scientist could

[48] This early cessation of interpretation is, of course, encouraged by the fact that energy is generally deflected from this necessary process of thinking and rethinking into irrelevancies which are interesting but less demanding intellectually, as shown above, chapter 5.

look into a microscope without knowing what things seen would be critical for his general hypothesis. Here, then, is the source of the much lamented gulf between the trivial precision of the linguist and the momentous subjectivity of the critic; for how can unguided observing be other than trivial, or undeveloped and unrefined hypotheses be other than subjective, that is, remote from the data?

A number of common oppositions of terms fall to the ground if seen in light of the view I have advanced. For example, "description" cannot be opposed to "interpretation," for the two terms refer to different aspects of the same process. Likewise, in literary study "analysis" should not be thought of as fundamentally unlike "interpretation";[49] nor should "logical" be opposed to "interpretative,"[50] and the "objectivity" of science should not be opposed to the "subjectivity" of criticism.

Many linguists[51] use an argument against critics which

[49] To regard interpretation as an artistic activity is, of course, to misconstrue investigation in general. Cf. Spiller, "Literary History," pp. 45, 55. At the opposite end of the spectrum, other critics on occasion grant interpretations a finality or obviousness that no explanation in any field deserves, e.g., Rodway, "What the Critics Really Need," p. 161; and Casey, *The Language of Criticism*, pp. 146–147. Linguists who pride themselves on their scientific objectivity, on the other hand, eschew interpretation of literary texts as an alien "subjective" element in their objective discipline. But all initial hypotheses are based on subjective impressions—it is only the refusal to develop and refine them that could count as "unscientific."

[50] This is the emphasis of Righter's work (*Logic and Criticism*).

[51] See, for example, Halliday, "The Linguistic Study of Literary Texts," p. 302: "There is a crucial difference between the *ad hoc*, personal and arbitrarily selective statements offered, frequently in support of a preformulated literary thesis . . . and an analysis founded on general linguistic theory. . . ." To be sure, it is ar-

sounds plausible enough, but which, in the context of the description of critical inquiry that I have outlined, needs serious revision: it is that critics generally refer to linguistic facts only to support some preexisting view, not in a spirit of objective investigation. Thus, the argument goes, their appeals to linguistic facts are not, in a sense, genuine: they have made up their minds what they think, and are just trying to get some support for their case. Linguists, on the other hand, must observe objectively, without prejudging the facts.

From the standpoint that I have taken, this argument against critics, with its characterization of what linguists do by contrast, is very misleading. Linguists are plainly wrong in thinking that it is possible to look at a text without any assumptions or "preexisting" hypotheses, and they misdescribe their own procedure if they think that any contrast exists between themselves and critics on this score. The focus of the objection should be elsewhere, and probably on three things: first, critics use facts selectively; second, they do not formulate them in the most intelligent way, consistent with the best analysis of language available; and third, their selective use of the facts prevents development and refinement of their hypotheses. In terms of scientific method, this would perhaps be thought of as inefficient and dishonest experimentation; but having a hypothesis cannot be thought of as a scientific sin. On the contrary, it is linguists who are open to criticism for refusing to acknowledge that they are working with a hypothesis based on their first impression of the text, and so failing to progress beyond

---

bitrary selectivity that Halliday objects to here: yet a "literary thesis" is not avoidable.

that impression. This is a most important lapse from scientific method. And so to summarize, the division of labor theory stops the inquiry at its beginning; the linguist will not allow his general conceptions to evolve because he will not acknowledge that he has any, while the critic glorifies his initial general conceptions as individual acts of judgment, which he will not put in their proper context in the logic of inquiry, and so he cannot give them precision or subject them to controlled development and modification.

There are a number of paradoxes to be seen in the critics' version of themselves as being quite unlike scientists. Take, for example, their insistence that they do not deal with the "certainties" of science. Since scientists grasped the fact that their views of a given area of nature were being upset at periodic intervals, they have become reluctant to talk about "truth" or "reality." In refusing to talk about the "real" state of affairs, they are, in effect, allowing the possibility that there is a gap between their abstraction and what is there to be abstracted from, so that further thought and investigation is never ruled out. It is ironic, then, to find that critics refer often to scientific certainty, while in their own practice in criticism they decline to operate with a view of criticism that allows for continual rethinking,[52] as scientific method

---

[52] Mowatt has shown that, in practice, critics are extremely reluctant to allow that certain widely held views (which he terms the "absolutes" of literary history) are anything less than certain. While in theory they defend themselves against scientific method by claiming not to be involved in scientific certainties, critics often hold so rigid a view of certain key propositions in their field that they will not allow them to be treated with that caution which is built into scientific terminology. See his "Lan-

does. Consider, for example, the rigidity of thought that is basic to the notion of form and content. "Content" is in practice a rigidified and unmodifiable abstraction from a text while "form" is all that has not yet entered into the abstraction. Content in a more adequate sense must be rethought and reabstracted, as more and more that had not yet entered into the first abstraction is assimilated to it.

Paradoxical, too, is the critics' notion that they deal not in facts, but in judgment and imagination; for it is precisely the failure to see how the imagination works constructively in science through a disciplined kind of activity that is the greatest loss to criticism. From the standpoint of scientific method, criticism must appear to be not a field that works with imagination rather than facts, but a field where imagination works defectively and inefficiently, using as its instrument concealed hypotheses or rigidified and absolute hypotheses.

The object of literary criticism, then, is an interpretative hypothesis as to the most general principle of structure which can be abstracted from the combination of linguistic elements in a literary text. The term "structure" is often used in literary criticism in a more superficial sense, to refer to one particular aspect of a text, for example, its natural breaks, its plot outline, and so on. I should propose to reserve the use of this term to designate the most general principle of organization which binds together and makes sense of all the detail of a text in combination. The most general statement of structure, in

guage, Literature, and Middle High German," pp. 74ff; and for a related argument, Dembowski and Mowatt, "Literary Study and Linguistics."

this sense, is equally a statement of thematic structure[53] and therefore of the meaning of the text. The test of statements of this kind is simply comprehensiveness—they must synthesize and thus make sense of as much as possible of the text. The application of this test is most obvious and comprehensible in works of a superficially loose and episodic outline: Goethe's novel *Die Wahlverwandtschaften,* for example, appears to be a collection of incidents, episodes, and characters where the coherence of the whole is difficult to see; an interpretation must arrange its diverse images and motifs, characters, and events, in such a way that their coherence in the one text becomes meaningful. It is easy to see the general procedure of hypothesis and experiment working here: typically, one abstracts a common thread from a few of these diverse areas of text and then looks at others in the light of it, allowing the first abstraction to be modified or even abandoned in view of what then appears. In this way, the episodic elements must be gradually absorbed into a more and more refined and developed view of the structure and meaning of the whole. It is unusually obvious that what this complex book needs is this progressive absorption of its detail: but the need is no less necessary for all texts. Every aspect of a text must be taken up into a general view, from the peculiarities of its clauses, through symbolism or imagery, to the major overt plot events themselves. Some allowance must be made in theory for those cases where this proves an impossibility. Cases are found in which the progressive attempt to absorb as much as

[53] Cf. the point elaborated in my *Kleist's "Prinz Friedrich von Homburg." A Critical Study* (Berkeley and Los Angeles, 1970), p. 11.

possible into a general overall view runs into a hard lump
that remains separate and refuses to be absorbed, however
we try; here we face the issue of a text that is not well
organized, and so is inconsistent and to that extent im-
perfect. But here the general framework I have proposed
is more necessary than ever, because in these cases, above
all, we must remember that our judgment is provisional
and hypothetical. It cannot be ruled out that someone
may still find the interpretation that can, to the satisfac-
tion of other critics, absorb the recalcitrant parts of the
text. As in the sciences, the degree to which other investigators are convinced by the suggested new interpretation
is the only measure of its value.[54]

[54] See the interesting controversy concerning the consistency or
possible inconsistency of Goethe's *Tasso*, in which the late S.
Burckhardt took the view that inconsistency or consistency must
always be a matter of critical hypothesis, while W. Silz insisted
that no one should doubt that the play was inconsistent. S. Burckhardt, "The Consistency of Goethe's *Tasso*," *Journal of English
and Germanic Philology* 57 (1958); W. Silz, "The Scholar, the
Critic, and the Teacher of Literature," *German Quarterly* 37 (1964):
118. In such cases, it is often the knowledge that the author
interrupted his work on the text that leads critics to judge all too
quickly that a puzzling feature is an error or inconsistency. In
Mark Twain's *Huckleberry Finn*, for example, Huck and Jim at
one point resolve to go north when their raft reaches a fork in the
river, but this intention is forgotten as the raft drifts south past
the fork. Critics who are impressed by the fact that the author
had broken off writing the book between these two points assume
he had forgotten what he was doing by the time he resumed work
on it. In the context of the book, however, there is nothing that is
necessarily inconsistent in an event that can easily be seen as part
of the gradual process of Huck and Jim becoming more and more
remote from the reality of society on the river banks, as they
"drift" downstream in more senses than one. Hard decisions (to
go upstream) about the "real" world are crowded out as their
existence on the river becomes a way of life.

It is only too easy to relate the theoretical issues I have been discussing to the weaknesses that can be seen in the practice of literary critics. The model of literary analysis, I have argued, should be that of a continuing cycle of investigation that moves from general notions to textual detail and back again, with continual refinement and development at each stage. A great deal of actual criticism can be characterized, in terms of this model, as presenting undeveloped and static ideas about texts. "Symbolic" interpretations, for example, usually operate on a level of generality that does no justice to the detail of a text. If they were viewed as initial broad speculative hypotheses about the text which would naturally need much redefinition, and if they were therefore thought of as exploratory tools in the light of which textual details could be examined, they might well be useful; but what actually happens is that they become too rigid too early, and remain crude and undeveloped accounts of the text.[55]

At the other end of the spectrum, criticism often refuses to make abstractions, and refers to the details of the text without employing any interpretative hypotheses. This is true, for example, of traditional plot-and-character analysis and equally of the kind of criticism which describes Goethe's poem *Auf dem See* as about being in a boat on a lake.

[55] Cf. A. E. Quigley's *The Dynamics of Dialogue in the Plays of Harold Pinter*, Ph.D. Dissertation, University of California, Santa Cruz, 1971, for a demonstration of how the common "symbolic" interpretation of bizarre literary material is often grossly inaccurate, reductive, and out of touch with the characteristics of the text. The point made in the text concerns only the common gross use of symbolic interpretations, and does not imply that appropriately controlled interpretation of symbolism is not important.

Both poles of undeveloped criticism to which I have referred could easily be the first stages of an investigation. That something more is needed than these undeveloped statements has probably always been felt; and this must surely be part of the reason why critics have so commonly turned to the context of origin of the literary work, in an attempt to find something more substantial. Unfortunately, it is precisely that attempt to provide a more developed criticism of texts that has been the strongest factor in its failing to develop beyond primitive interpretative hypotheses.

My conclusion in the second half of this chapter is that a general notion of critical procedure is possible and useful, and it does not differ significantly from the more general logic of inquiry; only a quite illegitimate contrast with a defective view of scientific procedure could have made things seem otherwise. The common insistence that critics cannot employ mechanical deductive procedures is an unwarranted brake on the kind of rational discussion of procedure that is pursued in other fields; a quite well-known and simple model of hypothesis and observation is sufficient to describe what critics do (or should do) and to give critics some confidence that they do not need to feel that a logical and rational procedure is inaccessible to them.

7: Generalizing About Literature

IN THE PRECEDING chapters I have discussed the logic of textual analysis and the nature of its results. I turn now to the logic of statements that have broader applicability than to a single text, and so to more general statements about literature.

The most important traditional question in this area of literary theory has been the question whether one can legitimately study individual works by themselves, without taking them together with other works by the same author and of the same period. Formerly, criticism of literature consisted mainly of volumes that surveyed a number of works, with relatively little detailed comment on each one. Literary biographies set comments about individual works in a general frame of reference which was the author's life, and literary histories strung comments on works together in the framework of historical sequence. Comments on individual works seemed to "add up" to something larger; history and biography seemed to offer secure general frameworks within which this accumulation of knowledge could take place and be justified.

The challenge to historical and biographical interpretation that first began to be seriously felt earlier in this century had the effect not only of shaking the accepted grounds for making interpretative statements about individual texts, but also raised a question about the basis for this kind of general account of literature; if historical and biographical circumstances are no longer thought to determine the meaning of a text, should we no longer generalize in historical and biographical terms? Over the last forty years there has certainly been an increase in the number of studies that have been devoted to individual works and which have made no attempt to set any results in a more general context. The complaint is now often heard that we no longer see the woods for the trees; the particular studies obscure the general picture. In one sense (the obvious one) this complaint cannot be justified: general works continue to appear in quantity, and they could, in theory, reflect the conclusions of the separate studies of individual works. But the basis of the complaint is probably a more serious, though unformulated, problem: the results of detailed individual studies have often made it harder to generalize about literature.[1] They

---

[1] This clash has often led historical or biographical critics to reject interpretative work on the grounds that its results are inconsistent with accepted generalizations about author or period involved; and yet it is only on the basis of synthesizing such results that the generalizations could ever have existed. This is not to deny that interpretative results can be questioned, but only to narrow the ground on which they can be questioned: they cannot logically be questioned on the grounds that they are inconsistent with a generalization that is an abstraction from all known results. To assert "this cannot be true of medieval texts," if there are no other grounds for the objection, is circular, in ruling out an instance that the generalization must include if it is to be valid.

have made distinctions between one century and another less easy to maintain; they have made it less possible to generalize about "classic" and "romantic" or about the niche traditionally occupied in literary history by certain great works. Close individual studies have, in effect, commonly introduced complexity and confusion into generalizations found in traditional survey volumes which had relied on a fairly cursory reading of the numerous works discussed. It is surely this kind of factor, not any absence of general studies, which is at the bottom of complaints about the appearance of analyses of individual texts.

In any field of study, one would wish to feel that particular statements are a contribution to a general field, capable of having a cumulative effect which would allow them to add to other statements, and so to lead to abstractions of greater scope and importance. But how is this possible within the framework of the analysis I have presented so far?

It is not necessary to think that generalization must be historical and biographical generalization; but this assumption is evidently built into another of the persistent noncontrasting alternatives offered by traditionalist literary critics: either we stop at individual interpretations of works or we go on to broader consideration of them in the context of author and period. Generalization is here taken to be identical with the kind of generalization traditionally favored; and the crucial question—What kind of synthesis?—has been prejudged before we begin to examine it.

Another important feature of this common misconception lies in confusing the two distinct issues of synthesizing interpretative results on the one hand, and of for-

mulating interpretative procedure on the other. The
traditional demand for a "synthetic" interpretation usually means putting works of literature together with events
from which they spring rather more than putting them together with other works of literature;[2] and the separateness objected to is separateness from local historical circumstances, rather than from other literary works. At
bottom, then, the issue here is one of theory of interpretation more than it is one of whether or not to generalize
results, and complaints against "individual" interpretations are generally complaints against the kind of interpretation rather than its not being generalized. Once
more, we see a familiar debate in literary theory being
fought ostensibly on one issue, but being really about
another; and again, this misplacing of the real issue has
impeded theoretical progress in both the ostensible and
the actual area of the debate.

In point of fact the traditional view actually works
against synthesis, and generally results in literary texts
being treated in isolation from other literary texts. If we
think of the generalization of individual results in any
other sphere, the process evidently involves putting comparable pieces of evidence side by side and then abstracting from a body of such comparable material. But that is
not the procedure being advocated by those who usually

[2] The title of Hermand's *Synthetisches Interpretieren* evidently
refers more to a synthesis of literature with political, social, and
historical facts and methods of study than to a generalization from
individual interpretations taken together; Hermand's work is a
typical and very conventional example of the antipathy of tradi-
tionalists to "Einzelinterpretation." The misconception that this
is a modern viewpoint is common in German criticism at the
moment.

complain about the lack of generalization in literary studies; what is advocated is not putting a number of comparable results together and abstracting to generalize, but putting literary statements together with other, quite different statements, to form a historian's synthesis. It is, of course, legitimate to urge writers of individual interpretations to synthesize, to generalize and abstract from a series of such interpretations, but in the corrective offered by those who most commonly urge synthesis, this is not in fact done, but instead the reverse: the traditional suggestion is in effect that literary texts be isolated one from another by referring each primarily to its context of origin rather than to the rest of the corpus of texts which function as the literature of the society, and through this to their general relationship to the whole of that society.

What, then, might a synthetic treatment of literary works do, granted that it were genuinely synthetic, and not just a defective interpretative theory in disguise? The most popular form of general treatments of a series of literary texts has been the literary history; but many other kinds of general treatments (literary biography, treatments of periods or movements in literature) share its theoretical assumptions to such a degree that for our purposes they can be considered as actual or potential chapters in a literary history. The question, What is literary history? can be approached in two ways: it can be answered in practical terms by investigating what such volumes contain, or in theoretical terms by asking what functions such a term might serve, and how useful these functions might be in the study of literature. In the latter case it will be relevant to look at the pronouncements of literary historians[3] as to what function they think literary history serves, though a discussion of the functions diagnosed by practitioners by no means exhausts the issue of the possible functions of literary history.

Literary histories generally include a number of different kinds of statements: names of authors and dates of composition, statements of historical and social circumstances, references to philosophical and aesthetic theories, brief evaluations of literary works, and also brief thematic or stylistic comments on them. Both texts that are a part of the literature of the community, and texts whose authors intended them as literary texts but which have never genuinely gained that status in the community are included. From such a collection of diverse statements, a dominant concern can easily be abstracted: literary history as practiced must be about the reconstruction of the local circumstances in which literary texts arose. As we have seen, this is subject to numerous logical objections: a limited context is wrongly thought to explain the existence of a work of literature;[4] the context of a text is wrongly thought to be a particular time and place instead of the whole culture; texts that are not the literary texts of the culture are included merely because their origina-

---

[3] Spiller's essay "Literary History" is an orthodox statement of what literary history is, and subject to all the criticisms in my text; how typical this position is can be inferred from the inclusion of the essay in the Modern Language Association's pamphlet *Aims and Methods*.

[4] Spiller, p. 48, "The ultimate and highest aim of the literary historian is therefore to help to explain the existence of masterworks." Note also his complete commitment (p. 43) to "such questions as, *How? When? Where? Why?*" These are all the questions of local circumstances of origin, irrelevant to literature by its definition.

tors intended them as such;[5] texts are interpreted by reference to biographical origin rather than general social function; and so on. In general terms, these concerns of literary history ignore the fact that determining the existence, value, and meaning of literary works is a matter of the whole culture rather than a local set of circumstances within it. But, even more important for our purposes in this chapter, we do not here have any framework for generalizing results; all we have is a chronological account that leads to local and particular statements of the background of each work, not to any general literary picture at all, though the illusion of it may seem to be given through a framework of general social history. In literary histories, great works of literature always appear unique and isolated; Goethe's *Faust* is too great to be spoken of in terms of an "explanation," looks like a black sheep in any social or literary movement, and any remarks on this work in literary histories look very ungeneralized and isolated indeed.

The contrast between generalizing and interpreting individual works has often been identified with "scholarship" as opposed to "criticism." While this opposition has usually referred, on the one hand, to the pursuits of literary history, and on the other, to those of interpretation, this particular pair of terms (scholarship and criticism) adds a new dimension to the opposition: for literary history now has assimilated to it the notions of reliability and careful weighing of evidence, while interpretation is

[5] It is doubtful whether such texts should ever be a part of the study of literature; if the definition given in chapter 2 is correct, they are indeed not literature at all. They may be of some use to the social historian—but that is another matter.

made by the contrast of the terms to seem more like the exercise of a talent, an individual act without a general framework. But this is another of the misconceived contrasts of critical theory: a given aspect of one pursuit is contrasted with a quite different aspect of another, and thereby this contrast—again really one of two stages of investigation—is illegitimately made into the contrast between two kinds of pursuit.[6] Literary history is no more scholarly than interpretation, nor less in need of imagination; in any inquiry, including literary criticism and interpretation, a familiarity with the concepts and methods of the field and its accumulated knowledge, built up by a succession of investigators, is unavoidable. Literary history and criticism are not to be differentiated by this kind of contrast.

So far, I have argued that the activity referred to as "history of literature" by its practitioners constitutes neither a general account of literature nor indeed an activity from which we can learn anything about literature. But is there any other sense of the term "history of literature" which could indicate a useful generalizing activity in literary criticism? The word "history" can function in a number of ways in designations of historical kinds of studies, as some paradigms will show.

In the most familiar sense, for example, in "the history of France," history concerns the sequence of events taking place in a particular geographical area, and historical study involves abstracting the most important outlines in these events. But this shows only one of many functions of the word "history" in phrases of the kind "the history

---

[6] On this occasion, Thorpe (*Aims and Methods*, p. viii) is correct: ". . . criticism is considered a form of scholarship."

of X." "The history of printing" concerns the evolution of a technique, its improvements, and technical discoveries. On the other hand, the "history of the Koh-i-Noor diamond" is not about changes or improvements in the thing about which the history is being written, nor does it study the sequence of events that constitute the subject of the history (as in the case of France), but rather what happened to that thing, itself changeless. A fourth possibility would be a history of clothing fashion. In this case we are not studying what happened to a changeless thing, nor the development of a technique, nor how a society evolved; we may be reduced to noting a simple sequence of one event following another without being able to use notions such as evolution or improvement at all. Change here may be arbitrary and difficult to abstract from.

It seems clear that the only idea common to all these usages is that of succession in time, and that otherwise the term "history" may involve many different kinds of study. Can any of these different notions sensibly be referred to literature? Take first the notion of the development of a technique (as in the history of printing). It is true that we can sometimes talk of the development of some aspects of the technique of writing—for example, the appearance of certain uses of the narrator in fiction. On the other hand, there are very distinct limits to this kind of thinking. In the development of a technique we think of one stage being an improvement on its predecessor, and so of the solution of a problem. But, for the most part, technical innovations in literature are new practices from among a range of possibilities that has always been and will continue to be available. One possibility does not supersede the other, and after an innovation by one author, another may return to a previously existing possibility. There is no necessary idea of sequence here; a particular author's individual innovation should probably be thought of as his characteristic expression, the reason for his achieving literary stature, not as his technical advance that will be used by all his successors. He has not solved a problem for all those who come after him. For this reason, it is preferable not to think of an author's technical innovation in historical terms. The cases that could be viewed primarily as technical progress are surely rare and of such insufficient scope that they would provide us with no reason to regard "history of literature" as a very important study if that were its only basis—certainly not as anything like *the* framework for the study of literature.

A history of literary study would be a possibility, and it would be analogous to the history of science; in both cases, the history of increasing understanding of phenomena is under investigation. But this would not be a history of literature. A curious fact emerges from this comparison: the history of science is not a prestigious area in the field of scientific inquiry—on the contrary, it occupies a very small space within studies in that field. Yet history of literature[7] occupies an extremely prominent position in the study of literature, even though its

[7] Colie's vague assertion that literary history depends on the assumption ". . . that the time when a thing was written has something to do with its nature" ("Literature and History," p. 9) is remarkably unhelpful. The crucial question remains untouched: is the work's chronology relevant to the interpretation of its meaning? "It is what it is because it was made when it was" is either trivially true of everything (and so has no special force here) or it is true in some special way with literature—but if so this is not explained by Colie.

rationale seems far less clear than is the case of historical study in the sciences.

If we take yet another of the paradigms set out above, that of history as the story of the fate of a particular thing, we should generate such questions as, How did Shakespeare's work fare over the years? But this is obviously not a general framework for literary study and is already recognized as a marginal pursuit.

Can we find a useful sense of "history of literature" in the analogy with the history of fashion? On the one hand, this might look promising in that it seems close to the use of "history" in the "history of taste," a phrase often used by literary historians. Yet the analogy is not a flattering one for literary history. If we think especially of changes of fashion in this century, a certain amount of fairly random sequence seems to be visible, in which the relation of one mode to the next, or to its social context, seems tenuous. The possibilities for abstraction and thus for historical study seem limited by the fact that much of this kind of change looks to be for the sake of change itself. We may have found a possible analogue for history of literature—but only at the cost of making it a trivial pursuit. Yet this example allows us to focus the problem more sharply: what is required is a sense of the term "literary history" which involves some kind of gain for literary study through the introduction of chronology; chronology in itself is of no necessary benefit to literary study until it has been justified.

The one possibility we have left is the use of history in the "history of France," where we are concerned with what happened in a particular place at a particular time and how it led to what happened next. But this model,

too, turns out not to be appropriate. The history of France
is an abstraction from a large sequence of events in France
over a long period of time. To be analogous to this usage,
history of literature would have to make abstractions from
a chronological sequence of literary events. As we have
noted, literary history usually focuses instead on historical
events in order to relate literary events to nonliterary
events.[8] But even if we tried to make literary history
fully analogous to the "history of France," that is, an
abstraction of dominant patterns of development in the
chronological sequence of literary events, we should still
find that the analogy would not hold in important respects. French society changes as one era dies and the
other is born, but Racine is still a fact of French culture
in the centuries succeeding that of his writing. If we take
the century of the origin of Racine's works as the locus
of Racine in order to show change, we ignore the critical
fact that literary texts continue to be literature, and that
they do not fade into the past. More texts are added as

[8] Cf. E. Vinaver, "The Historical Method in the Study of Literature," in *The Future of the Modern Humanities*, ed. J. C. Laidlaw (The Modern Humanities Research Association, Cambridge,
England, 1969), pp. 89–90: "there is a curious semantic anomaly
in the use of the term 'literary history.' When we talk about the
history of science, or of philosophy . . . the historical method consists in examining each of these things historically. . . . When it
comes to literature, however, the method is applied not to the
essentials of literature, but to its background, its antecedents
and its influence; it is focused not on what literature is, but on
what it has developed from or into. . . ." Part of Vinaver's statement is beside the point: historical treatment of anything is concerned with antecedents and influence. Yet he makes an important
observation here: much of literary history leads away from literature to nonliterary events, unlike history of science which relates different scientific events to each other.

years go by, but this is accumulation rather than development. Only by concentrating on the production of literature in terms of its context of origin can we make this kind of history; but if the making of literature is seen as the continuing social decision to respond to texts in certain ways, the production of literature has no relevant origin other than in that decision.

There seems, then, to be no sense of the term "literary history" which yields a study both intelligible and central to literary study. And if this is so, the question must arise: Why has literary history always been taken to be so central to the study of literature?

Two main temptations to gravitate towards historical treatment of literature can be diagnosed. The first of the two is the more trivial: to put literary texts side by side in any general way demands a form of organization and abstraction, and to string them together chronologically avoids the need for thought in such arrangement, for then chronology does it automatically. Inertia, then, would favor a chronological account of literature. The second reason is one that is more bound up with the nature of literature. The historical treatment is suggested, though not justified, by the sense that literary texts are the old and revered, the permanent texts of the culture, enduring through time. It is this sense of their being ancient wisdom, handed down through the ages, that brings in the notion of time and history. Both in Western and non-Western cultures, the "sacred" (not necessarily in an exclusively religious sense) texts are in an archaic language, conveying a sense of the permanence of a culture, and its continuity through the ages. Though this is the source of a sense that literature is "historic" it also shows, paradoxically enough, another reason why the historical approach to literature is a misconception: the historical approach to literature is predominantly concerned to rid us of this sense of pastness by recreating and placing us in the original present of the circumstances of the work's composition, so that we can understand it as a product of its age, as if we were a contemporary of its author. This procedure to be sure involves historical concerns, but in the sense relevant to literature it aims at annihilating our sense of literary texts as historic documents by making us treat them in present terms only—albeit a recreated present from a past time.[9] From that perspective, the text is not historic at all; the paradox is, then, that the defect of the commonly practiced historical approach is precisely that it does no justice to the historic quality of literary texts! It is antihistorical in the sense relevant to literature. Conversely, it is not an antihistorical view of literature to insist that we not pursue historical localization and explanation, but only a determination to preserve the sense of history in the experience of literary texts in the appropriate way.

To sum up at this point: there are recognizable temptations that have led to the use of literary history as a syn-

---

[9] Thus the arguments of Wellek and Warren (*Theory of Literature*, p. 31) against historicism are sound but not the most central, i.e., the arguments that (a) we cannot experience the work of literature in any other way than as the men of the twentieth century that we are, and (b) we should impoverish Hamlet if we restricted ourselves to the meaning it had for contemporary audiences. Shakespeare is indeed impoverished if only read in terms of his age; but even from our twentieth-century perspective we must preserve the sense of Shakespeare as part of the revered past of our culture, though that sense also includes an awareness of its continuing with ourselves as its current members.

thesis in literary studies, but no valid theoretical reasons that support it. Whether we look at theory or practice, literary history always entails seeking both cause and meaning of literary texts in their local circumstances of origin. Most other traditional syntheses suffer from the same logical error, usually because they have derived from literary history. Literary biography, for example, is logically a page from a literary history: its reductive and antiliterary assumptions are the same. I do not mean here that generalizations from the series of works of one author are not meaningful or useful, but only that in so far as they are worth grouping together for a synthetic treatment involving generalization, this will be a matter of their inherent nature, and of whether that nature lends itself to such treatment. The question of the comparability of different texts has nothing added to it by common authorship if texts by the same author are not inherently comparable in any fruitful way. (Authors do not always write about the same thematic issues.) The same reasoning applies to literary movements, that is, to grouping of texts according to relations between authors which are either assumed because of chronology, or because of explicit statements of a group of authors concerning their common views on literature. The result is such period labeling as "Romanticism," "Realism," and so on. Once more, a dilemma arises: either the texts suggest the grouping, in which case the historical facts are unnecessary, or only the historical facts (chronology or manifestoes or both) suggest the grouping, in which case it is pointless and distorting.

In practice, most "-ism" concepts result either from attempts to generalize from texts originating in the same era because it is felt that their origin in the same period guarantees their generalizability, or from literary manifestoes and catchwords popular at a particular time, which have been accepted as valid descriptions of the works concerned ever since. Many of these concepts are blatantly meaningless, as the long and rather unsuccessful history of attempts to define some of them would imply; "Realism"[10] is the most obvious example. If a term has to be found for a clear need, its meaning is determined by that need; but if a term is inherited, and a perennial debate ensues as to what it means, we must surely conclude that the whole situation is suspect, and that the generalizing term has resulted less from the series of texts than from the mistaken notion that they ought (for extraneous reasons) to be generalizable. Thus the mysterious quality of many of these terms comes from their origin in an attempt to create a general framework where none existed; their problematic nature is misinterpreted as an indication of their complexity and richness, a procedure all too common in literary theory.

Another drawback of most "period" generalizations lies in their tendency to reduce the possibilities of the human scene at a given time; there is more diversity in any

[10] See the analysis given of this term in chapter 1 of my *Narration in the German Novelle*. Here I argued that the term "Realism" indicated only the absence of any of the recognizable conventions of writing—so broad a framework as to be useless for a serious investigation. Manifesto words, such as "Romanticism" and "Realism," usually arose in historical situations because a writer or set of writers objected to a literary convention predominant among writers of their time. The "Realists" simply wanted no more of the "Romantic" conventions. But that does not mean that their work has anything in common other than not being Romantic.

group of human beings than they allow, and conversely more continuity in the range of human concerns from one age to the next. Changes from one age to another relate more to the nature of the problems set for human beings at that time than to their basic responses to problems; and so period concepts usually concern themselves with relatively superficial matters.

It is possible to state some simple propositions governing the use and usefulness of literary terms which function as general concepts:

1. If such concepts are valid descriptions and generalizations, they stand in no need of historical justification, and can stand on their own without reference to chronological contiguity of the works concerned.

2. The extra step of referring them to chronology introduces a historian's perspective (that is, What was happening in the society at a given time, in all areas of activity?),[11] and abandons that of a student of literature (that is, Is there a group of literary texts which can profitably be taken together?)

3. Manifesto terms are, in principle, dangerous since they have usually derived from texts that are forgotten (that is, not literature) rather than from the literary texts of the culture, and from reactions against what had prevailed hitherto rather than from adequate descriptions of the literary texts with which they are associated.

4. There is no reason why works originating from the same time should always be comparable, nor why works from widely different points of time should not be; the continuing similarity and variety of human nature is a far more important factor in generalizing about literary texts than any set of local historical circumstances.

[11] Such activities as literary history, the German "Geistesgeschichte," history of ideas, and so on, are therefore all simply history, though to be good history they would need to weigh literary evidence about a period carefully in the context of all the other available kinds of evidence.

Few, if any, of our currently used general concepts could stand scrutiny in the light of these principles; it would be wise to regard them all with considerable scepticism, and to start again.

The first studies to be both general and literary have been discussions of genre and literary conventions; but even here, there has been a strong tendency to lapse into a genetic and historical treatment by making the origin and development of the genre the focus of the study. By the same line of reasoning that I have developed above, it can be shown that such a treatment is not a generalizing one, nor is it central to literature. On the other hand, it would be profitable from both points of view to consider the possibilities of a genre, and so, for example, how the convention of the narrator can be handled differently for different kinds of purposes and meanings.[12] To be sure, different possibilities may have been pursued at different times in history; but in that case a history will only be interesting as a genre analysis if it turns out to have been an analysis of the structure of the genre, and once this is admitted, then it is best simply to start out to do just that.

A distinction must be made here between a mere classification of literary texts and a genre; the former is an abstraction, the latter a convention. The novel is a genre—that form of literature which has a distinct narrative voice, unlike poetry or drama. The convention of the narrative voice is invoked by any work within the genre; but the

---

[12] See, for example, such works as W. Booth, *The Rhetoric of Fiction* (Chicago, 1961); though, as I have argued elsewhere (*Narration in the German Novelle*), there are distinct weaknesses in this popular book.

classification "political novel" is an abstraction from those using this convention—not itself to be thought of as a convention. A genre form exists to be exploited; a classification exists after a number of works have made the abstraction feasible, but does not then become a usable convention, with all that that implies. Though different considerations apply to these two different cases, neither of them can finally be considered of the highest importance in the general study of literature. Let us turn first to genre. Beyond a certain limit, the study of how the possibilities of a generic form can be exploited will not encompass all that we feel important about literary texts. An analogous limitation can be seen in studies of ambiguity in poetic language;[13] they make us aware of the extra and special possibilities of expression that literature can exploit, and as such they resemble an exposition of literary grammar: we learn the forms and possible expressions, the basis of literary expression over and above that of ordinary language. And yet the character of the complex utterances that use this grammar is still to be examined; this kind of study may enable us to investigate more intelligently what literary texts have to say to us, but does not necessarily concern the central issue of the meaning of a complete text at all. Genre studies, therefore, do not *per se* involve generalization from one complete text to another, while that is what any important generalization of interpretative results would have to do.

There are different, but equally compelling, reasons to regard most classifications according to type (such as the "political novel") as no more satisfactory. The reasons

[13] Cf. W. Empson, *Seven Types of Ambiguity* (London, 1930).

are the same as those that occur in the kind of generalization attempted in discussions of motifs, of which "the child in literature" might be a typical example. It is always possible to pick up a word, an object, or a theme from everyday experience and make this into a general framework for the investigation of literary texts;[14] but this will always be an arbitrary and idle pursuit unless the framework is suggested by interpretations of complete texts and by the function of the individual elements within their various contexts—which is rarely the case.

The question still remains: What is an intelligent framework for the generalization of the results of literary interpretation, one that avoids the reductiveness and antigeneralizing tendencies of literary history, the randomness of motif and type investigations, and the equally serious limitations of genre discussion? To answer this question it will be necessary to return to the main thread of the argument of this book and to pass on to my next chapter.

In my discussion of evaluation, I have argued that the search for a necessary general feature of texts that guarantees their value is a mistake; no such feature exists, or is demanded by the logic of value. Instead, value categories are based on efficiency in a certain kind of performance. Investigation of what makes that performance

---

[14] This procedure is especially favored among German critics: see, for example, W. Kayser, *Das Groteske* (Oldenburg, 1957), or E. Staiger, *Grundbegriffe der Poetik* (Zürich, 1946). Both works take from ordinary language what are basically simple terms, and then make them artificially complex. Cf. this point further argued in Ellis and Mowatt, "Language, Metaphysics, and Staiger's Critical Categories."

possible, that is, investigation and analysis of valued literary texts, is an empirical pursuit in which many factors may be involved, not just one. It is in this proposition that we can find the necessary logical basis for the general investigation of literature and for the generalization of results of individual interpretations. An investigation of literary value, then, is an investigation aiming to find important general factors which relate to the ability of literary texts to function as literary texts. Such factors would be found by abstracting from adequate interpretative accounts of individual texts. Generalizing about literature is thus *the same thing* as investigating its value; the past uncertainties and conceptual confusions in these two aspects of theory are related to each other, in that if one theoretical problem had been solved, the solution of the other would automatically have followed. In investigating what makes literary texts valued and thus effective as literature we are looking for significant general patterns that members of the category display; and in making important generalizations about literary texts we must be making statements about how they function as literature. This leads to a further theoretical point: the investigation of the function of literature is the same thing as generalizing about literature. In one sense, the function of a literary text is to perform as a literary text; but the larger question of the function in human life of the category of literary texts is pursued when we analyze the empirical basis of the category and how what is found in it relates to human life in general. I conclude this chapter on the question of generalizing, therefore, by noting that my next chapter explores its more appropriate form: to ask for the most general statements about literature is to ask about its function in human life.[15]

[15] In this discussion, I have not touched on such terms as "Comparative Literature," "General Literature," and so on. In so far as these terms function as synonyms for the study of literature in general, they require no further comment; to the extent that "Comparative Literature" has had a narrower meaning, indicating a concern with international influences and sources, it was a more extensive literary history, which again needs no further comment. An interesting general framework would be the comparative study of the nature and function of literature in Western society as opposed to in a different kind of culture, e.g., China or a West African tribe. Literature may well serve different functions, and hence be something different, in different cultures.

8: The Function of Literature

THERE IS an ancient dispute as to what the function of literature is or should be;[1] the two sides have varied their terminology throughout the ages, but the opposition between them has remained essentially unchanged. On one side are those who have wished literature to have an immediate and identifiable purpose, on the other those who have argued that it should be an end in itself, for aesthetic delight. The second position varies little, for it simply clings to the idea that art is for art's sake. The first is inherently able to vary somewhat more, in that the purpose envisaged has been variously conceived. At times it has been simple moral instruction, at other times it has been the maintenance of the psyche in a healthy state. Evidently, the latter concept can also undergo much variation. Three different versions of it, for example, are those of Schiller, Richards, and Crews.[2] Schiller speaks of the

[1] Cf. the general account of this debate in the chapter "The Function of Literature," in Wellek and Warren, *Theory of Literature*.

[2] Cf. Schiller's celebrated essay *On the Aesthetic Education of Man. In a Series of Letters.* Ed. and trans. Elizabeth M. Wilkinson and Leonard A. Willoughby, (English and German facing). (Ox-

harmonizing of the psyche in eighteenth-century terms,
Richards, less interestingly, in terms of a rather elementary behaviorism, and Crews, in psychoanalytic terms;
but seen against the background of the centuries-old debate, the basic similarity of these positions will be more
obvious than their dissimilarities. Over the years, the two
sides have abused each other frequently and at length;
the dispute constantly breaks out again in new terms, but
with no basic change of structure. Crews's vehement attack on Frye on the grounds that Frye insists that literature must be taken on its own terms[3] instead of in the
context of its origin in life is a case in point; it is surely
necessary to see this dispute between the two not as
Crews sees it (as a justified attack on a currently influential book), but in much less local terms. The argument is
recognizably a variant of the age-old dispute as to whether
the experience of literature is merely pleasurable or
whether it has any useful function for us.

An important element of the situation, which must be
noted before we turn to theoretical analysis, is the central
role of literature in education; much time is devoted to the
study of literature and many voices are to be heard which
argue that the study of literature is the most important
kind of education.[4] It would certainly seem from this

----

ford, 1967); I. A. Richards, *Principles of Literary Criticism* (London, 1925); and Crews, "Anesthetic Criticism," II, e.g., "art uses
symbolic manipulations to reconcile competing pressures."

[3] N. Frye, *Anatomy of Criticism*, (Princeton, 1957); Crews's attack is in "Anaesthetic Criticism," I.

[4] Notably F. R. Leavis; Leavis's influence in Britain is obviously
a large factor in the rather moralistic strain in evidence in, for
example, the British contributions to the collection of essays, *The
Critical Moment. Literary Criticism in the 1960's* (London, 1964),
in which leading critical figures were invited to state briefly their

evidence that our society acts as if literature had some useful function.

In the verbal violence committed over the years by each side of the dispute on the other, the concept "aesthetic" has been central.[5] It has been used with both strong positive and negative force, as can be seen in the tone of its variants: aesthetic, aestheticism, aesthete.[6] Thus we hear it said that those who treat literature as having practical value have no aesthetic sense, while the counter-charge is that those who refuse to relate literature to life are "mere"[7] aesthetes. It is evident that any discussion of the function of literature must be much concerned with an analysis of this notion.

Another important general factor to be noticed before we begin our analysis is the way in which this old debate

---

critical position. Cf. such titles as "Are Purely Literary Values Enough?" and "Why I Value Literature" by W. W. Robson and R. Hoggart respectively.

[5] Cf. e.g., Casey's use of the word as a term in the usual opposition: "It has never been clear whether Arnold was a moralist or an aesthete" (*The Language of Criticism*, p. 179), and his continuing acceptance of the possible opposition of terms "aesthetically good but morally bad" (p. 193).

[6] Hermand provides an example of this negative usage: "Denn schliesslich interessiert uns an der Kunst wesentlich mehr als bloss ihre Form,—eigentlich alles, falls man nicht bereits zu 'ästhetisch' verbildet ist" (*Synthetisches Interpretieren*, p. 167). The concept has scarcely been more subtly employed than by Schiller, in his *On the Aesthetic Education of Man*; and it is therefore all the more surprising to see the popularity in the German-speaking world of a work such as Hermand's which abounds in such unsubtle use of the concept as that displayed here. For a lucid discussion of Schiller's usage, cf. the introduction to the bilingual (original text with facing English translation) edition of his essay by E. M. Wilkinson and L. A. Willoughby.

[7] Hermand uses the German "bloss" (mere, merely) very liberally throughout his argument, for example.

has involved the other areas of literary theory which we have already discussed. A theory of form and content tends to be built into it, for example, with the "aesthetes" concerned with form, their opponents with content. Likewise, a theory of critical procedure, too, becomes involved: not to be concerned with the historical and personal circumstances of the production of the work, the argument goes, is to be an aesthete who divorces literature from life, and prefers the external perfection of a literary work to its substance. I have already discussed these opposed positions which tend to be associated with the dispute centering on the word "aesthetic," and have typically found the oppositions between them misconceived. And here, too, I shall once again try to show that the traditional dispute as to the function of literature depends on opposing two positions that do not and cannot validly contrast with each other, once their logic is examined.

I turn now to the logic of the question as to the function or functions of literature. A simple example of an artifact and its function will serve as a point of departure. A doorknocker, by the use to which we put it just as much as by its structure and position, can be seen to have a clearly statable function. But now contrast with this the question as to the function of the bill of a toucan, with its exotic shape and color. Whether we look at its structure, or at its obvious uses, it will prove to be not only more difficult to state the function of the toucan's bill, but in many ways an entirely different kind of undertaking from that involved in stating the function of a doorknocker; and this difference is an important one for an understanding of the issues raised when we speak of the function of literature.

The doorknocker has one purpose, and it is apparent to the consciousness of its user. The toucan's bill, on the other hand, may have many separate functions: it may be that feeding, mating, and self-protection are all facilitated by it, the first and last most obviously so through size and structure, while color and visibility assist in sexual display. I do not say that all these factors are involved, or that others are not—only that many different areas of biological advantage may need to be considered. These functions need not be apparent in any immediate way, but only as the result of careful analysis and investigation; a simple notion of "purpose" would seem inadequate here. Another important distinction lies in the indirectness with which the bill may serve its function. The doorknocker's purpose is immediately and directly served when one uses it in the obvious way. But that need not be the case with the toucan's bill; its attractiveness may have indirect advantages for the species. A particular set of mating circumstances might have considerable advantage to the species, for example, and the bill, by facilitating those circumstances, would function indirectly, but still importantly, in a useful way.

The two cases I have considered are sufficiently different for them to be distinguished in terminology; I shall speak of the *purpose* of the doorknocker, but of the *function* of the toucan's bill, it being understood that a statement of that function need not be limited to a single factor. The question now arises: How do these paradigms relate to the case of literature? A good deal of the traditional argument was carried on in terms of the first: literature should serve an identifiable purpose, be composed with that in mind, and so function in an immediate and

direct way of which we are quite conscious. But it is easy
to see that the second paradigm is the appropriate one for
literature, not the first; literary works are not artifacts
made and designed for a specific purpose.

Nature does not generally leave advantageous behavior
to chance, nor even to intelligent decisions that follow
clear purposes; instead, it makes many kinds of advantageous behavior pleasurable. From this consideration
emerges the proper relation of "aesthetics" and function.
We rarely ask ourselves whether we need food, but instead experience hunger. Sexual behavior, too, does not
usually begin with a conscious decision to procreate. Our
most characteristic pleasures are dominated by the survival needs of the species. Such things are too important
to be left to rational choice (an unreliable factor), and we
are thus also impelled toward them by our experiencing
pleasure in them.

The experience of literature or of other works of art is
a powerful one which seems to contain its own justification, but that does not mean that it does not have important functions. No one in the state referred to as "in
love" thinks of the function of this state in terms of the
usefulness of a specific pair-bond in the human pattern of
child-rearing; it is for him a powerful and immediate experience which justifies itself. In both these cases, then, a
sense of powerful and immediate fascination is produced
and no clear and sensible purpose is directly visible for
the experience. Another analogous case would be children
at play.[8] Children are attracted to and happy in play, an

---

[8] Schiller was evidently much impressed with this analogy in
calling the aesthetic impulse the "play" impulse ("Spieltrieb").
But he might just as well have called it the "love" impulse; what

experience that seems for them an end in itself. As they mature, the situation changes. While their experience seems to justify itself, its biological function would appear to include the gradual exercising of the child's capacities before it becomes mature and must exercise them in "real" situations: its strength and judgment are developed in safe ways. The same phenomenon is known in species other than human. To children, play is a value in itself; to the biological analyst, it is functional.

We can, then, validly contrast behavior having a clear purpose with behavior that is experienced as an end in itself, but when we are discussing the function of behavior, nothing is an end in itself. Paradoxically, it appears that directly purposeful behavior is functionally more superficial, and that very basic functions are served by what is felt as "purposeless" behavior. And this makes sense: important functions are reinforced by enjoyment of the behavior fulfilling those functions, less important functions are not. From this point of view, literature would seem to be functionally important. Yet another general consideration would lead to that conclusion. In the study of biological structure and behavior, a significant guide to functional importance is simply the amount of energy devoted to a given structure or piece of behavior by a species. If the toucan's enormous bill did not

---

was needed was a term to generalize all those experiences in which we perform functionally vital actions impelled by a strong and immediate fascination rather than guided by rational control. These are all superficially purposeless actions that seem to justify themselves through the intensity of our experience, and play is only one of them, without that degree of significance within the group which alone could justify its name becoming that of the entire group.

serve a useful function, it could not survive competition with more efficient species. The human species devotes much energy to art in general, and literature in particular. In any statement as to the function of a piece of behavior, the energy involved and the importance of the functional advantage derived must stand in some reasonable relationship if that statement is to be taken seriously.

Let us now consider the traditional dispute in the light of my argument so far. The central contrast of this dispute—that between art existing for its own sake on the one hand, and having some useful relation to life on the other, is evidently misconceived: there is no necessary opposition or contrast between these views, which simply relate to different levels of analysis. One need not supplant the other, so that there is no need to choose between them. But the attempt to choose between the two inevitably distorted both. In maintaining that art should not have an overt, direct purpose, "aesthetes" have failed to think about the function of literature in our lives; it is indeed correct to reject any overt purpose for literature, but an error to think that, because of this, literature has no important social function. Meanwhile, the anti-aesthete is right to insist on a social function for literature but quite wrong to deny that the experience of literature is for the reader its own immediate justification; and this error leads him into the even greater error of conceiving the function of literature in terms of overt purpose. This, in turn, leads us to the original biographical and historical circumstances of its maker (because he, like the doorknocker maker, must have had that purpose in mind), and so to an unliterary attitude to the context of literature, and the fallacy of reduction to origins. In this way the function of literature becomes a local and trivial matter.

At this point, it will be seen, two different parts of my argument converge: the error of "art with a purpose" turns out to be the same as the error of historical and biographical criticism. But other parts of my analysis are relevant here, too. The results of my analysis of the definition of literature included the finding that literature is what functions as literature, not what is made as or intended as literature; that is, it is unlike doorknockers. And in my discussion of evaluation, specific single criterion theories of value were shown to be erroneous, and the causes of literary value to be many and various; the related conclusion of this chapter, though developed in a different argument, has been that literature has no one overt purpose, but instead a number of possible functions. I concluded also from my discussion of evaluation that performance as a literary work is literary value; in an analogous way, my conclusion here is that aesthetic response is primary and that a search for the functions of literature is an *analysis* of that response—not something separate from it, or to be opposed to it, as is the case in the traditional argument. One last area of the argument of previous chapters provides confirmation, and also clarification, of my analysis of the notion of "aesthetic" response. The conclusion that there is no need to distinguish what is said from how it is said also strikes at any distinction between the "aesthete's" retreat from the world to a concern with form, as distinct from the artist *engagé* being concerned with content and the problems of the real world.[9] It seems likely, in fact, that the second distinction creates the first; once two different modes of responding to literary texts are postulated, and a dispute is started as to which is correct, the next stage would seem to be to postulate two different objects (form and content) for the two kinds of response to relate to.

An "aesthetic" response must surely be conceived of as our immediate expression of all that makes an impact on us, consciously and unconsciously, in a piece of literature, including its elements traditionally thought of as content. A difficulty that is often raised for such a view lies in the typical assertion that we can appreciate a piece of literature aesthetically, yet dislike its content or philosophy. And this can seem like saying that we respond positively to the form, negatively to the content. But this analysis is dubious; the "negative" response to content is usually superficial. For example, we might say that we respond negatively to Mozart's *Don Giovanni* as regards

[9] I choose Hermand (pp. 168–169) once again, to exemplify a very open statement embodying this error: "Suchen wir daher ihr Faszinans nicht an falscher Stelle: in der formalen Stimmigkeit, der äusseren Perfektion, sondern in der inneren Fülle ihrer inhaltlichen Bezüge und Evokationen. . . . Und doch sind es letztlich Werke wie der *Wilhelm Meister*, der *Grüne Heinrich*, die *Buddenbrooks* oder der *Mann ohne Eigenschaften*, die uns auf viel mehr Ebenen ansprechen als das perfekteste Gedicht. . . ." The view of poetry expressed here may seem a caricature, but it is unfortunately fairly close to the kind of commonly stated opinion found, for example, in the writing of the eminent critic E. Staiger, e.g., p. 131 of his "Time and the Poetic Imagination," in *The Critical Moment. Literary Criticism in the 1960's*: "*Wandrers Nachtlied* is beautiful only because it is a harmonious whole." Staiger sees the value of literature as a matter of "unity in complexity." It should be noted that Hermand does not reject this silly notion of the value of poetry—he accepts it and therefore rejects poems.

its moral "content" (in that only Don Giovanni himself is musically exciting, and those who are morally superior are musically less sparkling) while aesthetically we respond positively. Yet the aesthetic response surely does take all factors in, and contains a significant amount of fascination with the Don's freedom from the inhibitions that we need for a cohesive society, but which are not without their personal cost to all its members.

Richards was surely right to say that literature had much importance for the psyche—the energy that goes in the direction of literature is evidence enough. But he was mistaken to think that he needed therefore to denounce "the phantom aesthetic state";[10] all that we need to do to reconcile the two positions is to think of the aesthetic response as the end product, in our immediate conscious awareness, of all that impresses our minds, consciously or unconsciously, in works of literature.

If we look at the old formula that defines the function of literature as "instruire et plaire," then the history of the subsequent argument can be described as an attempt to choose between two factors instead of seeking their correct relation, which would naturally have involved making the description of each side a good deal more complex.

At last, we are in a position to approach the question, What are the functions of literature? But that is where the concerns of this book stop. A logical analysis seeks to understand the nature of the question and to disentangle its logical structure, but the pursuit of the now clarified (and, be it noted, plural) question is an empirical matter. It is a question of research into the structure of society and into the relation of that social structure to the struc-

[10] Richards, *Principles of Literary Criticism*, pp. 11ff.

ture of literary texts, in which the usual empirical methods of investigation and relevant abstraction must be used; purely conceptual analysis can go no further. I shall nevertheless conclude this discussion of the function of literature by offering some observations based on my own experience of analyzing and teaching literature as an example of what seem to me to be some profitable empirical beginnings.

Human beings live in an unusual social situation. Man lives in social units composed of large numbers of his fellows, and yet remains an ingenious, opportunistic, aggressive individual, quite unlike the typical herd animal in nature. His behavior is in many ways like that of more solitary territorial animals, who do not get on well with their fellows. And yet, he must live in a large, precarious, and unstable social unit. There are one or two ways in which literature may well help to preserve the equilibrium of this unstable situation. For example, there is no scope for the exercise of all man's capacities in his typical social situation; it would be very dangerous for all of us to live the life of daily danger and seizure of opportunity that we are genetically fitted for. On the other hand, to have our capacities too much out of step with our actual lives is dangerous too. Perhaps, then, one of the outstanding functions of literature is to deal with this situation; it can offer us dramatic and violent experiences without the actual drama and violence that would threaten the stability of our society, and in more general terms can increase the content of our experience to compensate for the reduction it must suffer if we are to live together in such potentially dangerous social groups.

Another function of literature appears to be to assist

in creating a sense of the cohesion of a social unit the extent of which is invisible to the individual. We commonly speak of national identity involving prominently the literature of a country; the permanence and immutability of the social unit is suggested, again by the sense of the revered past conveyed in the archaic language of literary texts. Here, then, is a factor that tends to hold an unwieldy social unit together.

Among "primitive" peoples, the stories told in the community commonly have an obvious educative function; they impress on children in a forceful and yet palatable way the values of the tribe, its social system, and the chief dangers of its environment. Things are not quite so clear in this respect in Western societies. It is certainly evident that literature is considered a very important part of education; but it is probable that we should conceive of this in a broader way than merely as the transmission of the values of the society. A more important function of literature in education is likely to lie in the development of the important power of the imagination.[11] It is to be expected that literature in Western societies will have a somewhat different set of functions from those prevailing elsewhere; it may well be, as time goes by, that the functions served by literature in Western society will become less those predominant in earlier stages of civilization, and more concerned with how man can deal with increas-

[11] L. C. Knights, in his "In Search of Fundamental Values," in *The Critical Moment. Literary Criticism in the 1960's,* p. 80, says that "It is, then, simply in the growth and strengthening of the imagination that the value of literature resides." But his word "simply" gets the point out of focus; there is no one function of literature, and one need not think of the development of the imagination as a candidate for that unique position.

ing amounts of leisure time in such a way that he exercises his remarkable capacities without danger to himself and his fellows.

What, finally, are we to make of the common demand, most commonly made by Marxists, that literature serve an ideological purpose? In so far as this is part of the dispute in which the socially committed are on one side, and the formalists and aesthetes on the other, I have already dealt with it as a misconceived opposition: a mode of apprehension is not sensibly to be contrasted with what is apprehended.[12] What should really be contrasted here is a kind of social relevance that goes to an immediately felt, particular social problem, as opposed to social relevance of a much broader kind. If an immediate particular social need is pressing enough, one may indeed try to enlist the aid of everyone and everything in sight. If one is convinced that society needs rapid and fundamental reshaping (as, say, Marxists do) there is nothing inconsistent in demanding that literature help to promote this; in a rainstorm one might shelter under a parasol, and at Dunkirk pleasure boats were used to rescue sol-

---

[12] There is therefore no justification for C. L. Wrenn's statement that Western admiration for Pasternak's *Dr. Zhivago* was based on "non-literary causes," because the book lacked structure. (*The Idea of Comparative Literature*, Cambridge, England, 1968, pp. 9–11). Here we have a good example of the destructiveness of the crude opposition of local social relevance (exposure of Soviet Russia) on the one hand, and formal perfection of structure on the other. Either way, the impact of this impressive book is sadly reduced by such attitudes, and the critic only hinders the reader of the work. In a literal sense, nothing "lacks structure"; what must be at issue here for Wrenn is a certain kind of symmetry that he approves, but which cannot be justified as a criterion with which to judge works of literature.

diers. But nothing is derived from such incidents about the normal function of parasols, pleasure boats, or literature. When the immediate local needs are past, literature will still continue to function socially as before in a variety of ways, some of which are probably known already and others still to be discovered.

9: Literary Study Among Other Disciplines

THE BROAD question of the relation of literary study to other kinds of study breaks down into a number of more precise questions: What are the closest relatives of literary study? Are there any disciplines from which literary study must learn in order to progress and achieve all that it can achieve? Is the study of literature a branch of another discipline, or are its results a contribution to any other kind of study? Serious analysis of these questions is generally hampered by the laissez-faire attitudes that I have discussed earlier; if an approach to literature from the standpoint of any other discipline is just another approach to literature, no further thought seems necessary.[1]

[1] Something of the kind is explicit in Thorpe's introduction to *Relations of Literary Study*, p. xi: "We call the essays which make up this book by the name of 'relations' of literary study in order to suggest that they represent members of a family. . . . It would be a mistake to insist on the exact kinship even of those seven members who have been invited to make an appearance here." The notion of "family" here is essentially antitheoretical, suggesting the indivisibility and unanalyzability of blood-ties, and a warm, cozy atmosphere which we can find comfortable, but should not try to understand.

Much of the analysis presented in earlier chapters relates to the questions that I now raise, and to answer some of them I need only to refer briefly to matters already argued. Contrary to the popularly held view, for example, it will already have become clear that history is not an important relative of literary study; the same is true of biography. These two kinds of study dwell far too much on a set of particular circumstances, and too little on the general character of human behavior, to be able to contribute much to the study of literature. The disciplines that would appear to be most useful to literary study must be those that will assist us in analyzing both literary texts and their function in human life and society. Linguistics, as the study of an especially relevant branch of human behavior, and of the material of literary texts, will naturally be an important related discipline; and in order to pursue the question of the function of literature we can hardly do without that group of related disciplines that deal with human behavior and social organization, such as biology, psychology, and social anthropology. The relations within this group of disciplines are evidently uncertain, and may be more a question of the historical origin of the three than of any genuine theoretical differences between them in terms of the nature of their study. The student of literature can only wait for developments in the fields to see how perceptions of the relations between them change, for those perceptions are quite clearly in the process of change. Meantime, I shall refer to the whole group as human biology, in a broad sense, and shall now turn to the relation of that group of disciplines to the study of literature.

There are two distinguishable ways in which human

biology is relevant to literary study. First, it may contribute to the question of the function of literature in human social groups, and second, it may contribute to the analysis of how the individuals depicted in literature function and relate to each other. The general shape of the first of these considerations will have become apparent in the preceding chapter; only as more understanding develops of the peculiar nature of man as a species, and of the social organization that is at once the expression of this nature and a means of accommodating it, will it be possible to say more about the place in this whole complex of the behavior relating to literary texts. No doubt this area of study will be much affected by knowledge of a series of different kinds of social organizations and their different literatures. When we compare the differences in the literatures of a Western European country and a West African tribe, and relate those differences to their different social organizations, we shall have made significant progress in understanding the functions of literature. And this will be a more fundamental exercise in "comparative literature" than is ever involved in relating the literatures of two Western European countries. In biological terms, this common exercise might be thought of as one of comparing two sub-species of the common crow as a means of generalizing about and understanding birds.

The second area of relevance to literature offered by human biology is of more direct use in the interpretation of texts: as biologists analyze and discover more of the fundamental patterns of human behavior, we shall be able to understand the behavior of literary characters in new and more adequate ways. Take, for example, the case of the modern playwright Harold Pinter. Pinter's characters seem on the surface to indulge in much pointless speech, and it is difficult to see any coherent design in the overall direction of their remarks. But if we borrow some notions from human biologists, it is possible to make a good deal of sense out of these superficially pointless verbal exchanges. They then appear to be perfectly coherently patterned as verbal gestures which attempt to dominate or to express acceptance of domination; which attempt to defend the particular character's concept of his self, or to browbeat the other into surrendering his; which attempt to enlarge the particular character's psychological territory, or to concede it to another. In this case, the notions of aggression and territoriality developed in human biology[2] provide hypotheses that can make sense of an enigmatic text.[3] But if we accept such concepts and use them, on the grounds that they provide us with the tools to make what seems to be a series of justifiable abstractions from the literary text, we commit ourselves to keeping an eye on just how these concepts fare in their own special fields, and how knowledge in those areas progresses; otherwise, we shall be left cling-

[2] See, for example, the popularizations of these scientific concepts in such works as Desmond Morris, *The Naked Ape* (London, 1967), and *The Human Zoo* (New York, 1969); and Konrad Lorenz, *On Agression* (New York, 1966).

[3] I give here only as much comment on the interpretation of Pinter as is necessary to make the general point relating interpretation of literary characters to analyses of human behavior that derive from general biology. For a more detailed analysis of Pinter (and the source of the example that I use here) see Quigley, *The Dynamics of Dialogue in The Plays of Harold Pinter*.

ing to a set of concepts that are part of the history of science, and no longer part of the best analysis available of the field concerned.

From this point of view, it is unfortunate that Freudian psychology[4] has been the only area of human biology that has been imported into literary criticism in any extensive way, and that has provided abstract concepts dealing with human motivation very differently from our everyday way of speaking of such motivation. For literary Freudians have indeed clung to concepts that are part of the history of science with great tenacity, and have viewed the originator of those concepts more as a religious leader[5] than as a man who made some interesting beginnings on the task of thinking about human motiva-

---

[4] Freudians are, in practice, nearly always concerned with the mind of the author, and so are also guilty of taking literature in the wrong context. Cf. the example cited above, chapter 5, n. 20.

[5] Crews's "Literature and Psychology" provides us with a fine example of the religious character of Freudianism. He ostensibly writes on psychology and literature but quickly narrows the field to Freudianism; his framework is a discussion of the persecution of Freudians, and of common attacks on the Freudian position. His bitterest remarks are reserved not for the unbelievers, but for the heretic, Jung. There is condemnation of the intolerance of the unbelievers, but no inconsistency is seen between this noble plea for tolerance and his own righteous attacks on the faithless— a standard religious paradox. The faithless are not just intellectually mistaken people, they are morally corrupt, the defenders of vested interest against the true morality, the scribes (scholars) and pharisaic high priests of old orthodoxy; one reason why they will not accept the faith is that it tells of their sinfulness. The full martyr complex emerges in Crews's claim that controversiality guarantees that Freud was on to something; he cannot have been all wrong if he can provoke the "defenders of literary tradition into outbursts" (p. 75). I must make it clear in this context that I am using the term "Freudianism" not to refer to Freud's thought but instead to the group of critics who now base themselves on Freud.

tion. And so, Freud's writings have been viewed as sacred texts, and his concepts made rigid and immutable. It should be possible to question or suggest modifications to those concepts in any normal field of inquiry, and such an activity would usually be accepted as the normal search for progress by which the sciences advance knowledge.[6] But that kind of activity is taken by Freudians to be an attack on Freudianism, and a failure to accept the faith; and the same kind of loss of scientific perspective is displayed in the common claims that to reject Freudianism is to reject talk of unconscious motivation. Crews even goes so far as to say that "the postulates of Freudian psychoanalysis . . . alone have weighed the motivational effects of man's emergence as a species. . . ."[7] To judge from these impossible claims to exclusive possession of certain areas of motivational research, literary Freudians choose to live in the past and to avoid all that has been going on in human biology, so that the divine status of

[6] A major revision of Freud, for example, is suggested by the fact that inhibition and displacement are now known to be common in the animal world, and not exclusively human; it is, therefore, not possible simply to say that man's neurosis (self-disgust, etc.) comes from the interference with "animal" function. Freud evidently regarded animals with a kind of Rousseauism. A scientist's reaction to this kind of development in knowledge will be one of curiosity and interest; it is safe to say that a literary Freudian's response will be defensive and hostile. A further example of the failure of Freudianism to progress beyond the historical situation in which Freud wrote emerges from the assumption that to reject Freud is to ignore any sexual content of literature—true then, but surely not now, when it is evidently the adequacy of the Freudian account of this issue that is involved.

[7] Crews, "Anaesthetic Criticism," II. To be sure, Crews's setting of literature in the context of human biology here is most welcome; it is only a pity that the Freudian version given has not benefited from modern biological research.

their leader and the literal truth of his texts can be preserved with their fundamentalist zeal. None of this should take anything away from Freud himself as an extremely interesting stage of thought about human motivation. One need not believe in the immutability of Darwin's concepts to consider Darwin a great figure in the history of biology, and to suggest that some of them need to be modified is to look for progress, not to reject Darwin; and anyone who now used the original Darwinian system would look oddly rigid and old-fashioned. Literary Freudianism thus represents the fossilization of a stage in the history of biological research which gets more and more remote from current research as its adherents attempt to preserve the faith.

The relationship of linguistics to literary criticism is in many ways a special case; the claim is often made that the study of literature is a part of the discipline of linguistics, and, irrespective of the merits of this claim, it is certainly true that the largest new element in the sphere of literary theory in the last twenty years has been the considerable concern with linguistics applied to literary criticism.[8] My earlier chapters have already touched on several issues in this relationship, but I shall now bring together these scattered threads to round out the general picture.

A major motive for the interest in linguistics applied to criticism has been a general desire to set criticism on a more secure, "scientific" basis. To search for a more firmly based, precise, and reliable criticism is certainly reason-

[8] The Modern Language Association's *Relations of Literary Study* ignores the relation of linguistics to literature, yet another indication of the pamphlet's inadequacy.

able, though this does not necessarily in itself take us in
the direction of linguistics. Unfortunately, the only notion of "scientificness" that could seem to lead of necessity toward linguistics is that popular misconception
about science that we have discussed above, one that involves a narrowly deductive procedure and the accumulation of isolated definite facts, and that does not allow
for hypothesis or imagination. The result has been that
little has been achieved in the attempts to investigate
literature through the methods of linguistics; indeed,
these attempts have in the main served only to exagger-
ate the defects of the already poor model of critical procedure prevalent in criticism. The gap between facts and
judgments, which has always seemed a problem in criticism, has now been made so great that linguistics is identified with the former and criticism with the latter, a division of function that has rendered both sides helpless.
In practice, linguistic approaches to literature, dominated
as they are by this procedural misconception, have been
a positive menace to criticism, and have done a good deal
to earn the contempt with which critics commonly regard
them.

But the disastrous situation that now exists tells us
nothing about what the relation between linguistics and
literature is in theory and should be in fact. Neither does
the common syllogistic argument: Literary texts are language, therefore their study is linguistic. For this argument rests on the misuse of the verb "to be" which I have
commented on earlier; by means of it one can prove almost anything: for example, literary texts are historical
documents, therefore the study of literature must be historical; or literature is human behavior, therefore its study

is psychological. But in this case, the proposition "literary texts are language" can be reformulated to bring out an important fact that does not owe its existence to logical sleight-of-hand: the material from which literary texts are made is language, and they are always exploitations of the conceptual possibilities of a given language. From this it ought certainly to follow that our understanding of how language works in general, and of the particular language of the texts, must bear some important relation to our ability to analyze literary texts.

This proposition may sound all very well in principle, but is it of great importance in practice? The question is important because it has not been uncommon to treat in far too pretentious a way linguistic analyses of a very ordinary kind. We can all identify nouns, verbs, and so on; it does not take linguistics to do that, but only the ordinary knowledge of English grammar that we are all taught at an early age. This is no longer true, however, when the best available analysis of a language reaches well beyond that which is popularly known and accepted, and when central perceptions about a literary text cannot be made except in terms of improved analysis. For example, the important pattern of deictics in Yeats's "Leda and the Swan" can scarcely be described except in terms of an account of English that is a considerable improvement over anything available to the critic ignorant of modern linguistic research; and from M. A. K. Halliday's analysis of the poem, it emerges that this aspect is of great importance.[9] When one comes to patterns of sound in poems, the point is even more obvious. To talk

[9] Halliday, "Descriptive Linguistics in Literary Studies," in *Linguistics and Literary Style*, ed. Freeman.

in terms of the repetitions of letters, or of the "same kind" of sound, is evidently much less useful than a competent phonological analysis, with relevant abstractions being made in terms of phonemes and formants.

It is probably best to regard meter in a similar way, that is, as an extension and exploitation of the properties of a given language. In Latin, meter is a schematic device that emerges from the clear contrast in that language of linguistically long and short syllables. The classical meters systematize the patterns of long and short syllables, so that certain short sequences of them (called "feet") become standard, and then certain sequences of such "feet" become standard kinds of lines. In contrast, the Germanic languages do not permit the clear contrast of linguistically long and short syllables; meter in the Germanic languages is a systematization based on the possibilities of stress and intonation in that language group. This means that meter in English has nothing to do with meter in classical languages; the two cases involve extensions of quite different features of two quite different languages. To use the terminology of classical meters is therefore fraught with danger when we discuss English verse, and much nonsense has been talked of "iambic pentameters," "feet," and so on, in this sphere. The methodological error here is unquestionably one of inadequate linguistic understanding; it results from the failure to see that "meter" is not one thing that can appear in many languages, but something that has its origin in the systematic extension of the possibilities of a given language. Understanding the metric system of a given language must therefore involve the best understanding possible of the relevant feature of that language, and of how the basic feature itself is then extended and systematized for metric purposes.

There seem to be adequate grounds, therefore, for saying that anyone who wishes to analyze the literary texts of a given language would be well advised to be conversant with the best available analysis of that language; and that, in effect, means that he must command the methods and language of modern linguistic research.

So much for the analysis of the particular language of the given text; but still to be considered is a much broader aspect of linguistics, which is of even more importance for the study of literature, namely, the general theory of language and of how language functions. Most critics of literature, like other people, operate with the common-sense theory of language, the reference theory. Not surprisingly, the limits of their ability to deal with literary texts are often the limits of the reference theory. This has been particularly noticeable, for example, in criticism of certain kinds of modern drama.[10] In the work of such writers as Beckett, Pinter, or Ionesco, dramatic characters do not seem primarily to "refer to" things, talk to each other about things, communicate facts about things to each other, or to do anything else that the reference theory of meaning can explain. The result is a crisis of critical inability to talk about the function of language in these plays. We commonly hear it said that in such plays the emphasis is on language for its own sake; or that language breaks down; or that what is important here is unspoken, and "behind" the language; or that the point lies not in the content of the language but in its use. All

[10] See, once again, Quigley, *The Dynamics of Dialogue in the Plays of Harold Pinter.*

of these formulations are attributable quite simply to the floundering that occurs when the critic reaches the limits of what his implicit theory of language can deal with. A distinction is being sought but not found; it is that between a referential function of language and other functions. Because language is only conceived of in terms of one function, the second term in a distinction between two or more different functions of language is missing, and it is then substituted for with various unlikely and meaningless notions, for example, language for its own sake, what is behind the language, the break-down of language. All are in reality clumsy and unfulfilled attempts to say that what is happening is not primarily referential but something else. But this kind of drama is not impossible to describe and analyze if we work with a theory of meaning that is not limited to a view of language as communication and reference but includes, for example, the notion that language also functions importantly to control our world by organizing it in relation to our needs.

In the course of the fifth and sixth chapters of this book, a variety of other examples emerged of critical errors which were the consequence of inadequate notions about language and meaning. Biographical and intentional criticism, for example, was shown to be importantly related to the split made by the reference theory of meaning between denotation and connotation; a misconception concerning the distinctive use of language characteristic of one individual also led to intentionalism, and the study of variant readings evidently resulted in part from a lack of awareness that meaning was always a question of contrasting possibilities. I showed also how an uncertainty about how to handle the degree of openness or specificity of a piece of language led to the common critical practice of attempting to make the text more specific than it really is. The concept of style, likewise, is a relic of a poor theory of language. All of these hindrances to better criticism could be removed if critics were simply more proficient in talking about how language functions, and had a better conceptual apparatus available to them for handling pieces of language.

There is little doubt, then, that critics are severely hampered by an inadequate understanding of how language works. And yet it is a sad fact that knowledge of the most thriving branch of modern linguistic research would not have improved their position. The most important weakness of the position of Chomsky and his followers has surely been their commitment to a rigid and simple reference theory of meaning. In order to pursue what has remained the main interest of his group—syntactic research—Chomsky initially simplified the area of linguistic theory that interested him less, the theory of meaning. The ultimate success of syntactic work undertaken on the basis of this simplification is another matter; but one has only to look at the uneasy shifts of position on the question of semantics among his followers since Chomsky's first book (*Syntactic Structures*[11]) to see that the whole issue has been an embarrassment for them and him. The absolute distinction between well-formedness ("grammaticalness") and meaningfulness in language was always suspect, and younger transformationalists now at last see as much for themselves. Nothing quite so exposed the simple reality behind an elaborate

[11] N. Chomsky, *Syntactic Structures* (The Hague, 1957).

technical language, namely that Chomsky had assumed a very primitive version of the reference theory of meaning, as the article written by Fodor and Katz entitled "The Structure of a Semantic Theory."[12] For some time this article was widely regarded as *the* statement of the transformationalist position on theory of meaning, though a somewhat more realistic estimate of its value is probably prevalent by now.

However one regards the details of this sequence of events, one fact remains abundantly clear: the literary critic in search of a more sophisticated notion of how language functions could not have received enlightenment from the dominant school of modern linguistic research, for on this point, that school was a positive hindrance. The position taken by Chomsky's followers on the concept of style, too, represented a retrograde step rather than progress.

Overall, it would seem that the theory of how linguistics could be useful in literary criticism[13] is very different

---

[12] Jerry A. Fodor and Jerrold J. Katz, "The Structure of a Semantic Theory," *Language* 39 (1963): 170–210. The vogue of this article now seems to be over; but what it revealed about the school of transformational grammar—that it was prepared to accept this primitive theory of meaning—will long remain an embarrassment.

[13] I have not referred to the attempts of linguists to define poetic language, since that has been a relatively self-contained activity, without any effects on criticism; I have argued above (p. 50) that those linguists engaged in this pursuit have only been dealing at best with the minor problem of poetic license. And I have not discussed the common objection that undue concern with the language of a text is at the expense of concern with its ideas; chapter 6 will, I hope, have shown that such a dualism (language or ideas) is not profitable. Precise concern with the language of a text is simply a more precise concern with exactly what its ideas are.

from what has happened in practice. In practice, linguistics has offered critics a bad critical procedure based on a poor model of scientific research, a version of the concept of style more insidious even than the critic's own, and a primitive view of the theory of meaning and of how language functions. Yet in theory, a command both of the best available analysis of the language in which a particular text is written, and of the way in which language functions and has meaning, should be of enormous advantage to the critic. It can only be hoped that the practical situation slowly comes to resemble what in theory it might be.

Bibliography

I list here the books and articles to which reference is made in the text or footnotes of this book.

Adams, Hazard. *The Interests of Criticism.* New York, 1969.

Aiken, H. D. "The Aesthetic Revelance of Artists' Intentions." *Journal of Philosophy* 52 (1955): 742–753.

Altick, Richard D. *The Art of Literary Research.* New York, 1963.

Ayer, Alfred J. *Language, Truth, and Logic.* 2nd ed., London, 1946.

Bell, Clive. *Art.* London, 1927.

Bersani, Leo. "From Bachelard to Barthes." *Partisan Review,* 34 (1967): 215–232.

Bierwisch, Manfred. "Poetics and Linguistics." In *Linguistics and Literary Style,* ed. Freeman, pp. 96–115. New York, 1970.

Booth, Wayne. *The Rhetoric of Fiction.* Chicago, 1961.

Bowers, Fredson. "Textual Criticism." In *The Aims and Methods of Scholarship in Modern Languages and Literatures,* ed. Thorpe, pp. 23–42. New York, 1963.

Boyd, James. *Notes to Goethe's Poems.* 1. Oxford, 1948.

Burckhardt, Sigurd. "The Consistency of Goethe's *Tasso.*" *Journal of English and Germanic Philology* 57 (1958): 394–402.

Carr, E. H. *What is History?* New York, 1961.

Casey, John. *The Language of Criticism.* London, 1966.

Chatman, Seymour, ed. *Literary Style: A Symposium.* London, 1971.

Chomsky, Noam. *Syntactic Structures*. The Hague, 1957.

Cioffi, F. "Intention and Interpretation in Criticism." In *Collected Papers on Aesthetics*, ed. Cyril Barrett, pp. 161–183. New York, 1966.

Cohn, Robert G. *Towards the Poems of Mallarmé*. Berkeley and Los Angeles, 1965.

Colie, Rosemarie L. "Literature and History." In *Relations of Literary Study*, ed. Thorpe, pp. 1–26. New York, 1967.

Crews, Frederick C. "Literature and Psychology," In *Relations of Literary Study*, ed. Thorpe, pp. 73–87. New York, 1967.

————. "Anaesthetic Criticism," I, II. *The New York Review of Books* 14 (1971): 31–35 and 49–52.

Dilthey, Wilhelm. *Einleitung in die Geisteswissenschaften*. Berlin, 1883.

Edel, Leon. "Literature and Biography." In *Relations of Literary Study*, ed. Thorpe, pp. 57–72. New York, 1967.

Eichner, Hans. "The Meaning of 'Good' in Aesthetic Judgments." *British Journal of Aesthetics* 3 (1963): 301–316.

Eliot, T. S. *The Use of Poetry and the Use of Criticism*. London, 1933.

Ellis, John M. "Goethe's Revision of 'Willkommen und Abschied.'" *German Life and Letters*, n.s. 16 (1962): 14–22.

————. "Great Art. A Study in Meaning." *British Journal of Aesthetics* 3 (1963): 165–171.

————. "Reply to Rodway." *Twentieth Century* 172 (summer 1963): 112–14.

————. "Description and Critical Appraisal." *Mind* 73 (1964): 284–286.

————. Review of W. Righter, *Logic and Criticism*. In *Philosophical Books* 5 (1964): 17–19.

————. *Schiller's "Kalliasbriefe" and the Study of his Aesthetic Theory*. Anglica Germanica 12. The Hague, 1969.

————. *Kleist's "Prinz Friedrich von Homburg." A Critical Study*. Berkeley and Los Angeles, 1970.

————. "Linguistics, Literature, and the Concept of Style." *Word* 26 (1970): 65–78.

————. *Narration in the German Novelle. Theory and Interpretation*. Cambridge, England, 1974.

Ellis, John M., and Mowatt, David G. "Language, Metaphysics, and Staiger's Critical Categories." *Seminar: A Journal of Germanic Studies* 1 (1965): 122–125.

Ellis, John M.; Mowatt, David G.; and Robertson, Howard S. "A Closer Look at 'Aims and Methods.' " *Modern Language Journal* 50 (1966): 281–285.

Elton, William, ed. *Aesthetics and Language.* Oxford, 1954.

Empson, William. *Seven Types of Ambiguity.* London, 1930.

Enkvist, Nils E. "On Defining Style: An Essay in Applied Linguistics." In *Linguistics and Style*, ed. Spencer. London, 1964.

Fletcher, John. "The Criticism of Comparison: The Approach Through Comparative Literature and Intellectual History." In *Contemporary Criticism*, eds. Malcolm Bradbury and David Palmer. Stratford-upon-Avon Studies 12, pp. 106–129. New York, 1971.

Fodor, Jerry A., and Katz, Jerrold J. "The Structure of a Semantic Theory." *Language* 39 (1963): 170—210.

Foot, Philippa. "Moral Arguments." *Mind* 67 (1958): 503–513.

Fowler, Roger, ed. *Essays on Style and Language.* London, 1966.

Freeman, Donald C. Review of *Essays on Style and Language*, ed. Fowler, *Journal of Linguistics* 4 (1968): 109–115.

———. ed. *Linguistics and Literary Style.* New York, 1970.

Frye, Northrop. *Anatomy of Criticism: Four Essays.* Princeton, 1957.

———. "Literary Criticism." In *The Aims and Methods of Scholarship in Modern Languages and Literatures*, ed. Thorpe, pp. 57–69. New York, 1963.

Gallie, W. B. *Peirce and Pragmatism.* Harmondsworth, Middlesex, 1952.

Gardner, Helen. *The Business of Criticism.* Oxford, 1959.

Gregory, Michael J., and Spencer, John. "An Approach to the Study of Style." In *Linguistics and Style*, ed. Spencer, pp. 57–105. London, 1964.

Hall, Robert A., Jr. *Cultural Symbolism in Literature.* Ithaca, 1963.

Halliday, Michael A. K. "Categories of the Theory of Grammar." *Word* 17 (1961): 241–292.

———. "Descriptive Linguistics in Literary Studies." In *Linguistics and Literary Style*, ed. Freeman, pp. 57–71. New York, 1970.

———. "The Linguistic Study of Literary Texts." In *Proceedings of the IXth International Congress of Linguists*, pp. 302–307. The Hague, 1964.

Hare, Richard M. *The Language of Morals*. Oxford, 1952.

Harrison, B. "Some Uses of 'Good' in Criticism." *Mind* 69 (1960): 206–222.

Heller, Erich. *The Disinherited Mind*. Harmondsworth, Middlesex, 1961.

Hermand, Jost. *Synthetisches Interpretieren. Zur Methodik der Literaturwissenschaft*. Sammlung Dialog 27. Munich, 1968.

Hill, Archibald A., "Poetry and Stylistics." Address given at the University of Virginia, September 21, 1956, in the Peter Rushton Seminars in Contemporary Prose and Poetry.

———. "A Program for the Definition of Literature." *Texas Studies in English* 37 (1958): 46–52.

Hirsch, Eric Donald. *Validity in Interpretation*. New Haven, 1967.

Hoggart, Richard. "Why I Value Literature." In *The Critical Moment. Literary Criticism in the 1960's. Essays from the London Times Literary Supplement*, pp. 31–39. London, 1964.

Hough, Graham. *An Essay on Criticism*. London, 1966.

Hyman, Stanley Edgar. *The Armed Vision. A Study in the Methods of Modern Literary Criticism*. New York, 1948; 2nd ed. 1955.

Jakobson, Roman. "Closing Statement: Linguistics and Poetics." In *Style in Language*, ed. Sebeok, pp. 350–377. Cambridge, Mass., 1960.

Jessup, B. "What Is Great Art?" *British Journal of Aesthetics* 2 (1962): 26–35.

Jones, Huw Morris. "The Relevance of the Artist's Intentions." *British Journal of Aesthetics* 4 (1964): 138–145.

Juhl, Peter D. "Intention and Literary Interpretation." *Deutsche Vierteljahrsschrift für Literaturgeschichte und Geisteswissenschaft* 6 (1971): 1–23.

Kayser, Wolfgang. *Das sprachliche Kunstwerk.* Bern, 1948.

————. *Die Vortragsreise.* Bern, 1954.

————. *Das Groteske.* Oldenburg, 1957.

Kennick, W. "Does Traditional Aesthetics Rest on a Mistake?" *Mind* 67 (1958): 317–334.

Knights, L. C. "In Search of Fundamental Values." In *The Critical Moment. Literary Criticism in the 1960's. Essays from the London Times Literary Supplement,* pp. 75–81. London, 1964.

Koch, Walter A. "On the Principles of Stylistics." *Lingua* 12 (1963): 411–422.

Kuhn, Thomas S. *The Structure of Scientific Revolutions.* Chicago, 1962.

Lake, Beryl. "A Study of the Irrefutability of Two Aesthetic Theories." In *Aesthetics and Language,* ed. Elton. Oxford, 1954.

Leavis, Frank Raymond. *Revaluation.* London, 1936.

————. *The Common Pursuit.* London, 1952.

Lerner, L. *The Truest Poetry. An Essay on the Question: What Is Literature?* New York, 1964.

Levin, Harry. *Why Literary Criticism Is Not an Exact Science.* Cambridge, Mass., 1967.

Levin, S. R. "Deviation—Statistical and Determinate—in Poetic Language." *Lingua* 12 (1963): 276–290.

Lohner, Edgar. "Tradition und Gegenwart deutscher Literaturkritik." *Sprache im technischen Zeitalter* 3 (1962): 238–248.

Lorenz, Konrad. *On Aggression.* Trans. Marjorie Kerr Wilson. New York, 1966.

Modern Language Association Committee on Research Activities. "The Aims, Methods, and Materials of Research in the Modern Languages and Literatures." *Publications of the Modern Language Association of America* 67 (1952): 3–37.

Morris, Desmond. *The Naked Ape.* London, 1967.

————. *The Human Zoo.* New York, 1969.

Moulton, William G. "Linguistics." In *The Aims and Methods of Scholarship in Modern Languages and Literatures,* ed. Thorpe, pp. 1–21. New York, 1963.

Mowatt, David G. "In the Beginning was the First Version." *German Life and Letters,* n.s. 12 (1959): 211–221.

————. "Language, Literature, and Middle High German." *Seminar: A Journal of Germanic Studies,* 1 (1965): 69–87.

————. *Friedrich von Hūsen: Introduction, Text, Commentary and Glossary.* Anglica Germanica II. Cambridge, England, 1971.

Mowatt, David G., and Dembowski, Peter F. "Literary Study and Linguistics." *Canadian Journal of Linguistics* 11 (1965): 40–62.

Nowell-Smith, Patrick H. *Ethics.* Harmondsworth, Middlesex, 1954.

Ohmann, Richard. "Generative Grammars and the Concept of Literary Style." *Word* 20 (1964): 423–439.

Orsini, G. N. G. "The Organic Concepts in Aesthetics." *Comparative Literature* 21 (1969): 1–30.

Osborne, Harold. *Theory of Beauty.* London, 1952.

————. *Aesthetics and Criticism.* London, 1955.

Quigley, Austin E. *The Dynamics of Dialogue in the Plays of Harold Pinter.* Unpublished Doctoral Dissertation, University of California, Santa Cruz, 1971.

Richards, I. A. *Principles of Literary Criticism.* London, 1925.

————. *Practical Criticism: A Study of Literary Judgment.* London, 1929.

Richards, I. A., and Ogden, C. K. *The Meaning of Meaning.* London, 1923.

Riffaterre, Michael. "Criteria for Style Analysis." *Word* 15 (1959): 154–174.

————. "Stylistic Context." *Word* 16 (1960): 207–218.

Righter, William. *Logic and Criticism.* London, 1963.

Robson, W. W. "Are Purely Literary Values Enough?" In *The Critical Moment. Literary Criticism in the 1960's. Essays from the London Times Literary Supplement,* pp. 48–59. London, 1964.

Rodway, Allan E. "What the Critics Really Need." *Twentieth Century* 172 (winter 1963): 155–163.

Rowley, Brian A. "Psychology and Literary Criticism." In *Psychoanalysis and the Social Sciences*, pp. 200–218. New York, 1958.

Sartre, Jean-Paul. *Qu'est-ce que la littérature?* Paris, 1948.

Sayce, R. A. "The Definition of the Term 'Style.'" *Proceedings of the 3rd Congress of the International Comparative Literature Association*, pp. 156–166. The Hague, 1962.

Schiller, Fredrich. *On the Aesthetic Education of Man. In a Series of Letters*. (English and German facing). Ed. and trans. Elizabeth M. Wilkinson and Leonard A. Willoughby. Oxford, 1967.

Schreiber, S. M. *An Introduction to Literary Criticism*. Oxford, 1965.

Scott, Wilbur. *Five Approaches of Literary Criticism. An Arrangement of Contemporary Critical Essays*. New York, 1962.

Sebeok, Thomas A., ed. *Style in Language*. Cambridge, Mass., 1960.

Silz, Walter. "The Scholar, the Critic, and the Teacher of Literature." *German Quarterly* 37 (1964): 113–119.

Spencer, John, ed. *Linguistics and Style*. Language and Language Learning 6, London, 1964.

Spiller, Robert E. "Literary History." In *The Aims and Methods of Scholarship in Modern Languages and Literatures*, ed. Thorpe, pp. 43–55. New York, 1963.

Spitzer, Leo. *Linguistics and Literary History*. Princeton, 1948.

Staiger, Emil. *Grundbegriffe der Poetik*. Zürich, 1946.

———. "Time and the Poetic Imagination." In *The Critical Moment. Literary Criticism in the 1960's. Essays from the London Times Literary Supplement*, pp. 130–137. London, 1964.

Sutton, Walter. *Modern American Criticism*. Englewood Cliffs, N.J., 1963.

Thorne, James Peter. "Stylistics and Generative Grammars." In *Linguistics and Literary Style*, ed. Freeman, pp. 182–196. New York, 1970.

————. "Poetry, Stylistics, and Imaginary Grammars." *Journal of Linguistics* 5 (1969): 147–150.

Thorpe, James. *Literary Scholarship. A Handbook for Advanced Students of English and American Literature.* Boston, 1964.

————, ed. *The Aims and Methods of Scholarship in Modern Languages and Literatures.* New York, 1963.

————, *Relations of Literary Study, Essays on Interdisciplinary Contributions.* New York, 1967.

The Times Literary Supplement. *The Critical Moment. Literary Criticism in the 1960's. Essays from the London Times Literary Supplement.* New York, 1964.

Vinaver, Eugène. "The Historical Method in the Study of Literature." In *The Future of the Modern Humanities,* ed. J. C. Laidlaw. The Modern Humanities Research Association, Cambridge, England, 1969.

Watson, George. *The Literary Critics. A Study of English Descriptive Criticism.* Harmondsworth, Middlesex, 1962.

Weitz, Morris. *Hamlet and the Philosophy of Literary Criticism.* Chicago, 1964.

Wellek, René. "Closing Statement." In *Style in Language,* ed. Sebeok. Cambridge, Mass., 1960.

————. Review of F. R. Leavis's *Revaluation.* In *Scrutiny* 5 (1937).

Wellek, René, and Warren, Austin. *Theory of Literature.* 2nd ed. New York, 1956.

Whorf, Benjamin Lee. *Language, Thought, and Reality. Selected Writings of Benjamin Lee Whorf,* ed. J. B. Carroll. Cambridge, Mass., 1956.

Wilkinson, Elizabeth M. "Goethe's Conception of Form." *Proceedings of the British Academy* 38 (1951): 175–197.

————. " 'Form' and 'Content' in the Aesthetics of German Classicism." In *Stil- und Formprobleme in der Literatur,* ed. P. Böckmann, pp. 18–27. Heidelberg, 1959.

Wimsatt, William K. "Genesis: A Fallacy Revisited." In *The Disciplines of Criticism. Essays in Literary Theory and History,* eds. P. Demetz; T. Greene; L. Nelson, Jr. New Haven, 1968.

Wimsatt, William K, with Beardsley, Monroe C. *The Verbal Icon. Studies in the Meaning of Poetry.* University of Kentucky, Lexington, 1954.

Wittgenstein, Ludwig. *The Blue and Brown Books.* New York, 1958.

————. *Philosophische Untersuchungen/Philosophical Investigations.* Trans. G. E. M. Anscombe. 3rd ed. New York, 1968.

Wrenn, C. L. *The Idea of Comparative Literature.* The Modern Humanities Research Association, Cambridge, England, 1968.

Index of Names